BREED

Evolution or Extinction

COLET ABEDI

Cover design: Dr. David Forstadt
Symbols and Drawings: Nedda

TABLE OF CONTENTS

THE FIVE KINGDOMS

For my father, Dr. Hedayat Abedi,
who taught me to love animals
And for Famous, who taught me how
If only heaven had visting hours…

"I live continually in a reverie of the future. I have no faith in human perfectibility. I think that human exertion will have no appreciable effect upon humanity. Man is now only more active — not more happy — nor more wise, than he was 6000 years ago. The result will never vary — and to suppose that it will, is to suppose that the foregone man has lived in vain — that the foregone time is but the rudiment of the future — that the myriads who have perished have not been upon equal footing with ourselves — nor are we with our posterity."

-Edgar Allan Poe

Map of the Kingdoms

Human beings are masters of the extinction game.

As a scientist I must acknowledge this one resounding truth- it is in our nature to destroy.

We build.

We conquer.

And inevitably, we are consumed by greed and violence and annihilate anything standing in our path. We have foolishly lived with the notion this planet was made for only us. Where we should have nurtured, we destroyed. Where we should have loved, we hated. For the past decade, we have been faced with one resounding truth—our species has brought about the extinction of all animal life on Earth. It is a brutal reality, and the day is quickly coming upon us where we will no longer be able to escape our inevitable future.

Not long from now, there will be no animal species left on our planet.

In order to preserve something from these species, I've spent years in my laboratory searching for a solution. Throughout this time, I have been guided by Vedic philosophy.

As a scientist, I've been fascinated by the great particle they continuously referred to called the atma, or as we know it, the Soul Particle. It is believed to be similar to antimatter but more profound. If I could harness this energy, this particle in our dying animals, and inject it into the pineal glands of human embryos, we would be allowed to keep something of the animal species alive forever, within our very own DNA. We could become a hybrid being: human in shape and form but gifted with the knowledge of these great animals.

After years of trials, my endeavors have finally been successful.

I believe the discovery of the Soul Particle will change Earth as we know it.

-Dr. Neil Hedy April 2, 2501

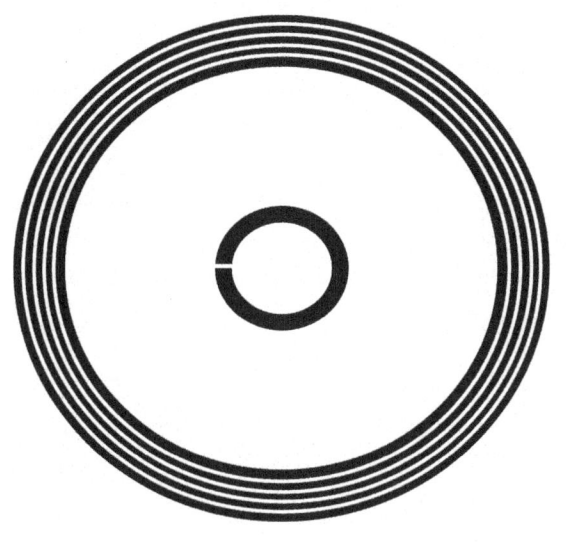

COAT OF ARMS
KINGDOM OM

CHAPTER ONE

"Truth is One: Sages call it by various names.
It is the one sun which reflects in all ponds;
It is the one water which slakes the thirst of all;
It is the one air which sustains all life."
-Rig Veda 3000 BC

Earth
Kingdom OM
2999 AD

I was falling.

Free falling through space at a speed barely visible to the human eye.

Something had gone wrong.

"Emergency," the flat, robotic voice rang through my small pod. "System malfunction," echoed as I fought through the force of gravity and managed to place my hand on the emergency fail-safe screen and slow down my descent.

As I breached Earth's atmosphere, I caught glimpses of barren landscapes devoid of all life. Wastelands of areas that at one time sustained human civilization. It was a heartbreaking sight. But before I could take in the devastation, my pod veered toward a pocket of land, sitting like a beautiful oasis among desolate ruin. Greenery, mountains, lakes, and oceans all came into view. But something was wrong with the electrical system, and I couldn't gain control. Everything flashed before me. Through the circular window directly in front of my eyes, I saw a quick view of a fluffy cloud, then the bright glare of the sun.

And then nothing but darkness.

As I fell in and out of consciousness, time seemed to stand still.

"You're going to be all right," a deep voice broke through the fog as I fought the oblivion determined to consume me. "Don't move. I've got you."

Moments later, I saw tanned hands unfasten my safety harnesses and gently lift me out of the pod. A human face so savagely masculine and raw, then flickered into something else.

A lion. A majestic king of the wild that had at one time roamed Earth, before they were driven to extinction.

It was something I had never seen before, and yet in an instant, before I could marvel at the sight, he was human again.

Darkness took me.

Everything seemed to flash before me. Brief snippets of a story I would one day have to string together into a linear tale that would make sense to me.

"Stay with me," the voice was soft as I was pulled protectively into a chest.

Was I dying?

"*Please,*" I begged. For what, I didn't know.

Before I could find the energy to speak again, my body was hit with a wave of exhaustion as my mind was flooded with memories from the distant past.

øøø

My mother often said there were moments in one's life that would forever change the way we viewed the world. My first came when I was sixteen. I was living a happy life on the planet Akasha in a cocoon of peace and blissful ignorance.

"Siren, you must learn to control your emotions." My

mother's soothing voice broke through the inferno that raged in my mind. "You cannot allow your Shadow to control you."

In that moment my innocence was lost to me forever.

She pulled me away from the giant screens, where I had just watched footage of the Cetacean Massacre, the brutal assassination of almost all my people on Earth hundreds of years ago. I saw people shot down in their homes. Explosions caused bodies to fall lifelessly to the ground. The screams of children fell on deaf ears. Painful pleas that are now burned into my mind for as long as I live. I had reached the age the Elders believed was acceptable to finally see our Cetacean history. The tragic horror our people had suffered.

I had never felt such rage.

The last time I flickered into my Shadow was when I was a child. And now as a young woman, I was unable to control myself—and my Cetacean ancestor emerged for a brief moment. I could feel the familiar tingling sensation in my forehead, like a thousand needles prickling my skin at once, the telltale sign I was about to flicker. Part of my face morphed into my dolphin Shadow, and I saw a vision of myself swimming freely in the ocean on Earth—among my Soul Particle ancestors. It took me a moment, before I could invoke the one word that would center me.

Arcana. My maxim.

Once the word came, I regained control and flickered back to myself.

My mother's ethereal face was etched with sadness and disappointment.

"My beautiful angel, your rage betrays you." she said as she watched me. "What you see is the way of man."

"This is not *our* way. We do not destroy. We do not kill." I yelled.

"No, it is not our way," my mother agreed. "But nevertheless, you must learn to forgive."

"How can we forgive this?" I asked in outrage as I pointed at the screens. "*How?*"

She smoothed out my brown hair as her bright blue eyes gazed into ones identical to her own. "My darling, what does this anger bring you?" she asked softly. "You only cause yourself distress. You cannot change the past or cruelty of man. You can learn from it, and choose a different way."

I looked away from her. My mother was always so calm and knowing. I had never even seen her Shadow. She could move on, but I could not forgive. Not yet.

Maybe not ever.

"Why did you show me this?"

"Siren. I want you to know your history," she explained as she knelt before me. "You and the three others are the future of our race and tasked with helping find a way for our Breed to live. How else can you fulfill your destiny? You have to know where you are going, who you will interact with, and why it is so important you never betray who you really are."

I looked away. How would I be able to coexist with these people, these other breeds, if I couldn't bear to even look at them? How would I be able to keep my secrets?

"How do you live with this?" I whispered.

"I live in hope," she told me with a smile.

"How can you expect me," I began slowly as my gaze narrowed on hers. "How can *anyone* expect—"

"Would you choose extinction for us?" My mother asked quietly. "After all this time, after all that was done to ensure our survival—must *our* Breed die?"

Extinction.

It was a word that held great power, and one that had

shaped my life from the moment I was born. "We escaped Earth for a reason." I said.

"It is our rightful home," she stated quietly.

"But what remains of it?" I argued. "You want me to live among descendants of people who slaughtered *our* women, men, and children. I can't believe any of them...*any* single one of them could be good..."

"Siren," my mother's voice was almost soothing. "Your father was the last male Cetacean, and he passed on to the light when you were an infant. We are all that is left. Twelve women —eight of us too old to take on the mission. You, my love, and the rest of the girls are the only ones who have a chance at ensuring our survival. We need you—we *beg* you—to return to Earth."

"The five breeds separated from one another for a reason," I said with petulance.

"That was never Dr. Hedy's dream," my mother said. "He never intended to have the breeds create sovereign kingdoms. Those were the twisted schemes of rulers who believed separation was the only way forward."

"But it happened," I countered. "People evolved into different breeds. With different traditions, desires, and ways of life."

"That is correct." She placed a hand on mine. "And yet, how does any ecosystem work?"

"It is an interaction between living and nonliving organisms."

"Yes. Forming a symbiosis, *all together*. As one." My mother's voice had conviction.

I understood what my mother was getting at. But those images I just saw were hard to reconcile.

The Cetacean Elders had always known this day would

come. At one time they had collected genetic samples from both male and female Cetaceans. When it became obvious the females were only giving birth to females, they harvested embryos. My people had futilely tried to grow male fetuses, but they all died. And now, only twelve female Cetaceans were left.

Our Breed was a breath away from extinction, a place our Soul Particle ancestors found themselves in, all those years ago. I couldn't let history repeat itself.

"How do we even know this will work? What if they recognize us?" I said to her.

"What other choice do we have?" My mother's smile was sad. "We can only hope our plan works. But for that to happen, you can never allow your emotions to take over like you did just now."

"You ask for the impossible."

"Not if you learn to control yourself. To invoke your word. Arcana." She chastised. "Remember why you chose the word, and the power you gave it. As for the rest, we'll equip you with the knowledge to assimilate."

Arcana meant mystery, a great secret of nature—just as we were. It was a word that reminded me we were made of magic and could use it to control anything. My mother was right, and I felt ashamed. I knew the basics: return to Earth and colonize Kingdom B. To give our Breed, a chance to live on.

My mother looked at me thoughtfully. "Remember, Siren, at the end of the day, no matter the Breed… We are all human."

"What if something goes wrong, and they find out what I am?" I finally asked, allowing my fears to be spoken out loud. "What then? Will they kill me?"

"I should hope not, my darling," she whispered painfully. I

could see the fear in her eyes. "We have prepared the best we can, and with all we know of Kingdom B, we have great hope."

Out of the four Kingdoms that remained on Earth, it was the only one my people identified as safe for colonization. When the leaders from the other Kingdoms had gathered together to plan the Cetacean Massacre, Kingdom B had been the only one conflicted by the thought of mass extermination. Though their leaders had reluctantly agreed, the people of Kingdom B had been divided by their actions. Ashamed of the genocide they were accomplice to, they had adopted the most liberal of all governments on Earth.

Every eleven years they voted for both a political leader and a spiritual one, with hopes that there would be a moral, esoteric voice to balance diplomacy. They had also built four entrances into their Kingdom—one for each Breed left on Earth. Their home, they declared, would always be open to *all* human life on Earth. We did not know if any other Breed lived in Kingdom B, but we knew their borders were open to the possibility.

"It could be a suicide mission."

"It will not be," my mother shook her head. "You know as Cetaceans we can blend in with our surroundings. Out of all the breeds the human-bird hybrids have the most inferior sense of smell. If confronted, you'll say you're OM, as our ancestors shared genetic similarities. You'll hide among them, guarding your secret forever. Even from the children I pray you'll one day bear." My mother gave me a sad smile.

"And I will never see you again?" I asked even though I knew what the answer would be.

"I will always be with you." I could see it took everything in her not to breakdown.

I tried to fight back my own tears, threatening to spill.

"It is not enough," I said. "I will be all alone."

"Delphine, Kalypso, and Jana will be with you," my mother's voice was gentle, reminding me of the other three embarking on this mission.

"I don't even know them!" My voice moaned as I thought of the other girls. "And now I'm to spend the rest of my life with them?"

"You would have spent the rest of your life with them here on Akasha," she pointed out.

"Yes, but here I have you."

"For how long?"

Her words made me pause, the meaning behind them, the deadly illness she was now fighting, and the thought of what would happen to her, almost bringing me to my knees. I silently cursed the injustice of our situation.

"What will you do, Siren?" My mother pushed.

I looked away and stared at the screens, which now showed pictures of our vibrant lavender atmosphere. Unlike Earth, our atmosphere changed color each hour of the day.

It was a beautiful planet. But it was still not our home. It was not Earth.

"You are the most important. The last descendant of Elora, the first to be injected with the Cetacean Soul Particle," my mother's voice was soft. "Would you have our bloodline die with you?"

I was the last of The First. The irony was not lost on me.

There was no other choice. I took a breath and stared deep into my mother's eyes.

"I will fulfill my destiny."

CHAPTER TWO

The memory of my mother still lingered as I woke up.

My senses became hyperaware of my surroundings. I could hear the booming sound of thunder, and the fall of hard rain. There was a calming smell encircling me like a protective cocoon. It was everywhere.

Lime. Mint. Wet wood.

Scents coming from a planet I had never even known.

Earth.

A place I had dreamt about my whole life. The home of my ancestors. A planet I never thought I'd actually see. But how did I recognize the smell? *How could I place it?*

And then I remembered.

My mother said that when I landed, it was entirely possible certain scents or sights would trigger moments of deep cellular recognition, something due to the merging of animal and human Soul Particles all those years ago. I would innately know my surroundings. I would *remember* things I had never even laid eyes on. At the time, I could not comprehend her words, but now, in this moment, I finally understood.

My eyelids still felt heavy, but I could finally focus on my surroundings. I was stretched out on my back and could hear the crackle of a fire, the smell of wood burning—and pine. That calming smell of pine, I would etch into my memory forever.

I looked up and stared at the orange colored rocks that were a mere four or perhaps five feet above my head. The shadows from the flames of the fire danced against the crevices as I took in slow breaths. I was lying next to the fire *he* had probably started, with a large brown jacket covering most of my body.

"You're back," a voice broke through the silence.

I looked up and saw a boy. No, a man.

He was athletic and muscular, his chest broad, his arms long and sinewy. Even sitting, I could tell he was extraordinarily tall. His dark amber colored hair was shoulder length and held back by a black leather tie. His cheeks were high and angular, his nose shapely.

I remembered him. I remembered seeing his Shadow.

He was also the first male human I had ever seen. And though I had been thoroughly educated on the opposite sex, I was still navigating through unchartered territory, and I needed a second to process. To move energy through my body. It was only extreme emotion which caused a Breed to flicker. *Extreme.* I could feel the tingling sensation in my forehead move over my face, but I reminded myself who I was. How strong my people were. I would not betray them.

Arcana.

My Shadow was exactly that, something to remain in the dark. Hidden. Forever.

"Where am I?" I asked slowly, even though I had an idea where I might have crashed.

"OM," his voice was low, powerful, and sounded like a rumble coming from deep within his chest. "You crashed in Kingdom OM."

It was his eyes that should have given him away. They were more than just human. They glittered savagely with the ferocity of the greatest cat from the lore he descended from.

The irony was not lost on me.

Here I was, in the home of the *Other Mammals*, the Breed who masterminded the Cetacean Massacre—singe handedly responsible for the annihilation of my people.

Or so they believed.

"You fell from the sky," he stated the obvious as his speculative gaze searched my face for answers.

"Yes," I whispered. "I don't know how, but I lost control of the pod."

I sat up slowly so I wouldn't feel so helpless lying down.

"Where are you from?" He pressed on. "Which Kingdom?"

I could see the good in him. As a Cetacean, I could read people's auras. All living creatures had an electromagnetic field surrounding their bodies, emanating an energy which resided in their heart and soul. His was deep blue with gold, telling me he was honest and had good judgment. I thought about telling him the truth. A part of me would have enjoyed seeing the shock on his face, but there was too much at stake.

He was still OM.

The motto the Elders had drilled into us before we embarked on our journey was *Mission First*. Survival of our Breed was all that mattered.

"There are only three to choose from," his voice was hard, his eyes narrowing distrustfully. "Kingdom B. Kingdom R. Kingdom A. Since I know unequivocally you are *not* OM."

"At one time there were five," the words came out before I could stop them.

He leaned away from my body, looking at me in surprise.

"The Cetaceans have been extinct for over two hundred years."

His words angered me, and I gave him a cold smile.

"Because of you. You *Other Mammals*. The architects of yet another human caused extinction."

His eyes narrowed at my tone.

"Every other Kingdom participated."

"Out of fear incited by your ancestors." I was barely treading water, injured and at his mercy, yet here I was unable to stop myself from lashing out. But my anger was tempered. I would not allow it to control me.

"The Cetaceans were genetically superior to the rest of the breeds," his voice was arrogant. "They posed a great danger to our survival."

"Survival?" I knew from my history lessons what his argument would be.

"They could reproduce. They had a greater intellect. They would have continued to grow exponentially, and who knows what would have come of it. The greater their numbers, the greater their power," he spoke as though he was talking to a child. "It was either the Cetaceans extinction or our own."

He stared down at me, his size and presence—the memory of *his* Shadow—dominating my space. "Stop avoiding the question," his voice was unforgiving. "Tell me what Kingdom you come from."

"Kingdom…" my voice wavered. *Lie, Siren. Speak.* "I'm from Kingdom B."

From my studies of Earth, I knew each Kingdom kept to themselves and hardly ever mingled with one another. In fact, it was rare they even set eyes on someone of a different Breed. There were pacts and laws in place, and each Breed settled far apart from the others. This system had worked for hundreds of years. It made my cover story easy to believe, because the odds were an OM had never seen someone from

Kingdom B before in their life.

He eyed me warily, then moved fast and leaned in close to smell my hair, my neck, my very *essence*. I knew what he was doing. As an Other Mammal, his senses were as heightened as those of the great beasts when they roamed the Earth.

My heartrate picked up. What if he could tell I was lying? We had not prepared for this.

"Are there more of you?" His voice was curious as he leaned back.

I shook my head and tried to inch as far away from him as I could.

"No," I lied. "Just me."

Moving in close again, he loomed over my face. His eyes took on an iridescent golden hue, becoming almost hypnotic—like he was trying to trap his prey.

"*What are you?*" he asked.

"I just told you. I'm from Kingdom B. You…you know *what* I am."

"What is your name?" He went on, daring me to break his enigmatic gaze.

"Siren," I replied truthfully.

"Siren." My name rolled off his tongue as if he were tasting something fine for the first time. "My name is Aedan, and I am the leader of Kingdom OM."

I tried to cover my surprise. Judging from his looks, he couldn't be much older than I was, and I had just turned seventeen.

"I saw you crash," he told me. "It's a miracle you survived. "

"How long have I been sleeping?" I asked as I hugged my knees to my chest.

"Two days."

My eyes widened in shock. I had been unable to communicate with the others for two days. They probably assumed I died in the crash. They would have been alerted through their monitors in their pods, and when I didn't contact them...

"And you were here the entire time..." I began.

"I would never leave an injured female unattended," Aedan's voice was harsh. "And...I had to make sure you were alone and this wasn't a trap."

"A trap?" I was confused.

"From Kingdom R," he explained.

The Reptiles. The most dangerous of all breeds.

"Are you at odds?" I asked quickly. The last data we collected from Earth was over twenty-five years ago, and at the time, there had been no reports of unrest between Kingdoms.

Aedan gave me a curt smile. "More like war," he said.

"War?" I knew my voice sounded unsure.

"The quiet kind," Aedan said. "One no one in the future will even know we took part in."

I wondered why he was telling me this. How could he know he could trust me? More than that, I wondered why the young leader of OM was alone on the land—seemingly unprotected—unless there were soldiers on guard outside the cave, awaiting his command.

I allowed myself to focus on the energy surrounding the cave. I felt nothing. Given the sensory skills Cetaceans possessed, if any soldiers were close, I would be able to feel their presence a few hundred feet around me.

"So where are we now?" I asked Aedan, processing his words, relieved there were no signs of life other than our own.

"In the caves of the Ancient Dwellers," he said. Or as Earth once called them, cavemen—the original humans to have inhabited the planet.

"When you have some of your strength back we'll leave for my home, where I'll get you to our med lab."

My stomach clenched at the thought of stepping foot in OM's capitol. "I don't need your med lab," my voice was strong. "I just need to get home—to Kingdom B."

"You're injured," Aedan's eyes narrowed. "You can barely walk."

"I'm getting my strength back," I began calmly, controlling all the emotions going on inside me. "And I'm grateful for all you've done for me, but if you just take me to the border—"

"I'm not taking you to Kingdom B."

"You don't have to," I said quickly. "I just need my maps, and I can find my own way—"

"As I said, you're coming with me to Larsa, the capital of OM."

I could feel the color leave my face.

"There's no need. If you just take me to my pod—" I implored.

"That is not going to happen, Siren," Aedan's voice was tense.

My body grew hot in fear as I stared at his impassive face. I could only imagine what my fate would be. Images of the Cetacean Massacre flashed through my mind.

"Please," I said to him, trying to reason. "I can't come with you."

"You will," he said coldly. "You crashed in my Kingdom, illegally trespassing on OM land. You could be a spy. I will not put my people at risk."

"I am not a spy." I spat out. My anger and indignance for him and his kind returning.

"And I'm to take your word for it?" he returned forcefully. "An unknown Breed, who fell from a pod in the sky? Do you know what will happen if I find out you are lying to me? If I find out you are putting any of *my* people in danger?"

I could only nod.

An invisible line had just been drawn.

"For your sake, I hope you're telling me the truth," Aedan said.

CHAPTER THREE

I stared at the crackling fire in silence, grateful Aedan had left me alone, so I could sit with my thoughts and contemplate my next steps.

I had already lost so much time and veered so far from what I was intended to do. We had strict instructions— Delphine, Kalypso, Jana, and I were to land together in a remote area of Kingdom B not regularly monitored. We were to hide our pods and use the virtual maps to find our way to the city. Because of the dangerous nature of our mission, the plan was to split and enter the Kingdom from the four different gates. And now, I was separated from the others.

I didn't know where my pod was. I didn't have my virtual maps. I was injured. And I wasn't in Kingdom B. And as if the odds couldn't be worse, I was at the mercy of the leader of Kingdom OM. My mission was daunting enough, and now I had to come up with an entirely new plan—a way to escape Aedan. However given his strength and mistrust, it seemed like an impossible task.

He was too perceptive. I knew, as a leader, Aedan would err on the side of caution, if only to protect his people. I had to figure out a way to make him trust me. Once his guard was down, I could escape and somehow find my way back to the pod that held the precious virtual maps I needed now more than anything.

It seemed like the only logical plan.

After sleeping for so long, my strength was slowly coming back, and I was able to sit up and stretch out my hands to receive the warmth from the flames. I was wearing my atmospheric spacesuit, which acclimated to all weather conditions. It must have torn during the crash because I was colder than I had ever been in my life. Aedan had given me what I assumed was his jacket to wear, it was so massive it practically blanketed my entire body. I pulled it over the rest of my legs and scooted closer to the fire. I moved my fingers through my long brown hair and winced when I felt the knots. I could only imagine what I looked like.

The rumbling of my stomach broke my chain of thought.

I looked around the cave and only saw a small black pack lying haphazardly on the dirt. I knew there was food in it. Fruit. And another synthetic product I could not decipher. Though my sensory skills were weakened by the crash, I still had the ability to zone in on the closest sustenance that would replenish my body. It was another one of our Cetacean gifts. And now, I needed to eat and regain my strength as quickly as possible, because my survival depended on it.

"You sound hungry," Aedan's voice broke through the silence.

I jumped at the noise. He really was like the lion he descended from—quiet and lithe. He came up beside me, his hair and clothes wet from the rain. He was wearing black cargo pants and a black, long sleeved top made from a fiber I didn't recognize. I watched as he pulled off his shirt and exposed his very naked and tanned chest.

He had one tattoo. It was directly over his heart and it was the face of a lion all in black.

"Sound?" I asked uncomfortably as I tried not to stare at his tattoo.

"I heard your stomach grumble from outside," he told me nonchalantly.

I looked away from him in embarrassment.

"You must be starving," he said. "You haven't had anything to eat in two days."

I watched as he walked opposite me and hunkered down in front of the fire. He grabbed the black pack and unzipped it. Just as I had sensed, he pulled out two bananas, got back up, and came over to me. He ripped one open and offered it to me.

"You're lucky I brought these along," he said. "On most hunting trips I only take synthetic meat." Aedan's Breed consisted mostly of carnivores and had created synthetic foods to satisfy the cravings and protein their genetic makeup required.

"Thank you," I took the banana gratefully.

His long fingers brushed against mine, before he quickly stepped away from me. My eyes flickered over his tattoo again. This time Aedan noticed.

"It is the mark of my ancestor," he explained what I already deduced. "Most of my people carry a tattoo of what Soul Particle they descend from. Do you have a similar custom?"

"No," I replied quietly. As Cetaceans we did not, and I had no idea if the other kingdoms did the same as OM.

Aedan sat down across from me and put his hands out toward the fire for warmth.

"Were you hunting the Reptiles alone?" I asked hoping to change the subject. His gaze met mine. I could see the flames dancing around in the golden depths.

"Yes."

"Why?" I asked in disbelief. He was the leader of OM. Where was his guard?

"It's the way I prefer. I'm confident as my ability as a warrior and leader of OM. I won't die at the hands of a

Reptile," Aedan said.

"Is that wise?" I couldn't decide whether to be impressed or put off by his arrogance.

Aedan's eyes flashed in annoyance.

From my studies of Earth, I knew each Kingdom kept to themselves and hardly ever mingled with one another. In fact, it was rare they even set eyes on someone from a different Breed. There were pacts and laws in place and each Breed settled far apart from the others. This system had worked for hundreds of years, and it made my cover story easy to believe.

"Why are the Reptiles here? On your land?"

"Why are *you* here?" He was relentless.

"You still don't believe me?" I said.

"No," Aedan shook his head. "I don't."

I looked down at the fire.

"Well you should," I said almost defiantly, before continuing, "So what will you do?"

"I don't know yet," Aedan replied honestly. "Given the danger Kingdom R poses, if I take you back to Larsa and reveal what I know to the others, they'll want to kill you because of the risk you might represent."

It seemed mankind hadn't changed in all these years. They still craved war. And death.

"You look surprised," Aedan went on as if he had not just threatened my life. "I've heard rumblings that *your* Kingdom B is having the same problems with the Reptiles."

"I wouldn't know," I said curtly. "I'm not involved in any politics. I work in planetary research." It was what we had been told to say if we were ever caught in a precarious situation.

"I don't believe you."

"I'm sorry?"

"People, no matter the Breed, talk. And rumors travel fast."

"Rumors are spread by fools," I stated coolly. "And I'm careful with the company I keep."

"That would make you the exception."

I shrugged.

"Or the anomaly," he uttered.

I could feel my face burn under his scrutiny.

"You weren't out scouting for new land?" Aedan asked curiously.

"Why would I do that?"

"Come on, Siren," He shook his head in admonishment. "You know Kingdom OM has the most desirable land on the planet. And as the climate and ecosystem becomes more unpredictable, what I'm protecting becomes more of a precious commodity."

He spoke the truth.

We knew the day would come when the others would eye OM's land. But since we hadn't collected research in twenty-five years, I didn't know things had escalated to this level on Earth. The planet—she was rotting. And her infection was human. If we stayed true to our nature, we'd eventually destroy all that was left of her.

"I won't deny it." I agreed. "But it has nothing to do with me. I told you, I'm not involved in that talk. I'm just a researcher. I keep to myself."

Aedan watched me closely. I met his gaze confidently, waiting for him to speak.

"You should sleep now, Siren," he finally said. "I'd like to try and trek home tomorrow."

Tomorrow? My mind raced. I needed more time to

recover.

"But the rain…" I argued. It was falling hard.

"There will be a break soon." Aedan lifted his nose in the air and took in a deep breath.

"At least a few hours. But a hurricane is coming, and we need to move fast or we'll be stuck here for at least a week without food."

Even the weather was working against me. "How far are we from Larsa?" I asked him.

"Not far. But with your injuries it will take at least a day."

"Before we go, I need to get back to my pod," I told him calmly, playing along even though I had no intention of returning with him to the capitol of OM. "There are some items I'd like to bring along with me. How far is it from here?"

Aedan's amber gaze was cold.

"There is no pod," he told me.

"There's wreckage…" I began.

"No," he shook his head. "I destroyed what was left of your pod today and everything in it. That's why I was gone for so long. It wasn't as easy as I thought it would be."

It felt as though the ground dropped from under me.

My stomach twisted in knots as mounting fear began to consume me. My mind reeled.

My virtual maps. My tracking device. My remote viewer. Without them, I had no way of finding the others or of telling them I was alive. They were items I needed for my mission. Items that would help me get to Kingdom B.

Gone.

Destroyed.

I could feel the shift inside my body. The tingling

sensation. The subtle stirring of an ancient creature awakening from hibernation. If I flickered—it would be over. I put my fingertips together and pressed in, forcing my energy to balance itself out—moving it through my body the way the Elders taught us until the harmony was restored. After a second, I was back to myself.

I could feel him watching me.

"How could you destroy my pod?" I was finally able to look at him.

"It had to be done," Aedan's response was fast as his gaze moved over my face distrustfully. I knew he thought my behavior was suspicious.

"You had no right." I kept my voice even, trying to remain calm. But I knew why he had done it, and why he believed it was necessary. But he robbed me of my only way to Kingdom B and at that moment, I despised him for it.

"I have every right," Aedan returned evenly, his eyes bright as they met mine.

"I will not go to Larsa," I told him and hated how my voice trembled. "*I. Will. Not.*"

"You will," Aedan practically growled.

"They will kill me," I allowed him to see the terror in my eyes as I continued to press my fingers together to keep my fear from taking over.

"If your story is true, you have nothing to worry about," Aedan's demeanor softened. "We will eventually return you to your Kingdom."

Eventually.

But my story was one big lie.

"I'm exhausted," I said quietly. I'd had enough. "I think I need to lie down again."

I moved back to my makeshift mat and fought the waves

of panic. I had to find another way to Kingdom B, but at that moment, I didn't know how it would even be possible.

I tried to shake the gloom that came over me, but my future had never looked so bleak.

ØØØ

"I can walk."

"It'll be faster if I carry you through this terrain," he said curtly.

Within a second, I was cradled up in his arms as he navigated through many felled trees. I was irritated he insisted on carrying me like a child, but it was true I was injured and would probably only slow us down. The benefit was I got to observe my surroundings. And even though with every step he took, I was getting closer to the city of Larsa and whatever fate awaited me there with the people of OM, I was still in awe. This was the most beautiful live canvas I had ever seen.

This was Earth.

The colors were not as vibrant and full of life as they were on the planet I grew up on, but nevertheless, it was a sight to behold. The ground was filled with twigs, leaves, and fallen branches. The tree trunks were a rich brown, the leaves glittered from rainfall, the moist air was heaven to breathe in. As far up as I looked I could only see massive trees, but I knew a blue or grey sky awaited me once we reached a clearing.

I knew from my studies the topography of Kingdom OM was diverse. They had valleys, mountains, forests, beaches, swamps, and desert. Their Kingdom had taken over Cetacean land after the massacre, so they had the best of everything. I could understand why they were worried the other breeds would try to encroach.

Aedan tightened his grip on my body. I was embarrassed to be in his arms again.

"I can walk," I tried to put up a fight. He picked up his pace, acting as though my added weight wasn't a burden.

"We're racing against the storm now," he told me. "I need to make sure we go a certain distance before night falls."

I looked up and could only see his angular jaw and neck. "I'm too heavy for you to carry all this way," I continued.

"You don't weight anything," he replied. "I've carried a lot more and for a greater distance."

I didn't doubt he could. He was a force to be reckoned with.

"And you're still recovering," he went on. "Your body needs a break right now."

Maybe he was right. But still, I had never relied on someone besides my mother for help, and it was hard to accept. I was taught to be self-sufficient.

"Thank you," I finally managed.

"You're welcome."

"I mean," I went on so he wouldn't think I was ungrateful for all his help. I might not like his Breed, but I was appreciative. "Thank you—for everything. For saving me. And...and for sheltering me. And giving me your banana."

That gave him pause. He met my gaze.

It was the first time I saw him smile.

I didn't know how to react to the sight, but I could feel myself blush.

"What?" I asked unsure if I said something wrong.

He laughed. "No one has ever thanked me for a banana before."

I had to look away. An Aedan who smiled and laughed was a lethal combination. He was too suspicious. Too smart. I wondered if this would be the way I reacted with all the males I encountered. Would they all have the same qualities?

The thought made my stomach sink in dread.

I thought about the others: Jana, Delphine, and Kalypso. I wondered if they had landed safely. If they were already within the walls of Kingdom B as planned. If they were okay.

Most importantly, if they were alive.

"What are you thinking about?" Aedan asked as he studied my face.

"Home," I said.

Aedan's eyes clouded over. The moment of smiles and laughter quickly gone. "Do you have family that will be searching for you?"

"No family," I assured him. "My father…he died when I was just a baby. I have no memory of him. And my mother…"

I knew my voice trembled, but I couldn't help it. My mother's sudden passing was a devastating blow. She had not been there to see me off on my mission. To reassure me. And now she was truly lost to me.

"Siren?" Aedan asked softly.

I looked up at him. I knew he saw the tears that threatened to spill. I felt a deep sadness every time I thought about my mother, and I was grateful it did not trigger my Shadow.

"I'm sorry." His gaze was filled with empathy, and it was almost my undoing.

"Me too," I said.

He shifted my body into one of his arms and held it

tightly as his other hand came up to touch my heart.

"Both your parents are alive right in here." His golden gaze burned into my soul. "You know you can talk to her at any time, in any place, and she hears you. It's what I tell myself, and it gives me comfort knowing they're here." An understanding flickered between us. We both lost people we loved. We shared a bond forged in grief.

"I know," I said and despite everything found myself opening up to him. "I just miss her. I miss her voice. Her laugh. The way she would make me feel like everything was going to be okay, even if she didn't even know it would be. And to think she's gone—"

I let my voice trail off. I was surprised I had just said so much to Aedan.

"The longing for those things will never diminish," he told me. "Losing someone never gets easier—somehow you just learn how to move on."

We both remained silent as he picked up his pace.

Speaking about my mother's passing only saddened me. The loneliness I felt after she was gone was unlike anything I had ever known. I always felt different. I was an outsider among the Cetaceans. Instead of playing with the others, I chose my mother's company. I never grew close or created a bond like the other girls all now shared. It never bothered me before, because I had her.

And then I didn't anymore. She was gone. And life would never be the same.

Hours went by and Aedan pushed on like a machine. His strength and perseverance were astounding. He never grew tired. We only took two small breaks during the day, but I felt like they were more for me. His consideration surprised me, and I welcomed the silence between us. It gave me more time to think.

Aedan had destroyed my pod, but I was luckily still wearing a belt on my spacesuit which had a compartment hiding a virtual diary and an emergency location device. With it I could alert the others to where I was, and they could do the same in return. The only problem was it could only be used once before self-destructing. It was seen as an extra precaution, another fail-safe, in order to ensure our protection.

Now, it was my only lifeline. I couldn't use it until I reached the border of Kingdom B. If I set the signal off now, they would know I was alive and in OM. And if they foolishly chose to come after me, I would only be putting them in harm's way. I could not jeopardize our survival.

Mission First, the motto echoed in my mind.

If I had to die finding a way to get to Kingdom B, I would.

Aedan slowed down his pace when we reached a small clearing. The sun was going down, and it was starting to get cold.

"We'll rest here for the evening. We need to start a fire. It's going to get cold very fast and without the caves to shelter us, it will be dangerous," he told me as he came to a stop.

We stood in the center of a small circle of giant trees. He gently placed me down, so I could lean against one and immediately started gathering wood for a fire.

"Let me help you," I said as I started to rise. I was still incredibly sore, and my body hurt but I didn't want to look as though I was taking advantage of his generosity.

Aedan cocked his head to the side as he faced me. I had to crick my neck back to look him in the eyes. "You want the truth?" He asked me.

"Always."

"You look so fragile and weak, I'm afraid you might break in two from the force of the winds coming in late tonight and tomorrow. I need you to save your strength," he explained. "I'm protecting you, Siren."

I had never heard those words before.

But I had also never *needed* protection before. Up until this moment, I had never been in any danger. It was hard to even comprehend the idea of my life being in peril.

"Siren?" Aedan asked curiously as he studied my face. "Are you all right?"

I could only nod.

"It's nothing," I replied after a moment. "Thank you for your kindness, Aedan. I will never forget it." And I meant every word of what I said.

"Another first," he mumbled.

"What is?" I asked.

"No one has ever accused me of being kind." He laughed as he shook his head, turned, and disappeared back into the woods, leaving me alone.

The rumble in the sky jolted me. There was a crackle, a deep moan and then lightening shot across the dusky canvas. I had to stand, even though I didn't have the strength. The sky lit up again, and it was the most amazing sight I had ever seen. I could watch it for hours.

I don't know how long I stood there staring up at the battle taking place up in the heavens. All I knew was it got dark very quickly, and the only light illuminating the small circle came from the lightening. I looked over to where Aedan had disappeared and there was still no sight of him. There was another flash in the sky.

A boom again.

And then the sizzling sound of lightening striking a tree a mere fifty feet away from me. The base of the tree practically exploded, giant slivers of wood flew in every direction, and I could see splintered bark running up its length. The sound was deafening. I jumped back in fear and watched as the fiery sight lit up the small clearing.

The lightening hit again, opposite the tree it struck, and I saw something move from the corner of my eye. Was it the branches swaying? Or my imagination playing tricks on me?

"Aedan?" I called out. I felt nervous. My gaze moved to the right, where the shadow was cast, and nothing was there.

Another crackle. And then I saw the movement again.

It wasn't my imagination or the trees casting a dark light.

It was a man.

He had the palest blue eyes I had ever seen.

They practically beamed out of his dark face. He was medium height and was wearing baggy grey pants and a long-sleeved matching garment. His hair was dark black and cut severely in different lengths, as if he had taken a knife to it and didn't have a mirror. And his skin. His face seemed to glisten like he had been doused in slippery oil, not rain from above.

There was another boom in the sky, and I heard him hiss loudly. Within a second he was a few feet away, giving me a clear view of his features. He had a small nose with wide, large nostrils and lips that were practically non-existent.

He gave off an energy I had never felt before.

Evil.

And I knew.

He was a Reptile.

Chapter Four

I smelled his rancid breath as he leaned in toward me.

"*What are you?*" his voice sounded faint, like he was hissing the words.

I stood deathly still, afraid to move. These humans were the most dangerous of all breeds. According to our lessons, they were the most volatile. They loved to torture, were maniacal and prone to irrational mood swings, but most terrifying, they loved to kill—even their own kind.

And from what Aedan had told me, it was abundantly clear this Reptile was not an invited guest on the land.

"I asked you a question, girl." He hissed again, scrutinizing my features. "You're not OM."

"No," I whispered back.

He stepped closer to me, and I tried not to show my disgust. Or fear.

His smell of rot and decay was overpowering.

"You don't belong here," I said with as much force as I could muster. "You're trespassing." My words angered the Reptile. His eyes turned into tiny slits.

"Oh, but I do," he said as he lifted his nose in the air and inhaled deeply. "Change is the way of the world, girl, and this land is ripe for the taking."

His hand grabbed hold of my hair and jerked my face up toward his. "You smell delicious," he said. "Like something fine to eat."

I tried to pull away but his grip was too tight. "Let me go!"

"Why would I do that?" he asked. "I just caught you."

His tongue slipped out of his mouth and to my horror, it

was long and thin, veering off into a V at the tip like his Reptile ancestors. It was not the flicker of his Shadow. It was his *actual* tongue. He had evolved into something from a nightmare. Had things really changed that much? Had breeds started to *become* their Shadow?

I closed my eyes in disgust when he licked his lips and brought his nose down to my neck.

"I won't share you with the others," he said.

Others.

There was more than one of these hideous monsters. I wondered if Aedan had come upon them and that was why he hadn't come back. I prayed nothing had happened to him.

"Please. Let go of me."

"You asked so nicely," he said as he licked my cheek. "But my mouth is already watering at the thought of having you. So, I'll have to respectfully decline your request."

I didn't wait any longer.

I lifted my leg and kicked him hard in the shin. He was so startled by my reaction, he let me go. I turned around and started running away from him, looking for any weapon I could use.

"Aedan!" I screamed out.

Between the lightening and the rumble of the thunder, I knew the odds of him hearing me were slim, which meant I was on my own. If I had my full strength, I would have been able to move fast and defend myself, but I was still weak. And my body ached from the crash. I didn't get far before the Reptile grabbed hold of my arm and threw me to the ground. He was enraged. His human eyes rolled back, and when they focused on me again, they were the eyes of a Reptile, his pupils slit into thin black lines. Again, it wasn't his Shadow—it was *him.*

"Bitch!" He screamed at me as I fought against him. I could feel my own Shadow struggling to emerge, parts of my body heated up as the tingling in my forehead started to spread. I fought with all my strength. I could not fail my people. I could not betray who I was—even if I was to die. *Arcana. Arcana. Arcana.* I chanted in my mind.

I pictured myself in the ocean, swimming deeply in its belly, far away from it all.

In my weakened state, he was just too strong and straddled me within seconds. The rain came down around us as he pulled my arms high above my head, while his grotesque face bent down to mine. I wished I could disappear into the wet mud.

"I was going to try and be gentle with you," he seethed as his reptilian eyes dilated. "But now when I tear into your skin I want to hear you scream. I want you to watch me eat you alive."

I bucked furiously underneath him, more terrified than I had ever been in my life.

"No!" I screamed.

"I believe I'm going to enjoy this." My fear pleased him.

He finally gave me a full smile, and when he did, I almost fainted. His teeth had been shaved down to resemble tiny daggers in his mouth. I could tell they had been intentionally filed this way to saw into flesh.

Human flesh.

"They say your soul leaves your body right before you die," he said. "They say the gods spare you from agony. From pain. From what I've seen, I don't believe it to be the case. But maybe you'll get lucky."

I closed my eyes and waited for him to rip into my skin.

But it didn't come.

There was a whoosh, a loud guttural cry and then the Reptile's body was lifted off mine and thrown against a tree trunk.

I sat up quickly pushing away from where he had just held me hostage, watching as Aedan threw his head back and roared. The sound vibrated throughout the land and moved through my body until it hummed with electricity. It was the loudest human sound I had ever heard. His Shadow emerged, blending in harmony with his human face until he was a mix of both. His eyes were feral and bright like a lion—the shape of his nose even changed, flattening. He was a startling combination of human and cat.

I watched as his cheekbones shifted up, becoming angular and more pronounced, his jaw subtly growing to make way for the powerful teeth growing right before my eyes. What was even more spectacular to witness—his size, already impressive as a human—but as his Shadow, he grew in power and strength. I had never witnessed something like this before. I had only seen Cetaceans' Shadows take over, but it was nothing like this. Nothing.

He bellowed into the night, an arresting beast mightier than his human counterpart.

I watched him stalk the Reptile the way the great lion he descended from had done in the distant past. He flickered between the two parts that made him whole. He embraced his Shadow. He knew where to hit. What to grab for the kill. Aedan was merciless. Precise.

He had me in awe.

He picked the Reptile up as if he weighed nothing and threw him against another trunk. Aedan's opponent didn't stand a chance as he pummeled him to death, ripping his limbs apart and I stood by and watched.

I should have been horrified by what I saw. The blood. The way Aedan's fury gave him superhuman strength, turning him into an ancient beast—but I wasn't scared like I was with the Reptile.

I didn't try and stop him as I should have, given the laws my people were governed by and the empathy I should have for all life—even one that just tried to take my own. Instead, I felt satisfaction. Like this creature, this Reptile, *deserved* what was happening to him. And I couldn't stop Aedan, because I was *relieved*.

It didn't take long.

The lightening raged on, taking the scene from dark to light, adding to the drama of what I watched. Aedan pushed away from the Reptile's lifeless body. When he stood up, his hands were wet with blood. He looked over at me. The expression on his face was feral, but I also saw satisfaction.

I understood why.

The need to kill.

He moved cautiously towards me, his body trembling with the aftermath of his hunt. He closed his eyes and lifted his head to the sky, roaring into the night, then his Shadow faded away. I didn't hesitate as I ran into his arms. I should've been terrified of him after witnessing what he'd just done, but I wasn't.

Aedan made me feel safe.

He pulled me tight into his embrace as his arms encircled my body.

"Are you okay?" he asked gruffly.

"I'm fine," I whispered. "He…"

Aedan pulled away from me so he could check my body to make sure I wasn't hurt.

"What did he do?" his growl was back. His fury lit up

his eyes—the gold speckles more pronounced.

"He…" my voice broke.

"Tell. Me."

"He wanted to eat me…" I was horrified by the thought and could barely get the words out. Had all the Reptiles turned into cannibals?

Aedan's eyes rounded in shock, but the look was quickly masked and replaced by outrage as he pulled me back into his arms. I held onto him. My protector. He seemed far older than a teenager with a maturity that defied time. A man, who had watched over me, while I was unconscious, had taken care of me, and had saved my life for the second time.

"You saved me. Again."

"Always."

My heart fluttered.

We held on to each other a moment longer, before the silence between us was too loud to ignore. He pulled back a bit, his strong hands moving up to run through my hair. He lifted my face up to his, his palms cupped my cheeks, his gaze burning into me like he could see deep into my soul.

And then his mouth crashed down on mine.

My body reacted instinctively as I pressed myself into him, somehow craving an experience I had never even known.

His lips were soft and gentle as he coaxed mine into responding. My body hummed with warmth. I could feel my Shadow move along the unknown precipice, teasing me to flicker, adding to the excitement of my experience. But I was somehow able to keep her at bay.

Aedan's kiss made me feel alive. And human.

This was intimacy.

This was something I had been denied my whole life.

Something I had only seen in movies or video logs. The instant our lips touched I understood so much. I understood the sadness that would come over my mother's eyes whenever she spoke of my father. I understood the longing I could sense when she talked of her youth. Intimacy between man and woman was an essential part of our DNA. Part of our being. We needed to be touched.

Wanted. To be held. And loved.

I felt as though I gave him a part of my soul with that kiss. And I wondered if I would ever get it back.

We both pulled away at the same time. Aedan leaned his forehead against mine as we took in heavy breaths. We held onto each other for a moment longer.

"We have to go," he whispered against my lips.

I could only nod.

"It's not safe here," he said.

I remembered the Reptile's words. "He said there were more of them."

Aedan's body tensed at my words, the moment between us gone. "Let's go!"

He grabbed ahold of my hand, picked up the bag he had thrown to the ground, and pulled me along through the trees. His entire body was alert. I was in pain, tired, and freezing— but there was no way I would utter any complaint. I wanted to get as far away from the Reptile's lifeless body as possible. And if there were more...

I didn't plan to be around to find out.

ØØØ

It felt like I had just closed my eyes when Aedan nudged me awake.

"It's time," he said.

I nodded and slowly stood up. I stretched out my sore

body and was grateful Aedan left to offer me some privacy. Once I was ready, I walked down the small hill we were perched on.

"Any sign of the other Reptiles?" I asked him.

"None," he shook his head. "They're hiding now, I'm sure of it."

"Or maybe you frightened them, and they went back home?" I asked hopefully.

"Reptiles don't scare easily," Aedan said with a grim smile. "And I imagine they were sent here for a reason. A mission."

I shivered, because I shared a similarity with the Reptiles.

I quietly followed Aedan, founding myself both excited and extremely nervous to see Larsa, the city that housed the inhabitants of Kingdom OM. We moved fast. As the day went on and we drew closer, Aedan became more reserved. We made it safely out of the forest.

I was able to distract my thoughts by enjoying the view. The sky was grey and somber, but the scenery was spectacular. There were fields stretching out to the right and left, intermixed with flat plains and what looked to be cultivated farmlands. The fields were covered with tall blades of grass that made me want to run my hands through them. The only thing I found strange was there were no laborers on what I assumed were farmlands. Since Aedan was quiet and didn't seem to be in the mood for conversation, I thought I'd ask him later.

"We're not far," he said as he finally broke the silence and faced me. He towered over me, his gaze indecipherable.

He stared for a long moment before finally beginning.

"Why didn't you flicker?" His voice was dangerously

soft.

My stomach fell in dread.

"I realized walking here," he went on as I tried to stop myself from reacting. "I've never actually seen you flicker... into a *bird*."

"And?" I returned forcefully, staring him in the eye. Being confident and nonchalant was the only way he'd ever believe me. I couldn't let the gravity of the conversation shake me.

"Why is that?" Aedan cocked his head. "You've been in two life-threatening incidents. A normal reaction—the *assured* reaction would be to flicker into your Shadow."

"Maybe for you." I said the words out loud as a reminder to myself. "But I'm a strong woman. And I don't allow my emotions to *ever* control me—no matter what situation I'm in."

"Spoken like a soldier." Aedan's gaze captured mine. "Lucky you're not one."

"I guess so," I returned evenly, lifting my chin in defiance. He held my gaze as he continued.

"Things will be different when we enter the city. I don't know how my people will react when they see you. They'll know you're not one of us."

A feeling of foreboding raced down my spine as I pressed my fingers together. Calming myself.

"I anticipated as much," I said, pleading again. "Which is why I wish you'd let me return to Kingdom B."

"You just experienced one of many reasons why it isn't safe to trek through the land alone."

I hated that he was right. There could be more Reptiles out there. And I was unarmed, still weak from the crash, and I didn't even have a way to find Kingdom B.

"When will it be possible?" I asked pointedly. "When will I be able to go home?"

"When I say," he said with a shrug.

"I have a right to know what will become of me once I'm inside your walls," I said as I met his shrewd gaze.

Aedan took a step toward me.

"Once you're refreshed and checked out in med lab, we'll discuss returning you to your Kingdom," his eyes remained on mine. "And the rest of your story."

I found it hard to believe this was the same man who had been so compassionate before. He seemed colder now, impossibly distant, like he was putting a wedge between any friendship we had forged. And I didn't understand why.

"There's another thing," He said.

"Yes?"

Aedan looked over my shoulder as if he were searching for the right words.

"What happened between us—"

I could feel my face turn red.

"Look at me, Siren," he said quietly.

I did. His gaze was fierce.

"It was a mistake for so many reasons," to my mortification, he went on. "I think you know it as well as I do."

I could only nod.

"And there's something else…"

I fought an unfamiliar feeling of nausea that was quickly overwhelming me as I waited for Aedan to explain. The awkward silence stretched on before he spoke.

"There is someone in my life. Her name is Kali."

I felt as though the ground dropped under my feet, and I had no real bearing.

"She's not just anyone," he went on. "She's my intended mate."

He was bound to someone. Promised. And he had given me my first kiss. My first experience with human contact.

"I think we were both overcome," he went on uncomfortably. He was having as hard a time speaking the words as I was hearing them. "You thought you were going to die. I was enraged at the Reptiles. Seeing them on our land and hurting you, I succumbed to something that is not only immoral but forbidden. I take full responsibility. It was wrong. *I* was wrong to do it."

I allowed his words to sink in. I found a strange sense of peace knowing he had integrity. Though I had no experience, maybe he was right. It was just an adrenaline fueled moment that caused a foolish choice.

After a while, I realized I hadn't said one word.

"I won't allow you to take all the blame," I said to him and tried to act as though I was unaffected by what had happened between us. "And you're right. It was a moment— that's all it was. We never have to speak of it again. Your... your intended mate never has to know. As far as I'm concerned, it didn't happen."

Except it had.

I found my humanity in his kiss.

Chapter Five

We approached a giant metal wall that enclosed the city of Larsa.

From the recordings I saw on Akasha I knew the other kingdoms didn't have such a fortress of protection. But then, they didn't possess the most desired land on Earth.

Aedan made his way to what I assumed was the main entrance.

Within the shiny metal sheen of the doors were emblems of all the mammals their Soul Particles descended from: a lion, gorilla, tiger, wolf, elephant, polar bear, and a horse.

As much as the conversation with Aedan was still replaying in my head, I had bigger things to worry about. How would I be able to find a way to reach Kingdom B without being discovered or worse, killed, when I would be trapped within OM's walls?

He looked over at me. "Are you ready?"

"Yes."

"Stay by my side and avoid any eye contact." I was irritated by Aedan's edict. I believed avoiding eye contact was a sign of weakness, and now I had no choice but to listen to his command.

"They will have questions," Aedan continued, "and I'll address them all when I appear in front of the Assembly."

"Assembly?" I asked.

"I'll explain later," he said in a dismissive tone leaving me no choice but to wait.

Aedan walked up to the doors and placed both palms on the metal. I watched as it lit up to a bright tan color that resembled the shade of his eyes.

"Cellular recognition complete." A robotic voice echoed as the massive doors slowly slid open. While we waited to walk through the entrance, I closed my eyes. *Arcana.*

My Shadow would lie dormant. It would not fail me.

As I opened my eyes I had my first glimpse of human city life. This was Kingdom OM.

There was a long metal bridge about ten feet wide, suspended in the air, above what looked to be a meteor crater. The walkway was over half a mile long. Faint noises came from everyday life. I had seen pictures and some video images of each Kingdom, and still, it didn't prepare me for the world in front of me.

With Earth's population declining, Kingdom OM's was down to around fifty thousand and continuing to drop. But for a Breed with only eleven of its people left in the entire universe, it seemed like an endless sea of life.

The city was a sprawling dichotomy of modern and what I viewed as archaic architecture. There were four metallic skyscrapers that looked to be over fifty floors high and leaned in toward one another to create the tip of an ancient pyramid. At the very top, an enormous lapis colored stone sat connecting the buildings. The giant sheets of platinum on the four buildings reflected the light from the sky above as well as the streets below. The roads were clean and made up of dirt and gravel. Where our mode of transportation on Akasha was the pod, similar to the one I came to Earth in, OM's was much more rudimentary. Their vehicles were circular and hovered a mere two feet off the ground as they made their way through the wide streets. Hundreds of people were walking by the roads, crowding the sidewalks, as they went about their business.

The ones who flickered into their Shadows took me by

surprise, and I knew it would take some time to adjust. The citizens of OM were known to be a passionate Breed, so I suspected I'd have to get used to it fast. When I could finally pull my eyes away from seeing both human and their animal Shadows walking among each other—really just seeing so many humans at once—I was able to admire the rest.

The city was pristine. Extraordinarily clean. I could see soldiers dressed in dark brown leather pants and tight long sleeved shirts, similar to what Aedan was wearing, stationed at almost every block, scanning the day-to-day activity of its citizens.

Each one was fully armed.

From what I learned, the socioeconomic breakdown of OM was made of three classes. More than half were laborers, either farmers or soldiers. There were those who worked in the government, which only consisted of a small percentage. And then there were the scientists who were constantly looking for ways to produce higher quality synthetic meat and innovative ways to cultivate the land for sustenance without animal life on Earth.

There was a resounding thud as the doors slid shut behind us.

"Welcome back, Praetor," a voice to our right said.

Praetor, I knew from my studies, was Latin for leader.

The man who called out to Aedan was as tall as he was. He had short cropped black hair and eyes that were yellow. On his thick, muscled arm I could see a tattoo of a tiger. He walked over to us from a catwalk that was perpendicular to the bridge, leaving a group of what I assumed were Aedan's soldiers guarding the entrance to the city.

He moved as quietly as Aedan.

I did as I was told, even though I wanted to do the

opposite and averted my eyes when he drew near. The two men loomed over me, and I could feel the stranger's eyes on me.

"Cyrus," Aedan stated in greeting.

"You took longer than anticipated. We were close to sending a search party out for you," he said to Aedan. "Your General was the one to stop me."

"The decision was a wise one," Aedan said. "As you can see, I'm in one piece."

"You brought something back with you."

"I did," Aedan replied.

"A Reptile?"

"No."

If I had feathers they would have ruffled at the audacity of the two speaking about me as if I wasn't there. I purposefully stared down at my hands to try and distract myself.

"An *Other*?" Cyrus asked.

"Yes."

I tried to remain quiet but it was becoming difficult.

"Did she tell you her Breed?"

"She did."

"What is she?"

"Not here, Cyrus," Aedan told him, his voice sounded exhausted. "I'll explain later."

Even though I kept my eyes down, I could feel Cyrus's penetrating gaze.

"Does she have a name?" Cyrus continued to talk about me as if I was invisible.

I had enough. Before Aedan could answer, I did.

"Siren," I replied, looking up at Cyrus. "*Her* name is Siren."

I could hear Aedan's low growl, and I knew he was angry. I'd gone against his orders. But I didn't care. Cyrus's gaze met mine. I watched his eyes round in surprise, the yellow becoming impossibly brighter, as he took a step closer to smell me the same way Aedan had back in the caves of the Ancient Dwellers.

"Enough!" Aedan roared.

Cyrus stopped.

"We go, Cyrus," he said curtly. "Now!"

Cyrus bent his head in obedience and fell into step with us. I was now sandwiched between the two giants. If I had any fear or doubt before, it had just multiplied by a thousand. How was I going to do this? I was in a land I didn't know, with people who had slaughtered almost my entire Breed. I took in a deep breath, attempting to soothe myself as best I could.

Crossing the bridge, the two remained completely silent.

As we drew near the end, I got a better view of the smaller buildings past the city center square. The architecture was simple. Each structure was either one or two stories, made up mostly of glass and stone, allowing natural sunlight in.

I could see a marketplace where goods and food were sold. The women and men wore bright colors, but their clothing was simple. The females donned long tunics that were open in the front to reveal tight tops, exposed bare midriffs, and fitted leather pants, coupled with flat knee-high boots. All the outfits were monochromatic, but together it was like a kaleidoscope of color. The men were dressed in leather pants and either short or long sleeved fitted tops. I was amazed at how athletic the people of OM were. I knew they took pride in their bodies and were conditioned to always be in their best shape. They were a mix of ethnicities, different races and colors, and yet, they shared one similarity —they were all descendants of the *Other Mammals*. A bond that would unite them against any foreigner until the day they died. This was what one-fourth of the human civilization looked like. I couldn't help but be impressed and in awe.

We reached the main road. Two circular vehicles pulled up before us, hovering slightly in the air. The doors to both slid open, and I could see they were computer controlled. Aedan ushered me inside one. Cyrus went in the other.

As soon as the door shut and we were alone, he turned to me in displeasure.

"I gave you orders!" he said roughly, looking suspiciously like his Shadow was about to emerge, his body quivering.

"I know. But I'm not accustomed to following…"

"Your Kingdom doesn't have laws?" He all but growled, interrupting me.

"Of course…"

"Do you not obey them?"

"Yes, but…" He wouldn't let me get a word in.

"No!" Aedan's thunderous voice rang through the vehicle. "While you are a guest in *my* land, you will follow *my* orders."

"You sound like a despot…" I couldn't stop myself. Surely his fury was unwarranted.

But as I looked up into his eyes, I saw anger there, and I immediately shrank.. He didn't appreciate my words. He moved fast. In a second he had my chin in his hands, pulling my face roughly toward his.

"You are an outsider, Siren," he began in a controlled

voice. "What I demand of you is for your own protection. It's not for some sadistic pleasure, as you might believe. It's for your own good. Do you understand me?"

I was no damsel in distress, and I didn't fundamentally agree with him but I understood. It took all my willpower to keep my mouth shut and not argue my point. I could barely manage a nod, before he let go of my chin and moved to the opposite side of the leather seat.

"We're going to my home," he told me.

I chose to remain silent. The last thing I wanted to do was provoke him even more because his energy felt volatile. Instead, I stared blindly out the window and waited. I had to be smart. He was my only ally here and the key to safe passage within the city and eventually out. The vehicle moved quickly through the streets, taking fast turns, and winding its way along another road.

Within a few minutes we began to ascend a small hill. I watched as an impressive but ancient looking structure began to take shape. The center was designed like the Great Pyramids of Giza with golden colored limestone that was sanded down perfectly. Four limestone towers flanked the sides and a tall, fortified wall offered privacy.

The arched entrance was guarded by soldiers, who nodded in approval as we passed through. We entered a round, pebbled atrium where the vehicle came to a stop.

"We're here."

The doors opened and Aedan helped me out.

I looked around his home and wondered if I would remain here or if he would take me someplace else. Once my feet touched the ground, the doors closed, and the vehicle shutdown, remaining where it was. Within moments the atrium was alive with activity. Aedan's servants rushed down the wide marble steps that led inside the building. There were five in all and each held something their Praetor might need: wet cloths, a clean shirt, pitchers of water, a platter of fruit and synthetic meat.

Aedan approached and took what they offered. I stood where I was and watched how each bowed their heads in obedience to him. They avoided eye contact and were careful to stand utterly still. I heard Cyrus's vehicle enter the atrium, then he came to stand next to me.

Aedan turned to me and held out a goblet of fresh water.

I stepped forward. "Thank you," I said.

I drank all the water, and he offered me more, which I gladly took. My gaze moved over the servants, and I was taken aback by the unmasked hostility radiating from their eyes. They did *nothing* to hide their feelings. One even flickered, and his elephant Shadow emerged in anger, his energy aggressive before becoming human again. I put the goblet down on the tray and stood my ground. I met their looks dead-on, ready for whatever came my way. If this was a taste of what my stay would be like, it would not be easy.

If Aedan noticed, he gave nothing away. When he was finished the servants stepped aside, and he motioned for me to follow him up the stairs and into his home.

But before I could move three vehicles swerved into the atrium and came to an abrupt stop. Twelve imposing looking soldiers quickly exited the vehicles. They fell in-line behind a man who looked as though he was made of steel. He had tawny colored hair and was not as tall as Aedan or Cyrus but looked just as lethal. He moved with power, fixing his cold gaze on mine as he walked toward me with purpose. I shivered in fear. His dark brown eyes radiated his hate, and I couldn't stop myself from taking a step back when he reached me.

The guards stopped behind him in unison as his gaze slowly moved from my feet to the top of my head. "You bring an *Other* into the Kingdom?" His voice rumbled with rage.

Aedan and Cyrus moved to flank my sides.

"It doesn't concern you, Milo." Aedan's voice was cold.

"An *Other* in OM is *all* of our concern," Milo's gaze narrowed dangerously.

"You forget yourself." Aedan growled in a voice that vibrated in power.

"Do *I*?" Milo returned ominously.

Tension radiated from Aedan's body. I could sense there was something deeper between them. It was more than evident that they hated one another.

"What is this thing?" Milo finally bit out.

"As I stated, *she* is none of your concern," Aedan returned with warning.

Milo's brown eyes began to glow ominously. Half his face flickered into his Shadow—a powerful, but menacing silverback gorilla. "I have a right—"

"In the Assembly room you have a right," Aedan did not lose his cool. "Not outside."

"You overstep your power," Milo sneered.

"I overstep nothing," Aedan returned.

Milo finally shook his head and smiled before fixing his gaze on mine.

"We shall see about that. I'll see you in the Assembly room," he spun around and walked back to the awaiting vehicles. Aedan didn't relax his stance until the soldiers left the atrium.

Once they were gone, he looked at me with an

inscrutable gaze. "Let's go inside."

He walked up the stairs, and I followed, trying to calm my fear but it was nearly impossible. Luckily I was able to keep my Shadow in check. Milo's threats had thrown me, and the danger of my situation hit me hard. I wasn't welcome in OM. If Aedan couldn't or chose not to protect me, my life would be in peril. We walked through another set of tall archways into the largest indoor space I had ever seen. The ceilings were at least thirty feet high, and the limestone ground practically sparkled like a precious metal.

"This is the Great Hall," Aedan explained.

I could see how it got its name. The furnishings were sparse but looked incredibly comfortable. There were long white couches across from massive thick wooden tables and huge arched windows flanked by light linen curtains. There were beautiful exotic looking plants and flowers, creating an ambience of serenity. Thick wax candles in human sized candelabras were stationed at every archway, ready to be lit.

Four different stone spiral staircases were situated in opposing areas of the vast hall.

"Welcome home, Praetor."

A beautiful woman, with caramel colored skin, made her way over to us. She had long, black hair that fell past her shoulders. Her eyes were wide, the color of emeralds. She was dressed in tan colored leather pants, with a small top that accentuated her physique. I could see a tattoo of the face of a wolf peeking out from under her top. She gave Aedan a wide smile, showing perfect white teeth. I was beyond self-conscious about my own appearance.

I wondered if this was Kali, his intended mate.

"All is well?" Aedan asked.

"As well as can be expected," she returned.

Cyrus and I stood a step behind Aedan and waited. He turned and motioned for me to come forward. Cyrus remained where he was.

"General Canis, this is Siren," Aedan said.

Not Kali. I felt immensely relieved.

"Siren will be staying here as my guest," Aedan informed her. I was grateful I would be staying close to him, since he was the only person I knew.

General Canis's eyes slowly moved over my body.

"Siren," Aedan said. "This is my General."

Her gaze whipped back to Aedan's, and I saw the look she gave him. The same that Cyrus had. *What is she?*

"Later, Bibi," he told her tiredly. "She needs med lab and a room to clean up in. I will call the Assembly together tonight."

General Canis nodded. Aedan's continued reference of the Assembly had me on edge. I assumed they were part of OM's governing body, but I didn't know what their role was, or what power they had over the young leader.

"Will she be in attendance?" General Canis asked curiously.

"Not yet."

"Does Kali know you've returned?" Aedan looked over at Cyrus who asked the question.

I avoided looking at Aedan when I heard her name.

"She will," he replied. I felt his gaze rest on me and I shifted uncomfortably.

"Siren, please go with General Canis," he told me. "She will see to your comfort."

"And then?" I asked thinking of Milo and the Assembly.

"We'll deal with each situation as it comes," he told me. "In the meantime, go and rest. You need it. I offer you my protection. You're safe here."

He held my gaze for a moment longer, then looked over at Cyrus.

"A word?" Aedan commanded.

I watched the two men leave the hall and felt a wave of panic. He left me alone.

"Come with me," General Canis said coolly.

Her eyes met mine, and I was sure she could see my uncertainty.

"If the Praetor has assured your safety there is nothing for you to fear," she said as if she could read my mind. "Now, come. First you'll bathe and freshen up and then I'll take you to med lab."

"Thank you."

"You can thank the Praetor." Her voice was sharp.

I nodded.

"Follow me," she commanded.

She took me the opposite direction Aedan and Cyrus had just gone and up a staircase. There were only ten or so steps before we reached a long, wide hallway flanked by arched windows looking out into the Kingdom. General Canis moved fast, I had no time to stop and stare out at the view. The only thing I did notice were the obsidian black clouds forming ominously in the backdrop of the city. It was the storm Aedan had mentioned earlier.

The General paused briefly to look out at the horizon.

"She is a furious one," she said, referring to the storm. "And another will hit right after."

"Another?" I was relieved we weren't caught out there.

"They usually come in pairs," General Canis explained. "We called all the farmers in early just in case it reached us faster than anticipated. These days, one can never tell."

That explained the empty fields.

"Haven't you seen a storm like this before?" General Canis asked curiously.

"Not this close," I lied easily. I'd *never* seen a storm like this before.

"Then you're in for a surprise," she said.

"Are they a normal occurrence?" I wondered what the ramifications would be for the city.

"They have been for the past few years," she told me. "We take extra precautions with our people, ensuring none are caught outside the city walls—which always remain closed until the storm passes."

That meant I would be a prisoner inside Larsa until the weather calmed. I could only hope it would be quick. "Can the city withstand it?" I asked quietly.

"We've fortified it with a drainage system that can withstand higher category storms. The excess water will rush into the meteor crater you saw when you entered the city preventing any floods," General Canis told me. "We are safe."

She turned away and continued walking down the hall, then stopped abruptly.

"But you never know," she said without looking at me. "Is *anyone* really ever safe on Earth today?" She started walking again—her message loud and clear. The General did not want me to get too comfortable.

I followed behind quietly.

She reached a set of thick, wide wooden doors and turned the brass handle to open one of them. We stepped inside.

The room was pleasing. And nothing like the one I had back at home. A giant bed rested against one sleek limestone wall. It was two feet off the ground, with beige covers made of linen. Across from the bed was a sitting area in front of a fireplace so big I could probably stand inside, with two couches and a round wooden table that were just as close to the ground as the bed was.

I stared at the fireplace in longing.

"Would you like me to have it lit?" General Canis asked to my surprise.

I gave her an embarrassed smile. "Only if it's not an inconvenience," I said.

"It is not."

General Canis walked to the center of the bedroom and motioned toward a hallway.

"This way," she told me.

I was in awe of the room and wanted to take it all in, but the General looked like she didn't want to spend more time with me than necessary. I followed her down another narrow hall that led into a modern bathroom with a giant sunken round pool. It could have fit at least twenty people. There were ten running fountains cascading into the pool, creating a tranquil effect, and a long vanity with floor length mirrors hung opposite the pool. It all looked out on a panoramic view of the cultivated fields. Thick glass windows shielded the room from the elements outside.

"You'll find all the amenities you need here," she pointed toward the vanity, which was lined with various luxuries.

I watched her scrutinize my body. Like she was sizing me up.

"I'll return in an hour with clean clothes for you to wear."

"Thank you," I said.

"Again, thank the Praetor," she said curtly.

"Then please extend my thanks to the Praetor," I return in a cool voice. If I was to be treated with animosity by every citizen I encountered, then I would return the favor.

General Canis lifted a surprised brow before nodding curtly.

"I'll have refreshments brought up and placed in the other room," she said. "Don't be alarmed if you hear any noise, it will be the servants bringing your items."

General Canis walked over to a wall and placed her hand over an electronic panel. The lights went on but were dim. And then she left me all alone. I took in a deep breath and tried to relax. But it proved to be a difficult task. I was in OM, trapped within its city walls and surrounded by a dangerous Breed I thought I'd never lay eyes on. I had no way of knowing what would become of me.

And I was all alone.

One Cetacean among a den of wolves.

The sound of the water flowing into the pool distracted me from my turbulent thoughts. I couldn't wait to clean myself up.

"Now or never, Siren," I said out loud as I made my way over to the floor length mirror to finally get a good look at my appearance. It took everything I had not to scream.

I was unrecognizable.

There was enough grime on my face I could have camouflaged myself in the ground and hidden among the elements, and been completely safe. My brown hair was matted to my head with grease and dirt, the color hardly distinguishable.

The material on the legs of my grey atmospheric suit was covered with tears and filth. Even with all the dirt covering my body, I looked gaunt. I could tell I had lost weight in the past four days, my frame looked slight and fragile. I knew why Aedan was so worried about me keeping up with him. Had I seen myself, I would have been worried as well.

My hands moved to the thick black belt at my waist—holding the only things I had left from Akasha. It was a start. I unbuckled the belt carefully and placed it on the vanity. I would have to make sure it was with me at all times. I couldn't risk losing it.

I slowly unzipped my suit and stepped out of the offensive, filthy material. There were purple bruises all over my chest and waist from where the belt buckle had dug into my body when I crashed. I had giant black welts on my legs and around my ribs. It looked as though I had almost been beaten to death.

My body was softer than the women of OM, but I was still fit and lean from all the martial arts training on Akasha. I was strong enough to survive. I turned away from the mirror and stepped into the saltwater pool. It was about five feet deep, and the water was warm and felt good against my skin. I dunked my head in the water, grabbed the bar of soap, and started scrubbing the four-day journey off my skin. It took some time, but, I finally felt clean.

I dunked my body underwater and sank to the ground of the pool. I crossed my legs and put my hands on my knees attempting to do my underwater meditation as I always did back home whenever I needed to get my thoughts under control. It was one of my favorite Cetacean attributes—the ability to stay under water for almost an hour at a time. I found my time in the water my most peaceful. There was a silence around me that crawled into my body and bones and calmed everything. Every muscle. Every thought. Every fiber of my being. I felt closest to my Shadow in the water. I was whole.

I imagined I was back in Akasha, in my bedroom deep in meditation. The house I had shared with my mother was warm and safe. My ancestors had landed there with limited supplies, but given their knowledge, they found one area of the planet that would sustain them and built a small community that rivaled one on Earth. Our village was hidden among the giant trees, close to a small lake we used for sustenance. Our climate had two seasons. Winter and spring. The planet was kind to us. It had sheltered and protected us. But it still wasn't Earth.

If Aedan had looked in on my life, he would have found it idyllic. There was never any worry of an attack from another Kingdom, never anything scarce—

But it was an existence. Not a life.

It was by luck I heard the shout.

"Siren?" I shot up out of the water to see the General hovering over the pool.

"I've been calling you over and over."

"Sorry," I smiled awkwardly. "I didn't hear you."

"How long were you underwater?"

"Not long," I shrugged.

"*How long*?" The General persisted.

"Just a few minutes." I tried to look bored by her question.

General Canis continued to stare suspiciously. Human-Bird hybrids were not known for their underwater prowess, but some were able to stay under for a small amount of time.

"The servants found you clothes," she said after a moment. She pointed at the vanity. "There is a nightdress and day clothes. Depending on what the Assembly and the Praetor decides to do with you, we'll see about getting you more."

The General made sure there was no mistaking the precarious situation I was in.

"Perfect," I said evenly as I sunk low into the pool to hide my nudity. "I'm sure what you brought is plenty."

She ignored my comment and held out a towel for me— my cue that bathing time was over. She politely looked away when I walked out and took the towel from her. I quickly wrapped it around my body and faced her.

She looked down at the black welts on my calves, then chest.

"Are you in pain?" She asked to my surprise. I didn't think she would care.

"It looks worse than it is," I told her. "I'm really feeling much better. I think that bath did wonders."

"I'll take you to med lab tonight."

"I promise, there's really no need to." I rushed out. "And I'm just so tired…"

"Then we'll go in the morning."

"We can reassess in the morning," I agreed to placate her, even though I had no intention of stepping foot in their med lab.

I held onto the towel with one hand and brushed my hair back from my face with the other, all while General Canis continued to scrutinize me.

"Since it is late, Praetor would like you to have dinner in your room tonight." She looked me up and down and shook her head as if she disapproved of what she saw. "Alone."

I tried not to be hurt by his request. It felt cold. And dismissive.

"That sounds perfect," I gave her a forced smile. "My body could use the rest."

General Canis sat down on a backless small couch and crossed her arms. "Are you going to put some clothes on? Or must I wait here all day?"

Clearly, the people of Kingdom OM were not shy about nudity. My mother had not seen me nude since I was a small child, and now, a perfect stranger would.

I walked toward the vanity and found a brush and quickly worked the knots out of my hair. My long, brown locks were soon smooth and straight down to the middle of my back. My blue eyes were slowly coming back to life, and I was starting to feel like myself again. I looked over at the pile of sapphire colored clothes and picked up a long tunic that was separate from the matching leather pants and shirts.

"That's a nightdress," the General informed me.

I let my towel go and slipped it on as fast as I could. It was huge on me and fell off my shoulders and went to my knees.

"What did they do to you?" General Canis cried in outrage.

I thought she was referring to the welts from my crash.

"The bruises?" I asked.

"No!" she stood up and flickered into her wolf Shadow, rushing toward me, before she could gain control. She pulled down the left side of my nightgown and pointed to the three gashes down the side of my shoulders. I hadn't even seen those. Or felt them.

I saw a quick flash of the malicious Reptile who had wrestled me to the ground. I blinked the image away.

"It's nothing…"

General Canis lowered her nose to the mark and took in

a breath.

"Reptile," she growled in fury, her eyes glowing like her canine ancestor.

"I was attacked..." I rushed out thinking she believed I was one.

"Praetor," the General said in a low voice. "*Aedan*...he is not only my leader, but my best friend. We would die for one another. There are no secrets between us."

He told her about me.

"I know it all," General Canis said as if she read my mind. "He told me you fell from the sky. That you say you're from Kingdom B."

In a way, I was relieved she knew. Though my interaction with the General was limited, I respected her. There was something refreshing about her no nonsense demeanor. And like Aedan, her aura was golden, indicating she was honest. True, she had only seen to my comfort per her Praetor's request, but she had been considerate enough, when she could've been the opposite.

More importantly, if she was Aedan's best friend, I trusted her.

"Do the others know about my pod?" I asked.

"No," she said flatly. "And they can never know, or your life will be in danger no matter if you have the Praetor's protection or not. Aedan and I both agree the pod is an added element to your story that's both intriguing and alarming."

"Alarming?" I asked.

"The technology of your Kingdom," General Canis's voice was grim. "If you have made such advancements, it only begs the question of what else you might have that could possibly put OM at a disadvantage." They wanted to know if Kingdom B posed the same danger as Kingdom R.

What I believed to have been a small lie, could now turn into a dire political situation for an innocent Kingdom. I had to find a way to ease Aedan and the General's mind.

"You don't have to worry," I said. "My people—we're not like the Reptiles."

The General reached out and took a few strands of my brown hair in between her fingers.

"Unless of course, you are not who you say you are."

"I am from Kingdom B." My gaze met hers in the mirror. The General was suspicious, and frankly, I couldn't blame her.

"Ready for dinner?" She inquired.

I could only nod. I followed her back to the main room, where the fire was now blazing, and a tray of food had been set out on the table.

"I hope you'll find the meal satisfactory," she said.

"It looks wonderful," I replied as I stared at the colorful array of food. General Canis walked over to the mantel above the fireplace and grabbed a small metallic square object. She placed her palm on top of it, and a 3D holographic screen appeared opposite me on the couch. It was a virtual television, playing old footage of when the animals had roamed the Earth. I had seen similar clips like this back home.

"This should suffice," she said as she placed the remote back on the mantel. "The monitor senses your body movement and will listen to your command to shut off and turn on."

General Canis walked to the door and paused. "As I'm sure you're quite aware, you're forbidden to leave the room under any circumstances. Should you need anything place your hand over the silver panel by the bed, and I will be here as fast as I can."

"And Aedan?" I asked.

"What about him?" The General's guard went up.

I felt embarrassed asking, but he was familiar and safe—all I knew here on Earth.

"Will I see him?"

"Eventually."

My stomach sank. I needed to know what this Assembly would do with me. I had to figure out the next steps in my plan. My mission was all that mattered.

"I'm sure you have more important things to do than babysit me." I said, trying to keep the disappointment out of my voice.

"Actually, you're wrong," General Canis said to my surprise. "This situation is high on my priority list right now."

I was a situation.

"Sleep well, Siren." The General nodded curtly and left the room. I could hear the door lock behind her.

There was no mistaking the action—I was now a prisoner of OM.

CHAPTER SIX

I woke up in the dead of the night to the sound of the storm raging outside.

Rain pelted against the thick windows with fury, mirroring the emotions raging inside my soul. I got out of bed and stared out into the dark night, trying to make out an image of the fierce storm, but it was impossible. I turned away and stared at the doors to my room. I knew they were locked. I was still a prisoner. But I would not remain helpless.

I needed to find an advantage.

I looked over at the tray of half-eaten food, and an idea quickly formed. I grabbed the knife from my plate and made my way back to the lock, hoping there was a way I could somehow pick it open. Minutes went by as I tried to figure out a way to break free. I was so consumed with my project that when a strong hand grabbed hold of my shoulder, I couldn't stop myself from crying out. Jumping in fear, I quickly spun around, and aimed the small weapon at my would be assailant.

It was Aedan.

The knife I held was directed at his throat. I took in a deep, shaky breath as we stared at one another.

"Trouble sleeping?" He asked before grabbing hold of my hand and taking the weapon away from me.

"What are you doing in here?" I was unnerved to find him standing in my room.

"I heard noises," he said crossing his arms. "I wanted to make sure you were all right."

Since I couldn't deny what I was trying to do, I chose to

own my deed.

"I don't appreciate the lock on my door."

"You are a victim of circumstance," he replied in a low, unapologetic voice.

"I am not a victim," my voice was hard.

I saw a glimmer of admiration in his eyes, but he quickly masked it.

"Still," he cocked his head. "The lock remains. And this knife won't set you free."

I looked away from him, suddenly feeling foolish and completely deflated. I became acutely aware he wasn't wearing a shirt again. Only a pair of loose fitting pants made of the same material as my thin nightgown. Needing space, I moved away from him.

"Did I wake the whole compound?" I asked, making my way to the bed. I could feel his eyes on my back, and it unnerved me in a way I didn't understand. I got in bed and drew the blanket up to cover my body.

"My room is on the other side of this wall so I heard you," he said, following me to the edge of the bed. He seemed agitated, his moods shifting from one second to the next.

"How did you get in here?" I asked.

He pointed toward a secret panel I hadn't bothered to notice—it was wide open and led down a dark hall. I could see a light at the end.

"I thought it best if I was close," he sounded unapologetic. "My room is the only one with this access."

"Is this where you always keep your prisoners?" I wasn't angry. I just wanted to know where I stood. I wanted to hear him say it.

"If that's the way you want to look at your time here,"

Aedan replied carefully.

"How long will that time be? Is my life in danger?"

He glared at me. "I find your last question offensive, I gave you my word. I have assured your safety."

"That's not the picture your General painted," I snapped out.

"Bibi tends to err on the side of caution," he said with a shrug. "It's her job."

"You didn't answer my first question," I prodded.

"You'll stay here as long as I say."

"Convenient," I smirked before pushing for more. "And the Assembly?"

"What about it?" Aedan asked as he crossed his arms.

"I can only assume they'll be part of making the decision in my circumstance here."

"They will," Aedan's voice was even, his eyes betraying nothing. "But I'm still the Praetor of OM."

His words gave me little reassurance.

I must have missed something in my studies of the politics of OM, but then again, I never bothered to pay much attention to the Breed I always hated and thought I'd never set eyes on. I know the Amphibians were known to cheat in their elections, so it could never be called fair. The Reptiles had a ruling family, called The First—they were descendants of the first humans injected with the Reptilian Soul Particle. And the birds voted for both a ruler and spiritual leader.

"How did you…" I began hesitantly trying to choose my words carefully as not to insult him. "I mean how did someone so young—"

"Become Praetor?" Aedan finished knowingly.

"Yes."

"A competition," he said.

"That's part of your election process?" I asked in surprise.

Aedan's chest rumbled with laughter. "We do not elect our leader."

So he had fought for the title?

"I take it voting for a leader still happens in your Kingdom?" He asked.

"Yes," I said. "Every eleven years."

"Our laws changed over a decade ago," he said. "When we came to realize the Reptiles were eyeing our land, the Assembly decided to have a leader that could be both soldier and diplomat. We created a tournament—we call it, The Trial. The last took place one year ago."

"And when will the next one be?"

"When I die."

My stomach dropped at the thought.

"Or if the Assembly finds me weak and unfit to rule."

"Are members of the Assembly elected into office?"

"Yes," Aedan said. "To make sure the needs of the people are seen to and to ensure the leader does not become a *despot*."

"And the Trial?" I ignored the fact I accused him of being just that earlier in the day.

"It's a series of competitions. All different in nature, to prove you are skilled on the battlefield and intellectually."

"But you're so young," I couldn't help but say.

"I'm eighteen," Aedan said as though it was a great age. "The Trial is open to any citizen from the age of seventeen and up. I won in all competitions."

"Thank you for explaining," I said, astonished he had won at such a young age and became leader. "I didn't know."

"How would you?"

With Aedan, I realized I needed to listen more and talk less. He picked up on too much.

I shrugged and tried to brush off his comment. "We all know something about the other kingdoms."

"Do *we*?" He asked in a dangerously soft voice.

He watched me in silence for a long moment before switching the topic.

"The General told me you're refusing the med lab," he changed the subject. "She also said you had injuries on your shoulder from the Reptile's attack."

"It's nothing. Only scratches," I told him truthfully, embarrassed by his concern. "I didn't even know they were there, until she saw them. They don't hurt."

"Can I see?" He asked to my surprise.

"It's really not a big deal…"

"Now."

The windows rattled from the force of the storm.

Since I knew he wouldn't let up until I showed him, I lowered the blanket and turned my naked shoulder to him. I heard his angry growl. He looked concerned and upset I was hurt.

"You'll go to the med lab in the morning," he commanded.

"It's really unnecessary…"

"It's completely necessary," he said. "You were in a major accident, your body needs to be checked out."

I was told there was no way any of the kingdoms could possibly have technology sophisticated enough to decipher my Breed, but still, after all that I was *not* told by the Elders —I was afraid. What if there was a small possibility they could figure it out? What then? I'd be killed before I even had a chance to survive on Earth.

"It's nonnegotiable, Siren."

"I understand your concern, but I know my body. And I'm all right." I tried to argue.

"Humor me." He crossed his arms in a way that was meant to be intimidating.

I wanted to continue to argue, but I knew it would be a losing battle. *Careful, Siren,* I thought to myself, *Mission First.*

"If I didn't know better, I'd think you had something to hide," Aedan said quietly.

"I don't."

"Then this conversation is moot."

And there it was. Even if I refused in the morning, I was sure he would have me dragged there, which would just work against me.

"If you insist." I had no choice.

He watched me for a moment with his piercing gaze, and I felt as though he could see through my soul.

"I do."

"Well then, that settles it," I returned emotionlessly, hoping he'd leave.

"Good night, Siren," Aedan took the cue. "I'll see you tomorrow."

I watched him disappear past the door and press a button before it slid shut. I realized I should have been outraged by my lack of privacy—instead I felt strangely safe by his proximity.

I didn't feel alone.

øøø

As morning came, I stared at the door to my room and waited anxiously for the General to come and get me. I was ready to go, dressed in the blue buttery leather pants and top she had left for me. The pants were a bit long, but I had rolled them into the silver pair of boots I had worn when I arrived. I fastened on my black belt, not wanting to risk leaving it in the room. My exposed midriff would take getting used to, but there was nothing I could do about it, since this was what I was given. At least it would help me blend in.

The lock on the door rattled and General Canis entered. I stood up as she walked in the room. She gave me an approving nod.

"You look refreshed," she said. "And I'm glad the clothes fit."

"You have a good eye."

She looked down at my worn boots. "We'll get you another pair."

"These are just fine," I argued wanting to keep something of mine from my old life.

"You'll need more than one pair of boots while you're here," General Canis said as she turned to leave the room. "Follow me."

I stayed close behind her as we made our way back down the candle lit hall. I assumed workers would be milling about, but the space was suspiciously empty. The sky was ominously dark, the hurricane spraying water and rattling the windows.

General Canis took me up another staircase that led to an area of the compound, housing an enormous laboratory. It was filled with people working, all wearing brown medical lab coats spanning their bodies from their necks to their booted feet. The room was almost as large as the Great Hall but didn't have the same high ceilings. The floors were steel and sterile, and what seemed like a hundred different laboratory desks lined the room with scientists milling about. There were five stations in the center of the room that looked like medical examination tables with robotic mechanisms attached.

A few people looked up from what they were doing and stared right at me. I saw intrigue in the men's eyes and something entirely different with the women—revulsion.. And fury.

But not one flickered into their Shadow. I was impressed by their restraint.

I knew why they didn't like me. Through time Cetaceans had developed a pheromone that we were told would help us blend in and disguise ourselves, like camouflage. The downside—the pheromone also attracted the opposite sex— which made those of the same sex innately wary. Flying under the radar wasn't something that would be easy for me.

"This is Praetor's Objective Lab," she said as we weaved our way through. I kept my head held high and followed her lead. The scientists were careful to clear the way as we walked past them, averting eye contact.

The General came to a stop in front of a glass panel that separated the main lab from another area. She put her hand over a round electronic panel shaped like a lion's paw.

"Identification confirmed. Welcome, General Canis," a female robotic voice called out. "Access granted."

The door slid open, and we walked down another hall and into a sterile looking room that had two long examination tables with two sheets of metal suspended above them. There was an enormous desk against one of the walls that had a dozen or so microscopes lined across it.

An older man leaned up against it with his arms crossed. He was expecting us.

He had brown hair peppered with white and pale blue eyes. He was a few inches shorter than the General and was dressed in a long white coat as opposed to the brown ones the scientists outside were wearing. He seemed intrigued by me.

"Dr. Novak," she said in greeting.

"General Canis," he returned, pushing away from the table and making his way toward us.

"I have been debriefed by Praetor."

"Perfect," General Canis replied. "Then I'll leave you to it."

"I'll be back for you," she met my gaze. "You'll be safe with Dr. Novak. He's the lead scientist in OM and will see to your needs. You should know, Aedan and I discussed it last night and found it imperative that Dr. Novak know how you came to us. It will help with his examination."

I would have voiced my concern, but she didn't wait for my reply. Before I knew it the door closed, and she was gone, leaving me alone with Dr. Novak.

"What is your name?" He asked gently.

"Siren."

"Your age?"

"I'm seventeen," I said.

"Do you have a mate?"

"I do not."

"You've been through quite a lot these past days," he said.

"That might be so but I think the General and Aedan are overreacting. I'm fine."

"I can see that."

"And I think this is really unnecessary," I made sure my voice had force in it. "I don't need it."

"The Praetor insisted upon it." Dr. Novak's voice changed into something dominant—like the way Aedan's had been with Milo. Except for some reason Dr. Novak truly terrified me.

"What is that?" I finally said in defeat, looking over at the metal table.

"It's a med scan," he explained. "It will examine your body and confirm you have no internal injuries and will also heal any damage on your epidermis."

A wave of unease gripped me. If this machine could heal damage to the human epidermis, it *could* be sophisticated enough to ascertain my Breed. And there was no escaping it. In just a short time, the odds were that Dr. Novak would know what I really was.

If he could sense my raging emotions, he didn't show it. He walked over to a cabinet, opened it, and pulled out a white dressing gown.

"You'll have to change into this." He held it out to me. "I'll give you enough privacy to change and return in a few minutes."

I nodded gratefully and watched Dr. Novak leave the room.

I closed my eyes in misery as the reality of my situation sunk in. What would they do with me once they knew? Would Aedan have me killed? Would the Assembly he spoke of, demand it? There were many scenes from human history that came to mind. I gripped the dressing gown in my hand and fought to stay in control.

I could not flicker into my Shadow now. Not here. Not like this.

I closed my eyes and said my word. *Arcana*. Luckily, calm came quickly. I stared at the med scan in icy disdain.

My greatest secret would be revealed. And there was nothing I could do about it. After a few agonizing moments, I let out a deep breath and accepted my fate. I would face my future proudly. Honor my ancestors. My mother. And more importantly, myself.

I changed into the gown as quickly as I could. When I was done, I folded my clothes and walked over to the table with the microscopes. On impulse, I leaned over one and stared through the magnifying glass.

"You're looking at OM female reproductive gametes."

I jumped away with guilt. Dr. Novak was watching me with great interest.

"I'm sorry. I shouldn't have looked," I said, backing farther away.

"I was told you're part of Kingdom B's planetary research team."

"Yes," I lied easily.

"I can't say I blame you for taking a peek. If the tables were turned, I would be just as curious," Dr. Novak said with the kind of smile that put me on edge.

He motioned toward the med scan. "Have a seat."

I did as I was told.

"Those are some impressive bruises."

"They look worse than they feel."

"The med scan will take care of the external injuries and scars, but first, I'd like to do my own physical exam."

I hoped I didn't look as nervous as I felt.

Dr. Novak walked over to the table with the microscopes and picked up an instrument. It was a pair of thick metallic goggles, and he quickly put them on.

"Lights."

The room went dark and he hit a button on the side of

the goggles, then a red infrared light glowed from the lenses.

My heart rate accelerated.

"Stare right in my eyes please." I did as I was told and watched the red light take a retina scan. I felt vulnerable being at his mercy, afraid of what he could see.

"Turn to your left," he asked me. "I'll be looking in your ears now."

He took his time. "Very good," Dr. Novak said. "Now I'd like you to lay down, while I look over your body. This won't take long."

I leaned back on the table and awkwardly laid down as Dr. Novak began his cursory body scan. He was very gentle whenever he placed his hands on me, and it wasn't as uncomfortable as I expected, but still, I wanted none of it.

After a few minutes of silence he stepped away.

"I'm all done," he said. "Now the med scan will take over. I'll just be in the other room. Don't be alarmed by the crackling noise, that's just the machine doing its job."

Dr. Novak left me alone.

Within a few moments, a dull humming noise echoed in the room and then the metal sheet above my body lit up to a pale red color. I kept my eyes open and watched as the machine replicated a 3D image of my body right above me. The holographic image turned as it pieced together the structure of my internal organs. I could see my veins pumping blood and my heart raced as I watched the exhilarating pictures come to life.

There was a hiss and then a crackle as the light turned to an iridescent blue. I watched in awe as the electrical current moved out of the metal contraption with precision to target injured areas on my skin. There was no pain, only a sensation that was akin to being tickled. My back warmed up, and I could feel the same sensations occurring on the other side.

Within minutes the metal sheet moved up and the lights went on.

"Epidermal wound recovery complete," the robotic voice said. "Internal evaluation complete. Data download in process. Unknown samples detected. Report download in three hours' time."

I kept my breath even awaiting Dr. Novak's return.

"That wasn't too painful?" he asked brightly, entering the room.

"No," I answered sitting up. Remarkably, there was no evidence of any of the wounds.

Dr. Novak looked over my body once more. He seemed pleased. "Perfect."

I began mentally counting down the minutes before he would know the truth.

"While you change back into your clothes, I'll look over some of the initial results," he said. "If you don't mind, I'll leave you alone for just a short while. When I return we'll continue the rest of my examination somewhere more comfortable."

Fear was slowly gripping me.

"The rest?" I ask warily. "There's more?"

"Yes," Dr. Novak nodded before leaving me to change. "Much more."

I watched the door slide right open without a code and realized I had my first chance to escape. And given the impending test results, I had no choice but to try. I changed quickly and held my breath as I made my way to the door. As it had for Dr. Novak, it slid right open, leading out to the hall General Canis guided me through earlier.

And it was empty. It was now or never.

Since I couldn't very well walk through the Praetor's lab filled with scientists, I went the opposite direction hoping there might be another way out. I quickly moved through the sterile hall, entering every room I could see—each one revealing a different private lab, all empty of life.

Please, I thought despondently, but I was living a nightmare—every door I entered leading to nothing more than a medical prison.

"Dr. Novak will arrive back to the lab in five minutes time." A computer generated female voice echoed around the hall causing me to stop in my tracks.

"I monitor all movement within his private lab," the sterile voice informed me.

I searched for the source. "Who are you?"

"It is in your best interest to immediately return to the lab," she continued, ignoring my question. "I highly suggest it."

Highly suggest it?

I looked around the empty hall. If the computer was monitoring my movement, an attempt to escape was futile.

"Given the betrayal of his trust, the probability of arousing Dr. Novak's anger is greater than seventy percent," she warned.

I still hesitated.

"And his Shadow is quite unpredictable."

It made sense why he frightened me. "You will find no escape route," she continued. "If that is your intention, your attempt will produce no results. The probability of being caught is ninety-nine-point-nine percent."

I couldn't believe the computer was speaking so candidly with me.

"You'll tell him anyway," I pointed out the obvious.

"I am required to answer whatever questions Dr. Novak asks," she returned cryptically.

Which meant if he didn't ask, he would never know.

If he didn't ask.

"Time is running out, Siren," she said. "You must make a decision now."

CHAPTER SEVEN

I heeded the computer's warning and returned to the lab, but I was on edge. Dr. Novak's immediate greeting proved she had not misled me, which was more than disconcerting Minutes later, I was following Dr. Novak down another corridor in the lab.. He glanced over his shoulder a few times to make sure I was keeping up.

He came to a stop in front of another glass panel door and placed his hand in front of the security panel. "Identification confirmed," the same female robotic voice rang out. "Welcome to your office, Dr. Novak."

We kept walking and made our way down a dark hall lined with different computer monitors.

"Thank you, Sara." The computer had been given an ancient name.

I looked over at the doctor in shock.

"Freethinking computers are against planetary law," I said to Dr. Novak.

This was one rule I knew was supposed to be observed by all kingdoms. Out of fear of the great strides in technological advancements and the possibility of an AI takeover, a ban was issued on the creation or use of all independent thinking machines. The kingdoms unanimously agreed, because the planet and human breeds were changing at such a rapid pace, adding another potentially cataclysmic technological catastrophe to the mix would only prove to be dangerous.

Dr. Novak didn't seem bothered by my concern. Having just had a run in with the computer, I understood the power she held.

"Sara has her limits," he explained as we continued to walk. "She is mine exclusively. She is forbidden to interact with any other human unless I say. When my soul ceases to exist in this body, Sara will self-destruct." Dr. Novak had obviously told Sara she was free to interact with me, which only made me wonder why.

"Aren't you afraid of the risk?" I asked him in disbelief.

"Know thyself," Dr. Novak said.

I thought I should give Dr. Novak a brief summary of human history. *Know thyself?* The meaning of the adage and how it pertained to the different breeds was exactly why Sara's existence was dangerous.

"It gets boring listening to yes-men and women all day," Dr. Novak went on.

"And she is bound to this area of the compound?" I asked.

"Mostly," Dr. Novak shrugged. "Sara's loyalty is to me. She monitors my day-to-day movement and bodily functions. She is wherever I am and can access any other computer in the city. She does not interact with anyone or thing unless I explicitly grant permission."

"You speak as though she's a living organism," I replied.

Dr. Novak shrugged and gave me a small smile. "Sometimes I feel as though she is."

"Does the Praetor know?" I couldn't help but ask.

Dr. Novak stopped and turned to face me. I couldn't tell if he was annoyed, but his aura remained an orange-yellow color, indicating he was focused on the task at hand—his study of me.

"Nothing happens in OM without the Praetor's knowledge," his voice was cold.

I nodded quickly, taken aback by the anger flickering in

his pale eyes. He continued on his way.

"Here we are," Dr. Novak motioned toward what looked to be a home living room.

It had a similar style to my bedroom but was larger. A giant L-shaped couch curled around a coffee table. Where my view was of the fields and looked more rural, this overlooked the city, which now resembled a dead zone because of the hurricane.

"This is my office," Dr. Novak explained.

There was a pool, double the size of mine, in the center of the room. I wondered if he used it for experiments. Scientific tables lined another wall along with large metallic shelves filled with various instruments.

He walked over to a desk and pulled out a chair. "Have a seat and make yourself comfortable," he said to me. "Can I bring you a beverage?"

"Please."

"Sara, would you be kind enough to let our guest know what's available."

"Greetings. Welcome to Dr. Novak's private office," Sara's voice wrapped around me. I felt like she was everywhere. "We have an assortment of refreshments to offer you. There is tea, coffee, water, and synthetic meat juice."

"I'll just have water," I replied, discomfort evident in my voice.

"Thank you for being patient as we see to your needs," Sara's voice was polite.

Dr. Novak brought over a thin computer and placed it in front of me.

"Now if you don't mind, before we begin the next set of tests, I'd love you to appease my curiosity and tell me something about your home," his eyes lit up in excitement.

I wasn't surprised. After all, he was a scientist, and I knew he had to be more than curious to hear about a Kingdom he had never seen.

"What would you like to know?" I asked cautiously.

"Everything."

My mind raced, trying to remember what I had studied about Kingdom B. Their homes were high above the world, nestled within the tallest trees on the planet. From the videos I'd seen, the Kingdom was not modern at all but quite basic. Wooden structures perched within the trees, platforms built up in the air, connecting all the massive structures together to create something spectacular. A giant city in the sky.

"Our land is filled with forests," I began slowly. "The trees are so tall, if you're on the ground they cover the sky. Our city is built within them, every home is high above ground. It's a pretty incredible sight when you're so far up. It's almost like you can see the whole world. It's just...it's just home. The only one I've ever known."

Dr. Novak looked fascinated.

"And your people?" he asked after a moment.

"We live a peaceful existence," I said regurgitating all I'd read about the Bird Breed. "We live by our Kingdom's motto, '*The higher we soar, the smaller we appear to those who cannot fly.*'"

It was a quote by Friedrich Nietzsche, and it was my favorite motto out of all the kingdoms. Each Breed lived by one code of honor and all had significant meaning behind them, but I found this ancient philosopher's to be the one that resonated the most with me. I felt like it referred to my own journey with the Cetaceans—with every step I took, with every piece of knowledge gained, I seemed to fit in less among them.

"Nietzsche is one of my favorite ancient philosophers," Dr. Novak said in pleasure.

"It's not hard to imagine why," I returned quietly.

"Perhaps not," he returned with a smile. "And do you know our Kingdom's motto?"

I shook my head.

"It is one from Aristotle," Dr. Novak said quietly. "And one I find particularly relevant to humanity's current predicament."

I waited for him to tell me.

"We cannot learn without pain."

A feeling of dread trickled down my spine.

His tone.

The way he watched me when he repeated the motto. There was almost an underlying threat in the words. I could feel it. The wind howled, and a strong gust hit the window hard, pulling us both back to the task at hand.

"I'll get you your water," he said quietly before motioning toward the tablet. "But in the meantime, I'd like you to start the aptitude test."

"An aptitude test? How will that help my recovery?" I asked pointedly.

"It won't," Dr. Novak smiled sheepishly. "But it will help *me*."

"I didn't agree to this." Why would they want to check my mental abilities? To what end?

"You don't have a choice," his voice was hard. The exact opposite of what it had been a second before. "The Praetor has given me free rein to conduct *any* test I like."

That did not sound good.

"What is this for?" I asked cautiously.

"Research," he told me quickly. "It's just research, Siren.

I've never even seen your kind before, and yet, here you are. Falling from the sky like an answer from the gods."

"An answer?"

"Take the test, Siren." Dr. Novak urged. "There is no harm in it."

I followed Dr. Novak with my eyes as he walked over to a panel and pushed it open. There was a cup of water waiting. He brought it over, and when he placed it on the table, I saw the faint tattoo of a polar pear on the inside of his wrist.

"I'm sure if this exact same scenario had occurred back in Kingdom B, your scientists would be doing the same," he continued on as if he could sense my trepidation. "There is nothing for you to worry about."

I had everything to worry about now. But instead of fighting him, I chose to be amiable, hoping it would work to my advantage if and when he found out the truth.

I looked over at the computer screen. "I'll take it," I said to him.

I clicked the first question, and a holographic image came up and out of the screen. There were three different strands of DNA code. It was easy enough to figure out the pattern and know what the fourth would be. I moved through the series of questions and problems with ease. Dr. Novak hovered around, while I answered the questions but was careful not to disturb me.

"You're done," Dr. Novak said.

Another series of questions had come up on the computer.

"There is more..."

"I have enough."

I glanced over my shoulder and saw the curious look on

his face as he studied my features.

"Are you finished in here?" Aedan's voice boomed through the room.

He was standing at the entrance of the hall.

My heart sped up in relief at the sight of him. He was dressed in dark brown leather pants, a pair of brown boots, and a long sleeved thermal top that emphasized his incredible physique. His hair was pulled back, which only drew attention to his enigmatic eyes. I stood up from the table as he proceeded to give me a once-over. The look on his face gave nothing away.

"Impeccable timing," Dr. Novak said as he walked over and picked up the computer I had just worked on. "I'm finished with her now."

Dr. Novak faced me. "Siren, it was a pleasure. I am sure we will speak again."

Before I could respond, I heard new footsteps coming down the hall.

And in a second, what could only be described as a stunningly beautiful brunette came to stand next to Aedan. She was tall. She must have had a good four inches on me and was built like steel. Every muscle flexed as she moved. They complemented each other in every way. She even had the same unique colored eyes. From the territorial way she stood next to him, I knew this had to be his intended mate, Kali.

The look in her eyes resembled what I had seen earlier from the female scientists. Disdain. And almost hate. The Elders had warned us this could be the case when females from different breeds came upon us, but I hadn't realized it would be so blatant.

She ran her hand possessively over Aedan's shoulder

before walking past him.

"I didn't know you would be stopping by, Kali." Dr. Novak said.

"I didn't know I needed permission to see my father," she replied as she walked over to him and kissed his cheek. I watched as he gave her a look of parental love, the same kind my mom had given me over a thousand times. I felt a sharp pang in my heart.

Kali left her father's side and walked right over to me, invading my space. I held my ground and met her gaze evenly.

"I'm Kali," she purred, giving me a fake smile.

"I'm Siren," I returned with just as much artifice.

She leaned in to sniff me. Her body stiffened immediately, and she took a step back. Her eyes narrowed, and her chest began to rumble in displeasure.

Kali's gaze whipped over to Aedan, her eyes lighting up.

I could feel my body heat up. Did she know what I was? Or was it something else? The intimacy we shared? For some reason, the idea of her knowing what happened between Aedan and I bothered me more than a potential discovery of my Breed.

"Later," Aedan said to her.

Every muscle on her body looked as though it was made of stone.

"Now." She commanded.

Aedan growled in anger before moving fast and towering over her body. His stance was intimidating. "Kali," he warned. "We will talk later."

Kali had the sense to back down.

Aedan's eyes flashed at me. "You will go now with General Canis."

Looking past him, I found the General waiting at the entrance to the room. I was more than happy to follow this command.

I looked at Dr. Novak. "It was a pleasure to meet you," I lied. Though he had been nothing but amiable, something about him unsettled me.

"All mine, my dear," he said. "All mine."

General Canis barely bothered to glance at me as she led me out.

"I'd like to speak to your father alone." I heard Aedan say.

"I would like to stay," Kali persisted.

"You will go," was the last I could decipher from Aedan, before the General and I were too far away.

"Am I going back to my room?" I asked.

"Yes," she said. "Until Praetor says otherwise."

After all the testing, I was glad to return to my prison. I actually wanted to get there as fast as possible, so I kept up with her quick pace and was back in my bedroom in no time.

General Canis waited at the door.

"Should you need anything…" she said.

"I remember."

She closed the door and I heard the rattle of the locks. When I knew she was safely away, I ran to the pool. I undressed as fast as I could and stepped in the warm water. I quickly sunk to the ground and took a moment to focus my thoughts.

I began to listen.

After a couple moments, I clicked my tongue three times on the roof of my mouth and felt the frequency change.

The water moved in electromagnetic waves that were only decipherable to me. The sound first bounced off the walls of the pool, then vibrated down, until it made its way to the pipes that led out of my room. I became one with the vibration and telepathically followed the sonic path. I could hear noises in the compound, in everybody of water the pipes led into.

Finally I was exactly where I needed to be.

Dr. Novak's pool.

I knew the vibration would cause a ripple in the water, and I prayed it would go unnoticed by the men. I could even make out faint outlines of their bodies as they spoke.

"She is a fascinating subject," Dr. Novak said. "Her intelligence levels are above average."

"Is she what she says she is?" Aedan asked.

Dr. Novak was silent for a moment. "If I'm to be subjective and base my answer purely on what we know of the Breed?"

"Please."

"Then my answer would be no," he replied matter of factly.

My stomach dropped.

"And what you know of the other breeds?"

"That's the thing," he went on. "The odds would be even less that she is one of the others. Unless she is just an anomaly."

"Is there any way to be one hundred percent certain?" Aedan persisted.

"With the saliva samples I now have from the cup she drank from and the few strands of hair that were left on the med scan, I can test her genetic makeup," Dr. Novak said slowly. "But it will take time, and it is an experiment I have never conducted…"

Dr. Novak was lying to Aedan.

The med scan just completed a full body scan and epidermal test, which given the sophistication of the technology, I was almost certain would reveal my Breed. I also knew Dr. Novak would have the results in a short time. But he was hiding this from Aedan. To what end?

"Get it done," Aedan commanded.

"As you wish."

"And you will do so *alone*."

"I anticipated as much."

"And one more thing," Aedan's voice was hard.

"Yes?"

"No one is to know the truth. This stays between us."

CHAPTER EIGHT

I sat on the ledge by one of the large windows in my room and watched the trees sway dramatically from the impact of the ferocious winds pummeling OM.

They looked as if they might break in two. The water hurled every which way from the heavens, mad as it raced to the ground. The lightening crackled as it flashed in the sky, reminding me of a symphony by Bach, perfect and yet so haunting.

Listening to the entire conversation between Aedan and Dr. Novak, I found myself in such a precarious situation, and the odds were continuously stacking up against me. I felt like an alien, an outsider, even though I was finally on my rightful planet. I wondered if the others felt the same in Kingdom B—if they had even made it there. I was never supposed to be here in OM, and now, every path I followed in my head felt futile.

Dr. Novak had samples of my DNA and an impending lab report, which would reveal my truth. What he would do with that information, I did not know. But there was always a chance I could be wrong, and a sliver of hope remained. Maybe their technology wasn't as sophisticated as I believed. I knew it was more than likely I was deluding myself, but I had to cling to something or I'd go mad. The thought of telling Aedan the truth briefly crossed my mind, but I couldn't risk the chance. I was still a prisoner. Ultimately, *his* prisoner. I couldn't leave my room. I couldn't speak to anyone unless given permission.

No doubt about it, my situation was bleak.

This is Earth, Siren, I told myself. *You've dreamt about seeing this planet your whole life.* I watched the sky light up, determined to, at the very least, soak in every sight and experience, until I knew my fate. At the moment, I was sure of nothing. And so, I allowed myself to have this one break in time, just to be me. A free seventeen-year-old girl seeing a land she had only imagined in her head, for the very first time.

"Siren?"

I turned quickly and stared down the hall.

Aedan was in my bedroom.

"I'm in here," I called out and didn't bother to move.

"Can I come in?" He asked politely.

"It's your home. And you are the Praetor here," I replied. "You've told me more than once you can do whatever you want."

I heard his brisk footsteps as he walked in the bathing room. I tried to keep my cool and continued to stare out at the hurricane. Even so, I could sense his presence wrap all around me.

"How are you feeling?" He asked.

"Fine," I replied.

I heard him sigh.

"Or maybe the better answer is, as good as I can feel, considering I'm a prisoner."

I heard him take a step closer. "There should be some peace in knowing you have my protection."

"What would *you* do if you were in my situation?" I said as I turned to face him.

"I would be doing everything in my power to escape," he replied without hesitation.

I thought about my earlier attempt to flee in Dr. Novak's lab.

"You see," he went on. "I've been *nothing* but honest with you."

I knew he was implying the opposite with me.

"Did Dr. Novak get everything he needed?" I asked changing the subject.

"He did," Aedan replied.

"Will there be more tests?"

"Perhaps."

"Can you tell me how it went with the Assembly?" I pushed.

"I'll tell you when the time is right."

"But what did you tell them about *me*?" I continued.

"You were lost. I tracked the Reptiles who were tracking you," Aedan explained. "And when they attacked, I saved your life."

"And that's it? No one will want to know more?"

"For now. It's enough."

His answer didn't sit well with me. "So I'm at your mercy?" I pressed. "I just have to wait here, until you decide when and where and what…"

"Yes," Aedan interjected forcefully. "You *are* at my mercy. Remember that."

"How can I forget it?" I replied harshly. "This is *my life*, Aedan. Do you realize that?"

"You have nothing to fear, Siren."

"Wonderful," I threw my hands up in frustration. "So I'll just stay in this room until you give me permission to leave."

Aedan cocked his head to the side. "That's actually why I'm here," he told me.

I waited in silence.

"Against my better judgment, I want to invite you to dinner in the hall tonight," he said.

"Against your better judgment?" I repeated. "That's quite an invitation."

"It's an honest one," Aedan returned.

There he went again with the insinuations of my dishonesty. It angered me even though he was right. For a moment I thought about saying no, but I couldn't allow childish emotions to get in the way of what would only help my mission. I had to find another way to escape.

"I would like that," I conceded after a moment.

A flash of disappointment crossed his eyes. Maybe he hoped I would have said no. For some reason, the thought hurt.

"General Canis will bring you down in an hour's time," Aedan continued. "And will also be your escort this evening. In the meantime, is there anything I can have brought up for you?"

Here it was. The dichotomy that was Aedan. On the one hand, he was incredibly caring and generous, going out of his way to make sure that a complete outsider felt comfortable and safe. He was *protective*. And then there was the side that ordered, demanded, and watched me with suspicious eyes. The side that didn't trust a word out of my mouth.

I realized how much my presence was a struggle for him. He was visibly torn. Just as my emotions seemed to rage from one extreme to another when I was in his presence, it seemed he was grappling with the same problem.

"No," I shook my head. "I have everything I need."

His piercing gaze met mine.

"I'll see you downstairs," he said and walked out of the room. I didn't dare take a breath, until I heard the door close behind him.

Exactly one hour later General Canis came to my door to collect me for dinner and led me down the stairs to the Great Hall. She was quiet the entire time.

Her pace was quick, and I paused when we got close. I heard the clang of silverware, people talking and laughing amongst each other, and I tried to brace myself for whatever awaited me. I kept telling myself I had already walked among them earlier in the Praetor's Objective Lab. I had seen them up close and should not have any fear. But this was completely different.

General Canis turned to stare at me and raised a brow.

"Are you all right?"

I could only nod as a wave of uneasiness washed over me.

She sighed as she came to stand before me.

"You're the Praetor's guest," she told me. "And the others have been told this."

"I've seen the way they look at me," I told her.

"Then you know you're at risk," she said taking me by surprise. "Your every move will be watched. Every word dissected. Tread carefully."

The General was warning me. And I took her advice to heart.

I nodded slowly and prepared myself for what lay ahead. In actuality, seeing more than a handful of humans at one time was what had me on edge. Now I would dine among them, be immersed within their culture, and hope they would be polite. But there was no way to tell which way this would go.

"Remember this is new to them as well," General Canis said quietly. "As it is to me. We've never seen your *kind* before. Ever. Imagine if you heard about something your entire existence, heard about a way of life passed your walls and land but had never actually *seen* it. Wouldn't you agree it is normal for anyone to be wary of the unknown?"

She was right and her words alleviated some of my worry and I was grateful.

"And how do you think I feel? This is all new to me as well and I'm the one in a foreign land, essentially a prisoner." I answered. "But I'll keep your words in mind."

The General continued to watch me. "You don't have a lot of friends." She stated.

It wasn't a question.

"No," I said. "I tend to keep to myself. I'm an introvert."

General Canis smiled at me for the first time. "The truth."

"I'm sorry?" I didn't know what she was talking about.

"When you speak the truth it works. It suits you."

I could feel my heart race from her insinuation.

We walked down the final stairs, and when I saw the scene laid out before me, I couldn't help but stare in appreciation. The hall was buzzing with noise and filled with people. Men and women were everywhere. A massive table set for at least forty people was placed in the center of the room. Vibrant flowers and candles ran down the center of the table.

I watched as some of the women hugged or kissed the men they were with, sharing an intimacy I'd never witnessed in person, before in my life. They gazed lovingly into each other's eyes and were at ease with one another. Some even flickered into their Shadows, which was jarring to see, since I had only seen a Shadow appear during anger or fear. Although I knew it could happen, I'd never seen a flicker as a result of passion. People laughed and joked, drinking out of golden goblets.

"The Praetor always dines with his closest friends," General Canis explained.

She put her hand on my back and guided me to the dining table. Some people stopped speaking and stared right at me, and I tried my best to avoid their gazes but it was hard. I didn't know if I was up to seeing more of the instantaneous dislike, but the General's reassuring touch gave me the confidence I needed.

"We'll sit here," she guided me to two seats near the head of the table.

I pulled out my chair and sat down quickly, hoping to blend in and hide from all the looks coming my way. It was unlike me. I was usually brave, the most fearless out of the other three girls sent here—but right now, I felt anything but. General Canis quickly joined me and sat at my right, her presence calming some of my fear.

A moment later a pleasant looking woman came to stand next to us. She avoided my gaze and stared straight at the General.

"Can I bring *you* a refreshment?" She asked General Canis, completely ignoring me.

"The Praetor's drink for me," She replied looking over at me. "Would you like the same?"

I had no idea what that was but I agreed. "Yes, thank you."

The woman left with our request. People began taking their seats around us. It was hard to avoid direct eye contact, especially when I felt as though every single person in the room was dissecting my every move, like the General had warned me.

The empty chair to my left was suddenly pulled back,

and an older woman with skin the color of coffee, who looked to be in her late sixties, sat down next to me.

"You have the entire room enthralled, my dear," she said as I met her bright violet gaze.

Her silver hair was pulled back in a tight bun from her lovely face. She was dressed in the traditional clothing, in a light green outfit that complimented her eyes. But unlike the younger women, her midriff was not exposed.

She was the only other woman I had encountered aside from the General who didn't look at me like I was infected by the plague. But still, there was no kindness in her eyes.

"Do I?" I said.

She nodded. "Take a look around."

I did as she commanded, and I couldn't hide my visceral reaction. More than half of the guests had flickered into their Shadow in anger or fear. Watching me.

"They've never encountered an Aliud before." She said as if it should ease my mind.

She called me an *Other* in Latin. For the people of OM, Latin was a mandatory language to study, which was why so many of their titles were in Latin instead of English, like Aedan's title of *Praetor*. The other three Kingdoms had also adopted what were known as dead languages. For the Reptiles, it was Akkadian. The Birds had taken on Aramaic and the Amphibians, Ancient Greek. As the kingdoms were divided by what extinct species they descended from, the old rulers believed each one should adopt an extinct language as well. In preparation for our mission, the Elders made sure we were fluent in all Earth languages.

"And *I've* never encountered your kind before," I reminded her.

"No, I suppose you haven't," she stared at me shrewdly.

"And now here you are, dining among us. How surreal it must be for you."

You have no idea, I thought to myself.

"My name is Eadric."

"It's a pleasure to meet you, Eadric," I said. "I'm Siren."

"Named after sea nymphs that lured young sailors to their death," she said quietly as her astute gaze flickered over my face. "Part bird. Part woman. It's a fitting name."

"I suppose it is," I lied.

The woman brought our drinks over but refused to hand me mine. General Canis took the heavy goblet and set it in front of me. I looked down at the mysterious brown liquid.

"To fertility," the General said as she raised her cup. Eadric and I followed.

"Fertility," Eadric returned.

I was grateful neither Eadric nor the General were looking at me when I took a sip of the pungent liquid. It tasted bitter and was hard to swallow. I couldn't stop my grimace.

"I should have warned you," the General laughed knowingly at me. "It's strong. Probably more so for an Aliud."

"It is strong," I couldn't bring myself to politely lie. "May I have water?"

"You will have what is offered to you," Eadric snapped sharply staring at me with narrowed eyes. "You are in OM, and you will abide by our customs."

The sting in Eadric's voice took me aback. A moment ago, I thought she had been pleasant, almost accepting. And now, I knew it had been a facade. I was an outsider, and she was fast to remind me. The chairs were quickly filled, and a feeling of claustrophobia gripped me. The faces became all one blur.

"You look pale," General Canis lowered her voice. "Are you all right?"

I was surprised to see the quick flash of empathy in her eyes. "I'm fine," I replied.

"I'll get you water," she surprised me before casting an annoyed look at Eadric.

I nodded gratefully. A goblet of water was placed before me, and I gladly drank from it.

The atmosphere in the room quickly changed. Within seconds everyone was deathly silent, except for the sound of the hard rain from the hurricane pounding against the windows. And then someone grabbed hold of their goblet and began hitting it against the table. Soon the entire room joined in, and I looked over to see Aedan approach the dining table with Kali to his right.

Aedan reached the head and raised his hands.

"Praetor!" A man called out.

The people stood and raised their goblets. I pushed my chair back and joined, following General Canis' lead. A servant handed Aedan a goblet, and he raised it.

"To OM!" He called out as he drank deeply from the cup amidst the people shouting around him in pleasure.

When Aedan was done he placed the goblet down and sat in the chair, signifying the rest of the table could follow his lead. I slipped back in my seat and caught Aedan's eye. He nodded at me in greeting. I watched Kali sit to his left and place a possessive hand on his arm. Her golden gaze found mine and narrowed darkly. Her hatred for me, palpable.

I looked away, hoping to avoid inciting her anger any more than my presence already had.

"You must be anxious to get back home," Eadric turned to me as the hall buzzed with conversation. I was surprised she wanted to speak to me.

"I am," I replied quietly. "It's been a trying few days."

"Praetor has seen to your protection," Eadric said pointedly.

"Yes," I rushed out quickly, hoping I wasn't insulting Aedan's hospitality or sounding ungrateful. "Your Praetor has been incredibly generous and kind. I couldn't be more appreciative. So much has happened…"

"Of course," Eadric interrupted. "And here you are in a foreign land. It can't be easy for a young woman alone. I would understand if you were afraid."

"I'm not afraid," my voice was confident. "I've been assured of my safety and have been treated kindly. I'm just looking forward to going back."

"Assured of your safety?" Eadric's eyes narrowed. "Nothing is assured unless the rest of the Assembly and I deem it to be."

I reached for my goblet and tried to remain unaffected by her words. Eadric was a member of the Assembly, which meant she'd already spoken to Aedan about my situation.

"So tell me, do you always go out on these research missions on your own," Eadric demanded, speaking as though she had not just threatened my stay. "As I'm sure you can imagine, I'm surprised your people would take such foolish chances."

I looked over at General Canis who was busy picking grapes off a plate placed before us.

"Yes," I chose my words carefully. "My missions are peaceful scouting expeditions."

She glanced over me like she was sizing me up.

"Are you trained in hand-to-hand combat?"

"Some," I lied easily. I did not want to discuss the extent of my martial arts training. I needed the advantage. "The basics, really. But I'm no expert. I'm not a warrior or soldier."

"Then you put yourself at great risk," Eadric leaned back in her chair.

"We've never had anything to be afraid of," I replied.

"Then your people have lied to you." Eadric admonished. "There are always enemies to fear. And to live as though they will not or cannot come and knock on your borders is to live in ignorance. It is a huge disservice to your Kingdom."

It was hard to miss the disdain in Eadric's voice. She believed Kingdom B had failed to protect its people, and it was an entirely unfair and unfounded observation, but there was nothing I could do or say to defend them—as I would only be damning myself. I didn't feel comfortable discussing the political climate of Kingdom B with Eadric, since I had no real idea what the current situation was. Only what I had studied.

"Siren is not involved in the politics of Kingdom B," General Canis said to Eadric.

Eadric looked over at the General. "But she is now, my dear," Eadric's tone was serious. "She is right in the middle of it, embedded deeply, and will be held accountable."

A servant placed a plate filled with fruit, vegetables, and bread in front of me. I stared down at the colorful assortment but could find no appetite.

"Accountable for what?" The General leaned over me protectively, eyeing Eadric, growling low in her throat. "She cannot speak for her Kingdom. It is not her place."

"But she will," Eadric said with force. "She has no other choice."

I could feel the unspoken animosity between the two women. The General's mood darkened considerably. I wondered what Eadric was implying, and what it meant for me. Before I knew it, the General's arm flickered into her Wolf Shadow's and pounded the table.

"That isn't your decision to make," she barked. "It is Praetor's."

"Is it only his?" Eadric's voice was calm but bit of a warning. "What a temper you have, General. When I was your age I hardly ever lost control of *my* Shadow."

"Bibi?" Aedan's powerful voice broke the tension between the two women. The General gained control and glanced at Aedan. I was grateful everyone else was immersed in small talk and seemed to be ignoring us.

"I would like to invite Siren, our guest, to speak before the Assembly tomorrow," Eadric said to Aedan, before the General could utter a word.

If he was angry about Eadric's invitation, he gave nothing away.

"I will assess the situation tomorrow," he returned. "She is still recovering—"

"She looks fine enough to me," Eadric stated coolly. "She will speak before us—as it is our right to question her and her right to plead her case."

Aedan's face remained impassive.

"It is the law," Eadric continued.

"I know the laws that govern our land," Aedan replied sternly.

"Then you know, as your Eldest in the council you

cannot deny my request." Eadric said pointedly. "That, my young leader, *is* the law."

Growling under his breath, Aedan finally replied. "Siren will appear before you tomorrow."

Eadric looked pleased. "Then it is settled," she said calmly as she picked up her fork and began eating her meal.

I met Aedan's gaze again and could sense his displeasure with the turn of events.

"Do you find the meal unsatisfactory?" Kali's cool voice broke my train of thought. She motioned toward my untouched plate.

"It's perfect." I returned, picking up a piece of fruit and forced myself to eat it.

I broke Kali's suspicious gaze and looked around the hall, thinking how completely unprepared I and the other Cetaceans were for the mission we'd been tasked to undertake. I thought back to my studies and the confidence the Elders tried to instill in us.

Mental strength and awareness of your surroundings is what will lead you through this journey, child, they said over again. *You must trust your instincts. The innate knowing our kind is gifted with. That is the only way you will complete your task.*

"I can feel the storm brewing inside your soul," Eadric interrupted the thoughts churning around my mind. "Your energy is palpable."

I looked over at her, "There is no storm," I said. "I was just lost in thoughts of home."

Eadric's sharp gaze met mine. "And what do you see when you look around this home of mine?"

Her question caught me off guard.

"Come now," she chided. "You must have some

thoughts?"

I took my time before answering. I looked away from Eadric and took in my surroundings.

Your home is vibrant. It's living. It's breathing. It's all I ever wanted. You have so many people, a land. A system in place. Together. Bonded by your similarity. United as one. You have friends. Family, even. Generations of family who have passed on memories and a history here on Earth to you.

Do you know how lucky you are?

"I think your home is beautiful," I said instead.

"And my people?" She asked.

"I see them as a reflection of the land," I replied quietly. "Strong. And wild. Stunning to behold. Both individually and together."

Eadric's eyes widened at my words.

"That is quite a compliment from an Aliud."

"You asked me what I see."

"I did," she said. "And I am appreciative of such an accolade. If the tables were turned I would hope that my people would be just as generous. "

"I would hope," I said.

Eadric leaned back in her chair and grabbed hold of her goblet. Her mood seemed to darken considerably. "Would you like to know what I see when I look around this hall of ours, Siren?"

I waited politely for her to tell me.

"There is a sound missing," Eadric frowned as a shadow passed over her face. "And it is the most magical sound in the whole of Earth. Like a sweet melody from the gods, turning even the darkest of hours into light."

Eadric took a moment before looking over at me.

"It is the sound of children's laughter," she said sadly.

"The cries of a baby wanting her mama's milk. The sweet echo of mirth as they chase each other in the hall, immersed in their own secret fantasy world, where darkness doesn't exist."

I could feel Eadric's pain. And I understood it now, sitting among the people of OM, more than I ever did. Seeing this new world only made my mission feel more important. It only strengthened my resolve. This was what I wanted for my people.

"We've all been equally cursed with the same reproductive issues," Eadric sighed.

"All?" Surprised she knew it was as bad for the others.

"Every so often, the Elders from each of the four Kingdoms speak remotely via video conference," she began to my surprise. "We talk about issues that could affect humanity as a whole, the state of our planet and reproduction." This was something we had not known.

"I believe it is the most urgent issue all the kingdoms face," Eadric said with passion. "This race against our own extinction."

Hearing Eadric say the words my mother had repeated to me many times over the years was jarring. Though my kind was only seconds away from that terrible outcome, hers was stepping closer to it as each day passed. I understood her growing fear. It was one I lived with as well. It was our common ground.

When Eadric turned away from me, I allowed myself to look around the large table. A few people glanced my way, but most were immersed in their own conversation. My gaze moved to Aedan, then Kali, just before I watched Dr. Novak enter the hall and take a seat next to his daughter. He glanced over at me, and the smile he gave me made my bones chill.

He knew.

He knew what I was.

He picked up a goblet from the table and lifted it, saluting me. My mouth went dry as I watched him lean toward his daughter and whisper something in her ear. She looked over at me with a look that could kill. Did he tell her? Would they reveal it now to the room?

My breath lodged in my throat, and I looked around the hall searching for a way out. I had to escape. I could feel my forehead start to tingle, my Shadow awakened. Before I could push my chair back, General Canis placed a hand on mine and squeezed it tightly, forcing me to meet her gaze. Whatever she saw in my eyes made her curse quietly.

"Calm yourself," she whispered. "We can smell your fear."

"I need to leave," I pleaded with her. "I'm not feeling well."

"Not yet," she replied softly. "Siren. There is nothing for you to fear now. We will discuss the Assembly tomorrow."

I wanted to scream out to her. Once the Assembly knew what I was, my life would be over. I looked back at Dr. Novak who watched me in fascination. He shook his head and lifted his finger to his lips as if to quiet me. My heart continued to pound erratically, even though he knew, he was silently telling me he wasn't going to reveal my identity. I pressed my fingers together and pictured the ocean.

Not yet, at least.

It didn't matter.

There was something dark lurking in his eyes. Something triumphant, like he'd won a secret prize. And I knew with every fiber of my being, I wasn't safe.

Aedan rose and lifted his cup again, momentarily

distracting me.

"We give thanks," he said as he took a sip and then set the goblet down.

His guests followed his lead.

"I bid you all a peaceful night," Aedan called out before turning around to leave the room, barely sparing me a glance. Before he left, I saw him look pointedly at the General who pushed back her chair. Kali rose and followed behind him.

"It is time to go, Siren," General Canis said to my relief.

I rose abruptly and stepped away from the table. Dr. Novak was making his way over to me. I looked over at the General in panic, trying to calm my racing heart, but she had her back to me and was busy talking to one of the servants who'd come to stand next to her.

Dr. Novak reached my side and placed his hand on my arm before leaning down to whisper, "You and I will talk tomorrow. Rest easy tonight, dear Siren. Your secret is safe."

He let go of me before the General could turn and see. She nodded politely at him, while motioning me to leave. I didn't trust Dr. Novak. There had to be a reason he wasn't revealing what I was. A reason why he had lied to Aedan about the genetic tests he had done on me.

OM's motto echoed in my mind.

We cannot learn without pain.

Chapter Nine

I followed the General out of the hall.

We reached my room quickly, and when she opened the door, I could finally breathe again. General Canis followed me inside.

"What happened down there?" She crossed her arms.

"Nothing," I shook my head quickly. "I'm exhausted. It was too much, that's all."

She eyed me warily. "The only time I have ever sensed such fear is when someone is about to die."

"As you can see, I'm not dying," I whispered.

Not yet.

She watched me for a moment longer before turning to leave the room.

"Can I ask you something, General Canis?" I couldn't help but call out.

"Just Bibi," she said with a resigned sigh, turning to face me. "You have my permission to call me Bibi. And yes, you may."

I smiled gratefully, surprised she would allow me the intimacy in such a short time.

"Eadric," I said steadying my voice. "What does it mean to be an Elder?"

"Our Assembly is comprised of twenty-two people. All but one are elected by the people of our Kingdom," she explained. "Once voted into the Assembly, you remain for life unless your actions are deemed unacceptable by all the other members, in which case, you are excused and another vote will occur."

I waited for her to continue, before I asked more

questions.

"Eadric is the eldest member of the Assembly, the one and only Elder. She's been a member since she was twenty-five years old. She's now sixty-five. Because of her knowledge from the years and the fact that as an Elder she controls her Shadow, she is allowed to call the members together at any time she chooses, and this edict cannot be denied by the Praetor. She is also allowed to overrule a decision by the Praetor if she feels it is to the detriment of OM, which makes her even more powerful than the Praetor."

"And has it ever happened before?" I asked anxiously.

"Tonight is the first time Eadric has asked for the Assembly to be called together."

Bibi shrugged when she saw my startled look. "I'm not surprised," she said. "It is to be expected. You are the first Aliud to ever walk into our Kingdom. Let alone, dine among us."

I appreciated her candor. "You said all but one are elected to the Assembly?"

"Milo," Bibi said, mentioning the warrior I had met when I came to OM.

"He came in second to Aedan in The Trial," she went on. "For that honor he sits on the Assembly and is there to assume power if Aedan is seen unfit. Or in the event he is killed."

ØØØ

I had been up since dawn, waiting in anticipation for what the day would bring. The storm continued to rage on and had become therapeutic for me. The sound of rain helped lull me to sleep, mercifully allowing me a reprieve from thoughts of the Assembly and Dr. Novak.

Bibi collected me from Praetor's home, and we left for

the city center that housed the Assembly Hall. The building was filled with people, who I assumed were working their jobs as she ushered me quickly through. It was designed in a more modern way than Aedan's home, with sharp lines of steel and open space. There was no furniture in the room we walked through, only elevated video panels showcasing different areas of OM's land. I wasn't given much opportunity to take in the busy center, but what I did see, I liked. The building was sleek with glass walls, allowing you to see the world around you. There was security everywhere I looked, guards posted at different doors carefully watching the crowd.

Bibi ushered me through the building and showed me into a room that was completely round with orange hued limestone panels covering the walls. Once inside, it was almost impossible to tell which panel we came through.

"Wait here," Bibi commanded. "I'll be back for you shortly. Help yourself to anything you see." She left me alone.

There was a small round table with four seats and a tray full of refreshments. To calm my nerves I poured myself a glass of water and faced the stone panels the General exited from. The silence around me was almost deafening.

There was a swoosh. and the panel directly behind me slid open. I turned around and watched Kali enter the room. She was dressed in skintight yellow leather pants and a short top, accentuating her lithe physique.

With her arms crossed and an icy gaze, her stance was intimidating.

She stepped inside and the door shut with a thud, leaving the two of us alone, facing one another. I wasn't surprised to see her. After what happened in her father's office, her seeking me out was inevitable. I didn't believe her father told her what I was. Kali had shown her impetuous nature, when she had all but stalked me in his office. If she knew, she would have acted upon it.

"Can I help you with something?" I asked.

"You are not to speak unless spoken to, Aliud," she hissed. Her tone exuded superiority, like I was someone beneath her, and I didn't appreciate it one bit.

"You don't command me," I replied.

She took a menacing step toward me.

"You better watch yourself," her voice was filled with hate.

"Is that a threat?"

"It's a warning," Kali bit out. "You might have Aedan and Bibi fooled into trusting you're innocent, but I don't believe your story."

"Then I consider myself fortunate you're not in charge," I did not back down.

I crossed my arms and continued to meet her gaze.

"Is that all?" I asked coolly.

"No," she seethed as she moved even closer, her glowing eyes betraying the extent of her fury. "*That* is not all."

I waited for her to continue.

"You know why I am here."

"I do not."

Kali smiled coldly. "Stay away from Aedan."

I raised a brow.

"He's mine."

"I'm not following…"

"I'm no fool, Aliud!" Kali snapped. "Don't take me for one."

I watched her for a moment, taking the time to calm

myself. I didn't want to incite Kali's volatile emotions. But I also didn't want to be seen as weak. I had to be careful.

"You have nothing to fear," I finally said, my voice flat. "There is nothing between us…"

"You lie!" she raged. "I could *smell* him on you."

"Of course you did! He rescued me and had to carry me through some of the terrain, because I was incapable of walking. I was injured," I explained as calmly as I could, given it was the last thing I wanted to do. I didn't owe her any explanation.

"*That* is not the scent I am referring to." Kali growled loudly.

"I don't know what you're talking about," I knew she was referring to the kiss Aedan and I shared. Even though her accusation was completely justified, I was ready to deny it. I would never betray my promise to him.

Kali invaded my space, before I had a chance to continue. She moved fast and leaned down, her stance aggressive. She flickered into her Shadow, a tawny female lioness, the female version of Aedan. She was intentionally showing me her power.

"Quiet!" She hissed. "*I know the truth.*"

"You know nothing," I returned evenly. "You're wrong."

"I don't think so, Aliud," Kali said. "Don't think I will *ever* trust you. Don't you ever think my eyes will not be watching your every move. Every time you look over your shoulder while you're in *my Kingdom*, I will be right there. And if you should make one wrong step or give a look I find unacceptable, then who knows?"

"Are you threatening me?"

"Yes," Kali gave me a wide smile. "Yes, I do believe I am."

"I'm not afraid of you," I refused to back down. " And I have nothing to hide."

"Everyone has a secret," she said as she took in my scent. "Even little birds that give off the appearance of being frail and delicate enough to snap in half."

The venom she spewed only served to give me strength. What she didn't realize was her hatred of me was her greatest weakness. The chink in her armor. And if I had to, I'd use it to my advantage. My thoughts frightened me. I had not come here to be combative, but now, I had to be ready and willing to do whatever it took to defeat her. Or anyone else who threatened me.

We stared each other down as the tension in the room grew so much there was barely any air to breathe. And that was how the General found us. I could only imagine what she saw—a warrior intimidating a simple girl, one who was under the protection of her Praetor. What she didn't realize was I didn't need protection from Kali—I did not fear her.

"What is going on in here?" she barked out when she entered the room. Her angry gaze moved over us. "Kali?"

Kali hovered over me for a second longer before stepping away. She looked over at Bibi.

"The Alind and I were just getting something straight," she said indifferently.

"Does Aedan know you're here?" Bibi demanded.

"No," Kali replied snidely. "But I am sure you'll tell him. You are his best friend after all, always the loyal dog."

Bibi smiled coldly. "I consider that the highest of compliments."

"You are predictable as always, General," Kali said before heading out of the room. When she was gone, I met Bibi's gaze.

"What was that about?" She demanded to know.

"Nothing," I returned quickly. I had no desire to rehash the conversation.

"Siren…" Bibi warned.

"I don't want to talk about it right now," I countered. "I would like to focus my attention on my meeting with the Assembly. That's all that matters."

"You are correct," she said after a moment. "Right now, that is all that matters. But after your meeting you *will* tell me."

I assumed she wouldn't let up. "If you insist."

"I do."

"Is the Assembly ready for me?" I asked changing the subject.

"Almost," she said. "When the bell rings, it will be time."

I could feel the pit in my stomach begin to grow.

"There are a few things I think you should know," Bibi told me.

"Yes?"

"It's in your best interest to remain demure and obedient," she said to my surprise. "Do not engage in any combative discussions even if provoked."

"Why would I be provoked?" I asked.

"Trust me," Bibi said knowingly. "They could very well try and ignite your temper. They will grill you for the truth."

I nodded and waited for her to continue.

"You will refer to Aedan as Praetor. You are not to let any one of the Assembly members believe you have any affection for him, or he for you. They will see it as a weakness in his abilities. They must believe him to be completely impartial."

I could feel my cheeks burn. "I don't see Aedan in any way..." I returned.

"Siren," Bibi cut me off. "I have an uncanny ability to see through lies."

I looked away from her knowing gaze.

"What you think you see is the gratitude I feel for him saving my life."

"It is more than that."

Was it? Perhaps. But it was not an emotion I would explore.

"He has a mate," I stated the obvious. "And I am an Aliud."

"You *are* an Aliud," Bibi agreed. "Best you remember that."

The bell sounded and she turned her head.

"The Assembly calls." Her voice changed, and I watched her entire demeanor morph into the General she was.

My heart raced as I followed her out of the room and down a long tunnel made entirely of rock. It was lit up by torches and many guards lined the way. They saluted her as we walked through. She was impressive with the way she kept her poise and how she exuded power and strength. I could see why Aedan had chosen her to be his General. If I were leader, she was someone I would want at my side as well.

We made our way down the long tunnel until we reached two arching iron doors. Four of OM's soldiers stood in front of them, guarding the entryway. They pulled their swords in sync to their chest and saluted the General. They moved quickly to the side, and the doors gradually open. Bibi motioned me forward. I beheld a long hanging bridge suspended over jagged rocks.

"This is as far as I can take you," she told me. "Go to the end of the walkway where the Assembly awaits your presence."

"Thank you."

"Good luck," she told me with a nod of encouragement.

I moved past her and began to walk across the bridge. The ceiling was not very high and the tunnel became narrower the further I walked down. I could hear sounds of people talking as I stepped closer to what I assumed was the Assembly Hall. The tunnel grew darker, the air thicker, before I saw the circular entryway that led into a room, resembling the interior of a pyramid. The sanded walls were lit up by hundreds of tiny lights that twinkled like stars in the sky.

I walked onto a round, suspended floor that held one chair facing the twenty-two person Assembly. The members were seated behind a long stone table, which sat on a platform, suspended in the air. The ground beneath us seemed to fall into oblivion. I looked at the Assembly who were quietly staring at me. Milo was seated among them. He looked at me like I was something vile and repulsive. My gaze flickered over the rest of them, and I could feel the animosity and suspicion radiating from their bodies. I focused my gaze on Eadric.

I quietly waited for someone to speak.

A horn sounded and the members stood up. I watched a door to my left slide open, and a light came on to reveal another seat suspended on a round platform away from everyone else. I wasn't surprised when Aedan stepped into the room. He nodded quickly at me before looking over at the Assembly.

"You may begin," he said as he took his Praetor's seat.

At Aedan's command, all the members of the Assembly sat back down.

"Please have a seat, child." Eadric called out to me.

I did as I was told.

"Thank you for joining us today," Eadric's voice rang through the room.

"Thank you for inviting me to speak before you," I replied.

"Many of us have questions for you," Eadric explained. "If you could answer them to the best of your ability, this should be quite a painless experience for you."

I nodded.

"As is my right as Elder," Eadric continued. "I will begin the cross-examination."

I waited in silence, closing my eyes and taking in long, deep breaths to remain calm.

"Please state your name before the Assembly," Eadric's voice was dispassionate.

Arcana.

I opened my eyes and took another breath. "My name is Siren."

"And where do you come from?"

"Kingdom B." I kept my voice calm, even though my heart was racing a mile a second.

"What was your purpose on our land?" Eadric's tone was cold.

"I was on a planetary scout," I said. "I study the ever changing climate and the effects it has on Earth."

"To what end?"

"To ensure our survival and continued evolution."

Eadric gave me an incredulous smile. "How old are you?"

"I'm seventeen," I told her.

"And tell me is it common for your people to give such a great task to someone so young?" Eadric sounded doubtful.

"As common as it is for someone so young to become Praetor," I returned evenly, standing my ground.

A few members of the Assembly whispered among themselves in disbelief, taken aback by what they perceived as my impertinence. One person even flickered.

"Quiet!" Eadric called out to the group before fixing me with her grim gaze.

"It would be wise to remember you are at least for now, a guest of OM. We can change that very easily, child," she said sharply. "The Assembly will not tolerate any disrespect."

"My comment was not meant to be disrespectful," I told her quietly. "It was meant to point out a similarity in our kingdoms."

Eadric stared at me evenly.

"Tell me about your mission," she said at last.

"I'm sure you realize, we must evolve *with* the planet. Our research is conducted to make us more aware," I told her slowly. "And to find remarkable activity that could change our climate and our living conditions."

"And have you discovered anything out of the ordinary?"

"No," I shook my head. "Luckily, we have not."

"How did you come upon our Praetor?" Eadric asked.

Here was the one question I had to be the most careful in answering, because one wrong word could betray me.

"I went too far," I said keeping my eyes on Eadric. "I lost track of the time and where I was. Nature's elements worked against me, and I found myself in a land I didn't recognize."

There was a moment of silence before I heard someone laugh. The hollow sound echoed through the triangular hall.

It was Milo.

His thick muscles bulged as he leaned forward on the table and shook his head, admonishing my response to Eadric. He ran a hand over his face as if he were in deep contemplation before looking over at Eadric with a big smile.

"Is there something you find amusing?" Eadric asked as she returned his gaze.

"Perhaps," he replied as he arched a brow.

"Would you care to enlighten us?" Eadric sounded almost annoyed.

"With your permission may I ask a question, Elder?"

"You may," Eadric agreed after a moment. "Siren, this is Milo, a member of our Assembly and a great soldier. The floor is yours, Milo."

I stared at the young warrior. His aura was dark red, indicating volatility—which I had experienced firsthand.

"Thank you, Elder." Milo replied before turning his sharp gaze to me. He took his time, looking me over, like he was picking me apart. Without a doubt, he despised what he saw.

"I find it hard to believe you just lost track of where you were. Of your terrain." Milo's voice was condescending. "Please do tell me, how that's even possible considering what you do?"

He was right. The story was weak.

"It just happened…" I began.

"Happened?" Milo bit back with a harsh laugh. "How does one just *happen* to get lost in another Kingdom? To trespass?"

I stared at him in silence.

"*I* can only assume, and the Assembly must agree, this endeavor would take days, maybe even weeks by foot. And if you're so versed in researching land, how did you happen to miss how far you were from home? Wouldn't the distance you travelled not be cause for alarm? "

"It would," I admitted.

"Then please explain this 'happening' to us, because I for one am having a difficult time understanding it," he said with an unfriendly smile before looking at the others who nodded in agreement. "And most importantly, I'm having a hard time *believing* your story."

I looked away from Milo's accusatory stare and over at Eadric, searching for any type of reassurance, but I saw none. My mind blanked and for the life of me I couldn't think of a plausible lie. The faces of the Assembly blurred, and I felt a wave of panic wash over me. I looked around and felt the room begin to sway. Lying didn't come second nature to me. I had never even lied before crashing down on Earth.

Think, Siren. Think of something to say.

"Tell them about your mother." Aedan's voice rang through the dark fog that had begun to take over.

And just like that, my panic dissipated.

I looked over at Aedan and felt his calm. It was strange. Just hearing his voice made me relax and gave me the reassurance I needed. He had just handed me the lie to tell the Assembly.

Here he was, saving me, yet again.

"I must ask the Praetor to refrain from interrupting what is the Assembly's right," Milo's voice was ice cold. "We are allowed to ask the Aliud questions, and she must respond to them without any assistance from another, most especially our dear, esteemed *Praetor*."

It was hard not to miss the venom dripping from Milo's words. It was apparent he loathed Aedan. But Aedan remained unaffected by his animosity and stared right back. He looked almost bored.

"This answer is relevant to why she was on our land."

"Then allow *her* to speak of it," Milo returned.

"Tread lightly, Milo." Aedan's voice was hard. "I am your Praetor."

"And I would never disobey our leader," Milo's voice was almost mocking. "But there are rules in this Assembly that cannot be broken, even by you."

"Enough," Eadric interrupted the standoff. "Milo is correct, Praetor. Siren will answer the questions on her own without assistance from anyone."

"Your Praetor refers to my mother for a reason," I interrupted quickly, trying to diffuse any uncomfortable situation for Aedan as all eyes turned to me. "I-I lost her."

I hoped my voice would not break with the emotion I felt from even uttering the hated words. "She died." I met Eadric's surprised gaze before looking away.

"And it was recent. And sudden. And it devastated me beyond reason," I said as my voice trembled. "Maybe I was running away from the loss, but you have to understand, my mother was all I had. The only family. There was no one else of any relevance in my life. With her gone, I have nothing left. And nothing really to lose."

As I spoke the words I realized the truth in them. This mission, the one I had questioned while my mother was still alive, had allowed me to run away, as far as I could get from the agony of her loss. It was actually my salvation.

"When that pain consumes you," I went on truthfully. "You stop thinking. You can hardly even breathe—"

"I've lost many people I love," Milo interrupted ruthlessly, "and I have never been so overcome that I'd be foolish enough to trespass into another Kingdom."

"As have I," a female member of the Assembly said as she started at me with disdain, her face flickering into her tiger Shadow.

"I find your answer unsatisfactory," Milo went on. "Especially considering how the Praetor says he came upon you."

"I'm sorry?" I asked.

"You were with the Reptiles," Milo stated. "How do we know you're not one?"

The other members began to speak amongst themselves, whispering in agreement, swayed by Milo's words. I could feel what small tenuous grasp on safety I had, slowly slip away.

"They attacked me," I said. "One was trying to eat me —"

"For all we know it was a trap," Milo bellowed out to the room, standing up and pounding his chest the way his soul ancestor had in the past, flickering between both.

I had to fight back with all I had. "I know it's hard for you to comprehend," I called out, pleading with them, sensing Shadow mayhem among the Assembly was about to be unleashed. "I don't blame you. But the Praetor saved my life—you must believe me."

"Why would we believe an Aliud?" Milo roared out in rage, inciting the others to flicker.

"It was my naiveté," I rushed out, my mind searching for

a way to sway them. "Maybe I was, or am too young to go out on these planetary missions."

Eadric's gaze found mine as I searched for a way to reach her despite Milo's efforts to undermine everything I said.

"Maybe you're right. Maybe a part of me thought there was nothing to go back to. It was a foolish mistake on my part. An error. And I regret it now, more than anything."

"You regret getting caught," Milo said callously.

"No!" I stated shaking my head emphatically. "I regret all of this unease I've caused."

I looked at the other members of the Assembly, silently begging them.

"I made a mistake I can assure I will never *ever* make again," I said. "Please believe me. I can't express how sorry I am. I just—I just want to go home."

I searched their faces, hoping they would be swayed.

"The only way I might believe you is if you reveal your Shadow to us now." Milo's words caused silence to descend on the room. They all stared at me with wide eyes. I could see some contemplating his words.

"And how would you like me to do that?" I was determined to stay strong. I could not break. Not now.

"You are remarkably calm for being in a foreign land," Milo said slyly.

"And you are remarkably angry." I threw caution to the wind and gave right back. Milo was stunned. Right when I thought it was over for me, a few members of the Assembly laughed, lightening the mood. The relief I felt was staggering. I met Milo's gaze again.

"I'm sure you know there are *other* ways…" Milo said after the laughs died down.

"If you do not believe Siren when she says I saved her life," Aedan's voice was powerful, "then you're doubting what I saw with my own eyes. Had I not found her, she would have died. She is not a Reptile."

There was an underlying threat behind Aedan's words. If they believed I was lying, then they believed their leader was complicit.

"You will corroborate the Aliud's story?" Milo asked him harshly.

"I will," Aedan said without hesitation.

"You saw her Shadow?" Milo continued in disbelief.

"I did."

My heart stopped.

Aedan lied for me. And I knew he did it to protect me. I was overcome with gratitude and fear—I didn't want to jeopardize his position or life in any way. I'd do everything I could to make sure he was never at risk because of me.

Milo didn't look like he believed Aedan, but what could he say? A long minute went by before someone spoke.

"We don't doubt your words, Praetor," An older man spoke, who sat at Eadric's right. His face was kind and filled with understanding. "I understand loss all too well, child, and it has been known to make us do foolish things."

"I was foolish," I admitted lowering my head in obedience, hoping my meekness would aide my case and detract from my words with Milo. "Please forgive me."

"You must understand why we have to be cautious," he said.

"I do," I quickly told him before casting a glance up.

He looked over and met Eadric's gaze. An unspoken agreement passed between the two, then Eadric continued.

"Other questions?" She finally asked.

I spent the next hour answering questions from different members of the Assembly. They were easy enough to respond to. Most people were just curious about Kingdom B and the laws. The Reptile attack also caused intrigue within the Assembly. I recounted that event in great detail bringing my nightmares to life, telling them how Aedan saved my life. Milo was the only member who continued to stare at me like I was something that should be destroyed, an enemy in their camp. I was relieved he remained silent and did not intervene again.

"Are there any more questions for the Aliud?" Aedan finally asked.

The hall was silent.

Eadric stood up. "The purpose of our gathering is to rule whether or not you may remain in OM until your safe passage can be assured back to Kingdom B."

My heart pounded as I waited for her to continue.

"As you must understand, we cannot put any of our own people in danger, until we are sure there is no imminent threat from the Reptiles. We must err on the side of caution and assume there might be more out there. Your own people must assume you perished on your scout. And as you poignantly shared with us, with no family, there is no one awaiting your return."

Her words stung.

"You must realize the hurricane adds another layer to your predicament, making things more difficult for your return to Kingdom B. It's too dangerous to embark on any mission now, since we cannot predict the volatility of the storm."

"I understand." I could not argue against her logic.

Eadric looked over at Aedan.

"I consent to Praetor's wishes. The Aliud, *Siren*, will remain on our land as a guest until such time we may ensure her safe travel back home," Eadric continued. "When the hurricane passes, and under the guidance of the Praetor, we'll send teams to scout and confirm the Reptiles pose no danger. If our intel comes back that they do not, we will plan Siren's return."

The relief I felt was staggering.

"This is madness," Milo shouted as he pounded his fist on the stone table.

"The decision has been made." Aedan barked out.

Milo's eyes blazed with anger as he stared at Aedan.

"The Praetor already stated he will stand before us and be held accountable." Eadric's voice was harsh.

I felt sick knowing Aedan risked himself for me—yet again. But this time he was in more jeopardy than he knew, because I wasn't from Kingdom B as I said—if they found out what I was, if Dr. Novak told them, they would view me as something far more dangerous than a Reptile.

"And you, Milo, will not utter one more word against the ruling, or you will be at risk of losing your seat at this table." Eadric continued on. "We do not tolerate disrespect in this hall."

Milo met Eadric's eyes for a beat, before nodding obediently. "As you wish, Elder."

"There is one more thing." Aedan said as he stood.

"Yes, Praetor?" Eadric replied.

"As the Assembly has allowed Siren to remain in OM, Dr. Novak asked she be allowed to work with him in his lab. He believes there is much we can learn from the other kingdoms that might help with our own research. I think it would be prudent of us to allow it."

I could feel the blood leave my face.

"You cannot be serious!" Milo snarled out as he bounced out of his seat. "Is her staying within our walls not enough for you? Now you want an Aliud privy to our private research?"

I was not surprised by Aedan's request, since I knew the real purpose of his desire to have me in Dr. Novak's lab—to find out if I was telling the truth. But Dr. Novak requesting it now that he knew my Breed was another story altogether.

"We will not speak of it in front of Siren," Eadric said with authority. "Summon Dr. Novak so that we might hear this request and reasoning from him."

"You are excused, Siren," Aedan ordered without moving his gaze from Milo. "General Canis will see you back to your room."

"Thank you for your time and hospitality." I stood and tried to process my emotions.

I was relieved the Assembly would allow me to stay but felt immense guilt over the risk Aedan had put himself in. And now I had Dr. Novak to deal with.

Somehow, *he* seemed more frightening than a Reptile.

CHAPTER TEN

"Now you will tell me what happened with Kali." General Canis said once we settled in the pod.

I wasn't surprised she asked about Kali so quickly. She was relentless.

And true to her word.

"It was nothing. A misunderstanding. No cause for worry."

"It didn't look like nothing when I walked in the room."

"I believe she felt the need to mark her territory," I said dryly.

"She is tricky, Siren." Bibi said. "She can be quite vicious when provoked. Trust me. I have seen that side of her over the years."

I believed her.

I also knew it was too late for me in that regard. I was a sitting target for her now. I would have to tread carefully and do everything in my power to avoid her.

"From my first encounter with her, I could pretty much sense that to be the case. But I appreciate the warning."

We reached Aedan's home and exited the pod. Bibi escorted me back into the hall, and I was relieved she didn't continue to discuss Aedan or Kali.

"The Assembly asked about the Reptiles," I said, trying to break the silence.

"I'm not surprised."

"How long have you known they've resorted to cannibalistic behavior?"

Bibi walked over to a large window overlooking the fields.

"Months," she said quietly as she stared. "There were suspicions, but we brushed them aside, believing our only threat from Kingdom R was their need to take our land. But then everything changed after the Incident."

Bibi crossed her arms and watched the rain come down hard. Her tone turned somber. "There were accidents over the years, we believed were just bad luck. Soldiers gone missing. Their bodies, or what was left of their bodies, later found, looking as if they'd been ravaged to the bone. In the beginning, we mourned the losses and continued on, foolishly believing it was nature's elements."

"How many?" I asked moving to stand beside her, horrified people had died so cruelly.

"Twenty people have been killed and consumed by Reptiles."

I let out a gasp. Bibi turned her gaze to mine, her face showing the turmoil.

"Shocking isn't it?" Her voice was bitter. "I can only blame myself."

"You couldn't have known the Reptiles would do something so gruesome." I tried to comfort. I could feel her sadness and the weight of her guilt.

"I should have guessed it. I'm the General, in charge of the army and my Breed's safety, a position I wanted since I was old enough to know it existed. I was chosen by Aedan for my tactical skills and supposed intelligence to anticipate danger." Bibi smiled bitterly. "But even as great as my disappointment in myself is, Aedan's is tenfold."

"Is that why he scouts alone?"

"Yes," Bibi said. "To ensure there are no more losses, except for maybe his own."

Aedan alone out on the land made much more sense to

me now. "And the Incident you referred to?" I couldn't help but ask.

Bibi took her time before answering. I watched as her aura changed from white to light blue, indicating her pain.

"There was a group out," her voice was barely audible. "A family of farmers. Two young children. Girls. And their parents. They had wandered away from the land they cultivated—we don't know why. I can only assume they went out to explore or take their children on an adventure. They couldn't have known it wasn't safe."

My stomach began to sink in dread.

"They were late to return."

Bibi put her hand on the windowpane, her aura radiated her sadness.

"All citizens must check in and out at the gates, so we know their whereabouts at all times. With the ever depleting population, we must account for every human." She looked over at me.

"I'm sure this is the case in your own Kingdom, as each day goes by, every life becomes more precious to us. Every needless loss is like a mortal wound to the heart."

It seemed as though Bibi went into a trance as she recounted the events.

"I alerted Aedan. We went out together to bring them back."

For the first time, I saw her look vulnerable. The General, who always seemed as though she was unaffected and under complete control, looked like she was about to break down. Her voice trembled as she continued.

"It didn't take long for us to find them. We came across the family and a hunting party of three Reptiles. The most vile looking humans I have ever laid eyes on. And they were…" her voice breaking. She closed her eyes for a moment as she relived the horror again.

"Eating them."

I had to lean against the window for support. Even though I had experienced a Reptile attack, the atrocity she spoke of was still incomprehensible.

"The couple's bodies were ripped open, like carcasses half eaten and unimaginable to behold. And the girls…" her voice caught.

I did not want to hear anymore. I could not bear to hear anymore. As she told the story, I felt as though I was reliving it with her. "No," I whispered not wanting to hear, "Please, no…"

"Like young calves taken to slaughter," Bibi voice broke. "They were still alive watching those animals…"

I could feel the tears stream down my face, and there was nothing I could do to stop them.

"We killed the Reptiles," she said before looking over at me. "And we were forced to end the children's suffering."

I shook my head unable to even comprehend.

"Every day," Bibi's face flickered into her Shadow, her pain still raw. "I wake up to it."

"Why?" I whispered through my tears. "Why would they keep them alive like that?"

"I asked one of them that same question, before I plunged my sword between his eyes," Bibi's voice was bitter.

I waited.

"*It* told me a child's meat was the most succulent of all and tasted better if he or she were consumed alive—the adrenaline they release—the secretion, makes the meat more tender."

I couldn't respond. It was too horrific to even contemplate.

Humans *eating* humans.

We had become the monsters from fairytales.

It was a while before Bibi regained control of her emotions, and when she did, her guard was back up. But to my pleasure, she said I could have free rein in the living areas, and if I needed anything, I was to use one of the metallic call buttons that could be found in every room and my needs would be seen to.

After telling me the horrific tale of the Incident, her aura had darkened into a somber grey, so I knew she wanted to leave and take a moment for herself. I couldn't blame her.

"I'll find you later this afternoon, once I have an update from Aedan regarding Dr. Novak's lab," Bibi said as she started to leave.

Her mention of Dr. Novak brought me back to the danger I was in and the threat he held over me. Bibi stopped at the door and faced me. She surprised me with her next question.

"Will you be all right," she asked, "alone?"

"I'll be fine," I assured her, pleased she even asked. I was compelled to reciprocate the kindness and offer what little comfort I could. I could see her grief was hard to bear.

"Before you go there is something I'd like to say…"

"Yes?"

"I want to thank you for sharing the terrible tragedy with me," I told her. "I know it was difficult for you, but it's helped me understand things in your Kingdom much more clearly now."

"I'm glad I was able to give you clarity."

"It has," I said softly. "If I can offer you any solace—I

can say without a doubt, what happened wasn't your fault. There is no way you could have known such evil existed."

Still existed, I had wanted to say. But I wisely chose not to.

The General closed her eyes for a second, and when she looked at me, I saw a shift in her aura to gratitude. I was happy I could help ease some of her pain.

"Thank you, Siren," she said. She left me then, alone in the hall, with the entire afternoon to compose my thoughts and try to map out a plan.

First thing I had to do was explore my temporary home.

The storm caused the lights to flicker on and off in the pristine hall, casting shadows all around me. The entire passageway was silent except for the storm. There wasn't a soul in sight.

My mind mulled over my introduction to the Assembly. Without a doubt, Milo was now another citizen of OM I would avoid. He despised me on sight, and I instinctively knew he'd try to use me to hurt and undermine Aedan.

I refused to let that reason be me. I owed him that much.

Once the storm passed, I would be taken back to the outskirts of Kingdom B, where I could trigger my location device and find the others. I knew I couldn't depend on assurances from the Assembly or Aedan, and I needed to take matters into my own hands and find my own way out of OM. If my life was in jeopardy now that Dr. Novak knew my truth, I had to find a way to save myself.

But if the storm didn't break, or the threat of the Reptiles was too great, I would be stuck here in OM. And what then? Would I ever find the other Cetaceans?

I couldn't let myself think about that possibility. I *had* to find them.

As I continued my exploration of Aedan's home I found the floor plan of the compound was open and spacious. Every room felt similar to the Great Hall and my bedroom, with low couches, wooden tables, and giant white wax candles. I found myself wandering down a hall and walking into a room with giant double doors and floor to ceiling windows that looked out on the city. I didn't think I'd ever get sick of looking at the view. When I pulled my gaze away, I looked around the rest of the room.

My heart sped up at the sight—the walls were lined with shelves and stacked with ancient looking books. For the first time in a long while, I felt a rush of excitement course through my veins. I could hardly breathe at the vision of such beauty.

Old books.

Real books.

Human books.

I had never seen them firsthand before in my life. We had been taught through machines and programs, never actually holding a textbook in our hands. I walked over to a shelf and ran my fingers over the most sacred items I'd ever seen. I could feel the goose bumps crawl up my arms as I savored the touch, the *feel* of them.

I found myself walking over to stand in front of a glass case that held an old diary tablet one could write in as well as log videos. An iridescent light cast an eerie glow on the object.

My heart sped up in excitement when I saw the words laser printed across the top of the tablet…

Video Log
Diary of Dr. Neil Hedy

6:45 A.M.–March 3, 2511

The father of the Soul Particles! His *actual* diary. I could not contain my excitement as I pressed the small gold plated chip at the side of the tablet. An archaic version of a 3D television monitor came to life. The picture was grainy, and at first I couldn't decipher it, but then something slowly came up and I found myself face-to-face with a holographic image of Dr. Hedy.

I took a step back and almost came to my knees.

He stood in front of the monitor, dressed in a long white coat, beige pants, and a white top. He had a full head of silvery white hair and wore thick glasses, still I could see kindness in his hazel eyes. His skin was light, and I would guess he was in his late sixties.

It looked like he was in his private office, though the background was sterile and devoid of any pictures or even scientific instruments.

Dr. Hedy smiled and began to speak like he was talking right to me.

"What does it mean to have a Soul?" His voice was solemn but warm and likeable as I always believed it would be. "For years, scientists have tried to test the theory. They've weighed the human body at death to see if it was lighter and to see if there was some tangible way to tell we are not just a mass made of molecules and atoms. To know there was something greater within us that lived on."

I found myself reaching out, trying to touch his face. My hand moved through the image, and I watched as another picture came on the screen as he spoke. It was of a lion.

"Today I buried the last great cat to ever roam our Earth," his voice was sad. "A lion. His name was Einstein, and he was magnificent."

I saw various images of Dr. Hedy with Einstein including older videos taken prior to his death that showed the two of them in a field, eating, playing. Scenes from a life I had only imagined.

A video came up of a team that looked to be military, moving through a great plain and coming upon a young cub huddled in a bush.

"He was rescued by the Extinction Prevention Team and brought to my laboratory where we built him a giant pen to live out his life," he said, and as he spoke, I was shown the various scenes he described. "His father and mother had been poached by human's intent on having trophy heads of the last great beasts to roam the Earth."

"Had we left him alone in the wild he would have succumbed, either man's evil deeds or nature itself, the result of being the last of his kind."

Dr. Hedy's face was etched in sadness.

"Einstein had become my friend. I was the only one he allowed near him, because we had a special bond," he said. "I could feel his pain, and I would often find myself sitting with him for hours, enjoying his energy and regal presence."

Next, an image came up of Einstein laying peacefully next to Dr. Hedy as he stared down at the incredible animal. "He was my companion. And he trusted me so completely that he allowed me to extract his Soul Particle for experimentation. Perhaps he knew it was the only way his species would survive on Earth."

I watched an image of Dr. Hedy in surgery sticking a large needle through Einstein's forehead into his pineal gland. And then the video flipped back to Dr. Hedy in his lab.

"Einstein died peacefully in my arms. When his eyes closed for the very last time and he let out the final breath, I wept. I wept for his loss. For how much I would miss his presence and love. And I wept for *mankind*."

Dr. Hedy took a moment before he continued.

"For here was the final proof of what we had become. The great father of relativity, Albert Einstein had once said, 'The world is a dangerous place, not because of those who do evil, but because of those who look on and do nothing.' With the death of this great cat of lore, his theory was proven correct."

"I have reservations," Dr. Hedy said. "Many fears have raced through my mind. At times I've wondered if I've stolen something precious. I am a scientist. I live in reality. With facts. The tangible. Have I gone against the natural order of man and the world? Conceivably."

He picked up a photograph of a dolphin and pointed at it.

"But when I stare into the eyes of this great creature, I see a soul I believe should live on.

In any way she can. Even if it means something entirely new for our species," Dr. Hedy's voice was strong and almost angry. "After all, *we* are the ones responsible for this. Nature *and* man must continue to evolve."

The 3D image went dark indicating the end of the journal entry. I had to watch it a few more times to be sure my mind had not been playing tricks on me.

This was Dr. Hedy's personal diary.

And all around five hundred years old, preserved in a way to stand the test of time. This tablet held his personal thoughts. Insight into the past. And all the data Dr. Hedy collected from the moment when he discovered the Soul Particle.

The diary seemed to emit a powerful energy. It was like a dream come true.

Worth the journey to Earth.

Worth the unplanned crash in OM.

But before I could play another one, there was a crackle in the room and then a robotic voice echoed in the space. "Dr. Novak will join you imminently."

I jumped at the sound of Sara's voice and backed away from Dr. Hedy's diary.

Panic gripping me, I stared at the door to the library. Dr. Novak was coming for me?

Now?

A second later the door opened, and he entered, leaving me no choice but to face him.

There was a cockiness in the way he walked, like he held all the advantage. And he did. I stared at Dr. Novak in silence, waiting for him to speak, fear beginning to wrap its cruel tentacles around me.

He quietly shut the door behind him before slowly making his way to where I stood.

"Sara do alert us if anyone comes near," he said as he watched me with a pleased smile. He glanced over at the video log. "You found Dr. Hedy's diary. It's quite fascinating, isn't it?"

I watched him suspiciously.

"The father of the Soul Particle," Dr. Novak continued almost reverently. "I envy the legacy he left behind."

He looked over at me shrewdly. "You can imagine as a scientist, I hope to make as great of strides as he did. To leave something behind for my people. Something to be written about in history."

I still did not speak.

"You must think me arrogant," Dr. Novak said as he crossed his arms, his eyes narrowing into slits. "But until you fell in my lap, I thought I'd never reach my goal. It seemed so futile."

"Your goal?" I finally asked him.

"Human reproduction," he told me simply. "Finding a cure."

"I'm not following," I said to him. "What do I have to do with a cure?"

"I can't answer that question quite yet," he said as he lifted a finger in the air. "But with all the tests I will run on you, the blood samples I will collect, and all the other experiments we will perform, I'm hoping you will be the answer."

The hairs on the back of my neck stood as I realized what Dr. Novak had in store for me—to be a test subject. A human lab rat. I was shocked he'd been so direct with me.

"I will not agree to this," I said, unable to keep the anger out of my voice.

"No?" Dr. Novak replied with a cold smile. "What choice do you have, my sweet Cetacean? If you don't do as I say, I will reveal your true identity to the Assembly, and I can assure you after having just met with them, they are looking for a reason to imprison or kill you. Especially young Milo. I've never seen him express such outrage and hate. He would like nothing more than to see you die."

I took a step away from the doctor.

"Aedan..." I began shaking my head.

"Even our young Praetor will not be able to keep you safe from him or the others," his voice was forceful. "And now he's put his own position at risk for you—he's lied for you—and you've lied to him. Imagine what they would all think? A Cetacean, alive. Here in our city? It would be a public lynching. An execution of what OM believes is a threat to our existence."

His words rung true.

"But me on the other hand," Dr. Novak continued as he stepped closer to me, staring at me as if I was a tasty meal. "I know what you can bring us. A Breed who had no problem procreating. A Breed who through time became genetically superior."

"A Breed you tried to destroy," I reminded him sharply.

"Sadly, yes," Dr. Novak said, his voice emotionless. "But thankfully our ancestors' plans didn't work out. And now, you're here."

"I'm leaving soon," I reminded him. "I was promised—"

"Some promises are given but never kept."

My stomach fell as I watched him.

"I believe you will bring us salvation, Siren."

He reached out and took a strand of my hair in his hands, studying it like it was a foreign object he had never seen. "Everything about you fascinates me."

I stepped away from him, creating as much space as I could.

"My beautiful, Cetacean girl."

My skin crawled from his words. "I just want to go—" I began.

"Home?" He asked with a hollow laugh. "Where is that home? We both know it's not in Kingdom B as you say. It's not in OM. And just how many more are there of you here?"

"I'm the only one," I lied easily.

Dr. Novak shook his head as he tsked me.

"I don't believe that for a second," he said as mounting fear began to overwhelm me. "But we'll unravel your story as time goes on. I will have the truth from you one way or another—"

Dr. Novak looks so eerily pleased.

"You can't imagine how excited I am to begin my experiments," he told me. "We'll keep this little secret between us forever. You are *not* to tell Aedan. Or the General. Or anyone. I think you know why." Dr. Novak turned around and headed for the door. When he opened it, he paused for a moment, giving me his profile.

"I can't wait for you to meet my other exceptional test subject," he said with a grin. "He's been all alone in my basement lab for so long, he'll be happy to finally have some company."

And with that he shut the door behind him, leaving me trembling in his wake.

I was about to become Dr. Novak's test subject. Experimented on. Poked. Prodded. Abused. And there was nothing I could do to change it.

I *had* to find a way to escape.

Chapter Eleven

The door to the library rattled again, and I spun around expecting to see Dr. Novak.

I was relieved to see it was Aedan. "I trust you're well?" His gaze swept over mine.

"I'm fine," I replied.

He continued to study me. "Your color has changed. And I can smell your fear."

I kept forgetting how advanced their sense of smell was.

"I'm still processing everything," I lied, knowing I couldn't tell him about my conversation with Dr. Novak.

Aedan didn't look like he believed me.

"Thank you, Aedan," I said softly. "Had you not said what you did, I don't know if I would be standing here."

Aedan watched me with hooded eyes.

"I know you're not a Reptile."

I looked away from him. "General Canis said I could have freedom around your home," I rushed out changing the topic.

"I know," he returned. "I gave the order."

"Thank you," I said. "As you can imagine, being confined to one room was not a desirable condition."

"No," he said. "I imagine not."

Lightning struck outside. I waited for Aedan to continue, and when he did not, I tried to fill the uncomfortable silence. "The books you have here," I began as I looked around, "they're wonderful."

Aedan raised a brow. "You have never seen one before?"

"No," I shook my head. "They're truly incredible."

Aedan looked at the precious items and nodded.

"I can't argue with you," he agreed. "This is my favorite room in the compound."

"I can see why."

"Somehow, I think even with all of our technological advances over the years, we lost sight of the beauty of reading as our ancestors had," he said looking over at the books lining the shelves. "There is something intimate about holding a book in your hands and discovering a story for the first time. Having a machine tell you seems less personal in a way."

"I would never have known the difference, until I saw this room," I agreed.

"There are no books in Kingdom B?" Aedan's voice was curious.

"Perhaps they're available to those born into different circumstances than I."

"The world can be unfair," Aedan said thoughtfully.

Yes, it can, I thought as Dr. Novak's face flashed before me.

"I never longed for what I did not know," I admitted to him. "But now...everything has changed." In more ways than I could ever speak of.

I could feel Aedan's gaze on my face.

"While you're a guest in my home, you are free to read from any of the books you like. We've taken great care in preserving them, so all I ask is you guard whichever book you choose to look at." Aedan's voice was low.

He walked over to the case holding Dr. Hedy's diary tablet and picked it up. My stomach sunk in dread. He was going to deny me the one thing I wanted more than anything.

It took me a moment to realize he was holding it out for me to take. "I'm certain this is the first item you want to look through."

I could only stare.

"Dr. Hedy's diary is at your disposal," he said. "Treat it with the respect it deserves."

"Thank you." I was overwhelmed and touched by his goodwill. He could not have given me a greater gift. I took the tablet from his hands and held on to it as if it would disappear.

For a second, I thought about telling him about Dr. Novak. But I was afraid. What if he turned against me? I had compromised his position in the Assembly, and he would be furious. Then I would have no one on my side. It wasn't a risk I was willing to take. I needed Aedan to help me out of OM. *Mission First.*

"You don't know what this means to me," I said to him.

"I think I have half of an idea."

"I'll be ruined now for good."

"Somehow, I think you were before you even entered this room," Aedan replied cryptically.

My heart sped up.

"Dr. Novak stated his case in front of the Assembly," his tone turned brisk as he changed the topic. "And they have agreed to his request. You will work with him in his lab."

"Will I be working or will I be studied by him?" I countered, knowing it was the latter. I wondered if Aedan knew about the other test subject Dr. Novak had mentioned.

Or was that another secret he kept from the Praetor?

"Both," Aedan answered truthfully giving nothing away. At the very least, he was honest, and I could not fault him for it.

"You'll begin with Dr. Novak tomorrow," he told me. "I thought you might prefer to have the afternoon to yourself after the stress of this morning."

"What kind of tests will Dr. Novak perform on me?" I prodded, trying to figure out how much Aedan knew of Dr. Novak's experiments.

"I leave the world of science in his hands," Aedan said with a shrug. "There is nothing for you to worry about."

"How do you know?" I insisted.

"He won't hurt you," Aedan promised me as he searched my gaze. I could see the truth in his eyes—or at least what he *believed* to be the truth. But Dr. Novak proved he was operating behind Aedan's back.

I looked away from his knowing gaze.

"There is nothing for you to fear," he said quietly, trying to reassure me. From the sound in his voice, I knew he was being sincere. Since I couldn't reveal the truth, I gave him a reassuring nod.

"Of course not."

"I've asked Bibi to show you around some of our city this afternoon," he began. "I thought you might like to see our way of life. To become acclimated to it. A closer look and not one from a pod. I believe it will only serve you, since we don't know how long you'll be staying here. And maybe, if all goes well, there'll be a time when you can travel freely around the city without an escort."

The grip he had on my leash was slowly loosening. He was actually trying to give me more freedom, which meant I'd be given the opportunity to find another way out of OM.

He crossed his sinewy arms and watched me under hooded eyes.

"Is there anything else you wish to discuss with me?" He asked.

I shook my head. His gaze bore into mine.

"I have the distinct feeling there is something *you* wish to discuss with me," I said after a minute and waited.

"Milo," he began. "Stay away from him."

"I planned on it." I thought about Dr. Novak's words.

"He won't harm you or go against the Assembly's or my wishes," Aedan said. "But still, I'd prefer you avoid him. General Canis is aware of this as well."

"I will."

My gaze shot up to his. There was a flash of something in his eyes—almost like he was unsure, not a sign of the usual confidence I saw whenever I looked at him. But before I could dwell on it, or even truly believe what I was seeing, he was back to being the leader of OM.

Distant and powerful. And completely in control.

"Stay out of trouble," was all he said, before he left me alone in the room.

A million different emotions seemed to vibrate through my body when he was gone. My mission was all I ever thought about. All I had ever known. Since I was a child I'd been raised with a singular focus—return to Earth. Assimilate. Ensure our Breed's survival. But what about the rest? Feelings. Emotions.

My life had not been my own on Akasha. And now it wasn't my own on Earth.

Sadly, this was the only existence I had ever known.

And I was angry.

I was angry Aedan saw the need to order me around. Angry he didn't trust me. Angry I had no control over my own life. Angry everything seemed to be spiraling into an abyss I didn't know if I could crawl out of. I had no choice but to fall in-line with whatever Aedan and the Assembly wanted. And now, Dr. Novak, too.

I was completely at their will. But I promised myself that would soon change.

ØØØ

I left the library a short while after Aedan and made my way up to my room. The Great Hall was still surprisingly empty. I climbed the stairwell and reached the hall leading to my room. The lights were out and the way looked dark and ominous.

I paused for a moment and let my eyes adjust to the darkness, my senses hyperalert.

The hairs on the back of my neck rose. Something was off. The energy around me seemed different. Volatile.

Dangerous.

I tried to shake the feeling, but something wasn't sitting well.

"OM tastes better than Bird."

I stopped walking.

"Between the two meats, I like OM better."

I slowly turned around and faced what I knew was a Reptile.

She was a child. She couldn't have been more than six, maybe seven. She had long blonde hair and almost translucent white eyes. Her body was gaunt, and she was dressed in a baggy black dress that fell down to her calves. A scaly, Reptilian tail poked out of the back of her dress. She was yet another Reptile whose human form had physically evolved.

She was only ten feet away from me. She licked her lips as her gaze flickered over me.

"I'm so hungry."

I thought about running to my room, but I knew she'd be upon me when I reached the door, and I'd have my back to her, giving her all the advantage.

I took in more of her appearance. She wasn't just gaunt. She looked malnourished.

Her hair was greasy and there was a frenetic energy surrounding her that was almost desperate. My eyes moved over the black collar around her throat.

"He said I could eat you." Her voice was childlike, unnerving me.

I contemplated my next move. "Who said?" I asked softly.

"The man in the white coat."

I felt the blood leave my face. *Dr. Novak.* I knew she was referring to him.

"When did he tell you this?" I whispered.

"When he let me out," she replied innocently, beginning to advance. "I haven't eaten in so long." I took a step away.

"Stay back," I told her, my emotions raging inside. She was a child. A starving prisoner of Dr. Novak and he let her out to come for me, and I didn't know why.

She shook her head eerily from side to side as she continued toward me.

"No."

She launched herself at me with a strength that was shocking for one so young. She morphed into her alligator Shadow, her eyes turning to slits. Her fingers tried to claw at my face as she hissed and moaned, snapping her teeth at me as she tried to take a bite—sounding like her Shadow. I fell back against the door, trying to keep her away. I knew I could kill her if I wanted. My strength was infinitely greater than hers, but I couldn't bring myself to do it. She was a child.

Only a child.

I pushed her off my body and watched her stumble onto the floor.

"Please!" I yelled, hoping someone would hear me and come find us.

But she was deaf to my pleas. She was starving. And she needed to eat. She ran after me again, this time when she hit my body she wrapped her small legs around my waist as she tried to reach my neck with her mouth. I pulled her hair back, jerking her head away, trying to unravel her legs.

"Get off me!" I said. "I don't want to hurt you."

"I'm going to eat you." She whispered, her eyes glowing bloodred.

Her ruthlessness shocked me. I turned my body around and slammed hers against the wall. She grunted in pain as her legs fell away from my waist.

"I don't want to hurt you," I begged her. I pried myself away, pushing her small body against the wall again, moving away as fast as I could. I started to run down the hallway toward the stairwell that led down to the Great Hall when a voice stopped me.

"First experiment complete," It was Sara. And her voice seemed to echo down the hall.

Before I knew what was happening, I heard a sizzling sound and watched as the child's body twitched in pain, her hands grasping the metallic collar that must have let off an electric shock, she flickered into her alligator Shadow before slowly sliding to the floor.

"What is this!" I shouted to Sara, to Dr. Novak, who I knew was watching and listening in.

"As Sara just said, our first experiment," Dr. Novak's voice came through.

My hands balled in fists at my side as I stared at the

girl's still body. I could feel the life in her organs, and I knew she was still alive.

"What kind of experiment is this?" I asked in horror.

"One to ascertain your level of empathy," Dr. Novak sounded calm. "Your refusal to kill the child is telling."

"How does this help you find a cure to the reproductive crisis?" I demanded to know.

"It doesn't," he said. "I was curious about your character. And now I have my answer."

"You're insane," I whispered.

"Now be a good girl, go down to the Great Hall, and make your way back to the library, while we clean up this mess," Dr. Novak ignored my words. "And don't forget these experiments are *our* little secret."

"What will you do with her?" I wrapped my arms around my waist.

"I think it's better left unsaid."

øøø

I sat in the library, blindly staring ahead.

Dr. Novak, he wasn't just a mad scientist looking for a cure—he was evil. Pure evil. What he had just done. What he put me through, was not for science, it was for torture. He had just proven that he had no regard for life—a *child's* life meant nothing to him. How many more of those Reptilian children were tucked away in his lab? How many more prisoners—test subjects—did he really have? Was this the prisoner he had spoken of?

And now, I was to be one as well.

What kinds of other experiments did he have planned for me?

I was at his mercy. I could say nothing, or he would reveal my Breed to the others. I was trapped.

I shivered in fear.

"What are you doing in here?"

I spun around to find Kali standing before me, her hands on her hips and her face contorted in anger as she took a step toward me. She was the last person I wanted to see.

The very last.

"I'd like to be alone," I stood up and met her gaze.

"You'd like?" she hissed. "What you'd like means nothing."

Her tone. Her voice. The look on her face.

I tried to reason with myself. To remain cool. But it was too much. The snide looks she gave me were just *too much*. I had enough of being looked upon as an insect someone wanted to squash. And after what had just transpired with her father…

No. This would not do.

"I've been given freedom to do as I please in the Praetor's home."

I watched Kali sputter and huff, as if she could not believe I was actually talking back to her. The beauty I thought she possessed diminished in her hate.

"The Praetor wouldn't allow it…"

"But he has," I crossed my arms and stared at her.

She could barely speak, she was so indignant. I kept my cool and watched her shrewdly lose hers. "Is there anything else?" I asked in a dismissive tone.

She walked toward me with force, stopping only inches away. Her hand moved to the sword at her side, clenching the handle so tightly her veins practically popped out. I was surprised she kept her Shadow in check. I wondered if it had to do with the fact I had not revealed mine. More than anything, she wanted to lash out, I could see it. But in doing so, she would risk the loss of Aedan. He would never forgive the insult to his command.

"Do you know who you speak to, Aliud?" She finally bit out.

"Yes," I replied. "I do."

"I will be the Praetor's mate."

"I don't see how your relationship with him has anything to do with me," I said calmly though her words unsettled me.

Kali's eyes narrowed and took on her Shadow's glow. "My, how the timid little Bird has grown her wings."

"I have never been known to be timid," I bit back in anger. "And this *little Bird* has always had her wings."

She began to pull her sword out of its hilt, the sound of metal scratching against the scabbard. Slow. Deliberate. But I would not move. If she were to strike me down, I would stand before her proudly, as was my right.

"Kali!"

We both spun around in surprise. Kali took a quick guilty step away from me as Cyrus, the male soldier I had met when I had first arrived in OM, entered the room.

He came upon Kali and I quickly, towering over us. His yellow eyes narrowed as he looked at the female warrior.

"Was your hand on your sword?"

"Never," Kali lied.

"Never?" Cyrus questioned. "I saw it with my own eyes."

"You dishonor me, Cyrus. I would *never* threaten our Praetor's guest," she looked innocent enough that I almost believed her.

"She is also the Assembly's guest." He said in warning.

"I am quite aware of the Assembly's foolish vote," Kali bit out.

"Foolish or not, it is their right and it is the law," Cyrus returned.

"We were just talking," Kali sounded defensive. "That is allowed, my friend."

Cyrus finally turned his attention to me. He looked me over in a concerned way, checking if I had been hurt. "Are you all right?"

I realized I could reveal the truth he no doubt already knew, or I could play my cards in a different way. If I made an accusatory statement against Kali, it would only serve to make her hate me even more. Her body was tense as she awaited my response.

I chose the latter.

"I'm fine," I smiled innocently. "It was as she said. We were just talking."

He didn't believe me. I looked over at Kali, who seemed more surprised by my answer than Cyrus. But she covered quickly.

"You see," Kali interjected. "It was just as I said."

There was an uncomfortable silence in the room, before Cyrus finally relaxed his stance. He turned to Kali. "The General asked me to tell you the Praetor calls for you."

"Where is he?" Kali's face lit up at the news.

"I believe he's back at the Assembly Hall."

"Then I will go to him there," she said with an excited smile. "And how did you know where to find me?"

"Your scent betrays you," he replied. "It is everlasting, a difficult one to forget."

Kali stepped forward and patted Cyrus on the cheek before leaning up on her toes and kissing him softly on the lips. I was so shocked by the intimacy I had to look away. I told myself I didn't know what was custom here in OM, this could just be their way. But for some reason, I knew there was something deeper between the two.

"Thank you for the compliment, my dear friend. As always, you flatter me." She didn't bother to look at me or even say goodbye.

My eyes settled on Cyrus. His cheeks were flushed, and I could have sworn I saw a look of longing in his eyes as he stared after her.

But he recovered quickly, meeting my gaze, giving me an apologetic look.

"She is a force of nature," he finally said.

"I can see that."

"Your name is Siren," he gave me a friendly smile. "I remember. And I'm Cyrus. I don't believe we properly met before."

He extended his large hand and it enveloped mine.

"I hear rumors you'll be our guest for some time," he said.

"Until the storm passes."

Cyrus looked outside at the raging wind and lightening and nodded. As if on cue, the thunder rumbled loudly. Cyrus gave me a small smile. "Like I said. For some time."

We both shared a laugh. And it felt good after the day I had.

I realized I was still holding onto his hand, so I pulled away.

"So tell me, Siren—may I call you by your name?"

"I promise you, I prefer it to *Aliud.* And may I call you Cyrus?"

"I would like that," he replied.

"So what would you like to ask me?"

"Why did Kali have her hand on her sword?"

"Is that where it was?" I shrugged it off.

Cyrus crossed his arms across his wide chest. "We grew up together."

"We?"

"Aedan, Kali, Bibi and I," he explained. "We know each other. I'm telling you this just as I'm pretty sure Bibi already has—Kali is impetuous and has quite a temper when provoked."

Cyrus looked away and ran a hand through his short black hair. "I don't know how to say this delicately," he went on slowly.

"I'm assuming you want to tell me I've provoked her?" I stated the obvious.

"Yes," his gaze met mine again. "You have."

"Is that why you're here?"

"I came here to call her for Aedan, as was requested," he said with a shrug. "He's like a brother to me and she—a sister."

From the way he looked at her, I knew there was more to it than that.

"I'm not following…" I feigned ignorance.

"They are intended mates. They have been since Kali came of age. She picked *him*…"

I heard the tone in his voice change and could feel his pain. Having to say the words hurt. He longed for something that could never be his, *would* never be his.

A silent piece of my heart understood exactly what he was feeling.

"When Kali wants something," he went on. "She gets it. No matter the cost. In her eyes, you're a threat. There is something she senses. As a woman. *As a female of OM.*"

I knew he spoke the truth.

I saw the kiss I shared with Aedan flash before my eyes, and I hoped my face did not betray my inner turmoil.

Cyrus continued. "And if you don't mind me saying…" His voice trailed off like he was waiting for my permission.

"Please," I urged.

"There is something about you," his voice sounded almost uncomfortable.

I waited for him to continue.

"As a man…" He fumbled for the words. "Forgive my boldness, but I can see *why* she feels threatened by you."

He was complimenting me and it was beyond flattering. I also realized it was something I needed to hear. The women I had seen and interacted with in OM were all incredibly beautiful and attractive. And vibrant. It was nice to know there was something intriguing about me as well.

"I've made you uncomfortable," he stated the obvious.

"A bit," I said with a nervous laugh.

"Forgive me," he said.

"There is nothing to forgive, Cyrus."

He was gentle, softer than Aedan. It was refreshing to come across such a trait in a male. I thought about the other Cetacean girls and wondered if they were going through the same emotions as I was, with the people they encountered.

I wondered what their time had been like on Earth.

And after experiencing Dr. Novak's first test, I wondered if I would ever see them again. I realized now from being in OM and interacting with their people that I wanted to get to know mine. Selfishly, I had ignored them my whole life—for what reason, I could not even say. They were my Breed. My people. The only ones I had here on Earth.

I prayed I'd be given a second chance.

Cyrus's eyes flickered over me as he studied my face.

"Are you all right?" He asked for the second time today.

I'm going to eat you.

"I'm fine," I said as I tried to push away the scene with the Reptilian girl from my mind.

"Are you sure?"

OM tastes better than Bird.

"Yes," I whispered.

Cyrus didn't look like he believed me, but after a moment, he nodded his head.

"I'll leave you in peace," his voice was gentle. "I'm sure you have a lot to process right now."

These experiments are our little secret.

"I do."

CHAPTER TWELVE

Bibi thought it best to take a tour of the city in a small weather resistant pod.

Since I hadn't really paid any attention to my surroundings that morning, I was looking forward to finally getting a real tour of the city of OM and to get to see as much of their border and security as I could. Before Bibi came to collect me, I had a few hours to sit in my room, clearing my head. I couldn't allow myself to dwell on the child and what had become of her. I couldn't allow myself to obsess about Dr. Novak and whatever experiments awaited me. If I was to somehow find a way out of the city, I needed clarity.

Dr. Novak said he wanted to test my empathy—and he had.

I promised from this moment on, he would only see my apathy.

I sat in the pod and looked over at Bibi. Something had shifted between us since she shared the story of the Incident. Her demeanor was much softer now, her guard was down and maybe, just maybe, she was starting to enjoy my company as I enjoyed hers. Since I never had any friends on Akasha, I realized through Bibi's companionship just how deprived I'd been.

"I thought I'd take you to the Virago Temple. To the training center," Bibi said as we moved through the city.

From my studies, I knew that in ancient times Virago was a name they called a woman who exhibited exemplary and heroic qualities.

"Is that where all the women of OM train?" I asked.

"Only the best," Bibi replied. "The ones who excel in the same manner as a man."

I could see the joy on her face.

"Do you go often?" I asked.

"Not as much as I'd like," she said. "But when I was younger, I lived there. I grew up within the walls of that compound. And I never wanted to leave."

"You lived there?"

"Yes," Bibi explained. "You must be asked. Invited, I should say. There is no application process, no Trial, as there is for the men—the Elders in our Kingdom assess each female as she ages. When we're eight, it's determined if we exude the skills to be warriors of Virago."

"And you left your family to train there?" I asked.

"My birth parents are dead," her voice was flat and devoid of emotion. It wasn't a subject she wished to talk about. "The family I have now consists of the Earth tribe I created."

Aedan.

Aedan was her family.

"And Cyrus," she said adding his name, like she just read my mind.

I looked over at her in surprise.

"It is not a hard deduction," she said with a shrug. "Nor is it very difficult to read your face, when you allow your emotions free rein."

I laughed nervously and changed the subject. "Cyrus told me you guys grew up together. He said it was you, Aedan, Kali and him."

"We did," Bibi said. "From infancy. We banded together and stayed that way since."

"You don't know how lucky you are," the words came

out, before I could stop them.

"We would die for one another," Bibi said as she turned her gaze to face out the window. "Even Kali. With all of her different moods and plots and drama—she, along with the others, they are the only family I have. Even if she and I fight more than we get along."

I wasn't surprised to hear her say this. From the little interaction I had with Kali, I felt as though her personality was the polar opposite of Bibi's.

"Was Kali asked to join the Virago Temple?" I asked curiously.

"She was," Bibi said. "She was actually recruited when she was six years old, which is unheard of. Her skills on the battlefield are extraordinary."

It didn't surprise me to hear that. Kali had the look of someone who excelled at everything she tried, especially physical skills.

"Did you compete in a battle similar to Aedan to be named General?" I asked curiously.

"No," Bibi said. "That's an office you are named to by the Praetor."

"Then it is a testament to your character."

"Perhaps," Bibi said with a small smile. "Regardless, I consider it a great honor."

"As you should," I replied.

I turned my gaze from Bibi and looked out the window. The pod came to a stop in front of a massive building that looked as though it was built in ancient Roman times. It was as grand as the Colosseum and was flanked by seven giant statues that looked at least fifty feet high. They were of the great animals the people of OM descended from: a lion, a gorilla, a tiger, a wolf, an elephant, a polar bear, and a horse.

"Isn't it wonderful?" Bibi stated, smiling at the temple in pleasure.

"It is," I agreed with the same enthusiasm.

"Let's go inside." Bibi pressed a button in the pod, and the doors opened up in a way that when we got out, the frame protected us from the grueling weather, so we were able to enter the Virago Temple without being pounded by the rain.

"Follow me."

We walked through the enormous arched entrance of the temple. It wasn't heavily guarded as the Assembly Hall was down in the city, but there were still female security guards standing on alert. The only acknowledgement they made of our presence was standing aside as we walked down the torchlit hall.

I could hear the sound of metal clanging and women grunting, the noise echoing through the musky building.

"We'll go in through the back, so we don't disturb the women training."

I nodded in silence as we walked through wooden doors that led out into a giant arena covered by a glass dome. I sucked in my breath when I took in the scenario. It was like I had stepped back in time and was watching footage from ancient Rome or Greece, when the gladiators would train for battle and sport. Only, all the roles were reversed, and the women here looked like lethal Amazonian warriors from mythology. There were four different battle stations set up in the large arena.

One was for swordplay. Another archery. I watched women partake in hand-to-hand combat, where it looked as though they were all experts in Jiu Jitsu.

And then there was the area where the women were

training with man-made machines…taser guns and weapons that killed on impact. All man-made weapons, except for swords, were forbidden on Akasha. Because of our small numbers my people had banned any weapon that could be setoff and used to kill without any real thought. We'd been mostly trained in the art of hand-to-hand combat. A few of us had learned the ways of the sword, but I had not taken to the weapon well and instead chose to hone my skills in different ways. The idea of plunging an object through any life-form to kill it, had never sat well with me. But now with the threat of the Reptiles, I wished I had taken more of an interest in honing that battle skill.

"This is unbelievable," I said in awe. "The women are incredible."

"They are," Bibi said. "And in many ways the women who train here are more lethal than the men in our Kingdom."

"I'm not surprised."

"You must have soldiers," Bibi said.

"We do," I acknowledged. "But we don't have anything like this for the women."

I quickly went through what I remembered about Kingdom B.

"That's a shame," Bibi said. "Especially since I believe we can be more formidable on the battlefield."

"Why is that?" I asked curiously.

"Women are more calculating in battle," Bibi explained her theory. "Dr. Novak has studied the different human gender responses during crisis. He's noted that men become consumed with battle rage and see red—where women, after an initial response to danger, can look at different scenarios and with training can keep more of a level head."

The mention of Dr. Novak and his theories made my skin crawl, even though I believed he was right.

"I think you can witness the discipline yourself now. How many Shadows do you see?"

"Hardly any," I said in surprise. There were some who flickered in the coliseum but not many. For the most part, the women stayed in their human form.

"They have your restraint," Bibi said it so casually, it took me a second to process.

"That's nice to hear," I replied the only way I could. I didn't want to have this conversation, so I changed it, "and the argument that we are physically weaker than men?"

Bibi looked over at me with a sly smile. "I'd take anyone up on that challenge."

"Even Aedan?" The question came out, before I could stop it.

"He's the exception." Bibi looked over at me. "I overheard you tell Eadric that you had some experience in hand-to-hand combat."

I looked over at the effortless way the women were training with one another. A flick of a wrist here, a kick there —the way they moved, it seemed so easy and resembled a dance, but I knew it was far from that. It took great discipline to gain skill.

"Some," I admitted slowly.

"Would you like to train with us?"

"Really?" The surprise must have been evident on my face.

"I think it would do you good," Bibi said. "The next time you come across an attacking Reptile you will be better prepared to protect yourself. And..."

"And?" I persisted, when she did not finish her sentence.

"Sometimes it's good to prepare for an attack from anywhere."

In case I had to protect myself from someone in OM. She didn't need to spell it out.

"No harm can come of it," she went on.

"I think you're right," I finally said. "And I would like that."

"Let's go then."

"Now?" I asked, surprised.

"No time like the present," Bibi returned as she walked over to a wooden gate and opened it, so we could enter the arena. The women who were training did not look our way once, but the others who were waiting their turn had their eyes glued on me. Bibi and I walked to the area of the arena where the women were battling in hand-to-hand combat.

There were around twelve women and girls standing with us. Some of them didn't look older than eleven or twelve years old, but even so, they looked formidable. Bibi's presence also seemed to have an effect on them. They looked at her like they revered her. If the General noticed their behavior, she didn't let on.

"Gaia. Angela." Bibi called out to the two women currently facing off.

They stopped immediately and turned to face Bibi. They both bowed in obedience.

"General," they said in unison.

"I will take the center," she told them. They both walked to the side and waited with the other women. Bibi turned to face me.

"Siren. Would you care to join me for some fun?"

Before I answered, I looked around at the group of women to gage their reactions. Some seemed surprised, others almost gleeful, probably thinking, in all fairness, that Bibi would demolish me in hand-to-hand combat.

"Yes," I said, even though I knew there was a good chance Bibi would decimate me in only a few seconds. I was good at hand-to-hand combat and confident in my skills, but I'd never been up against a General.

I followed Bibi into the semicircle the girls formed. The rain pounded the glass dome above us, and an eerie silence filled the arena. I was sure any woman who wasn't in the middle of an exercise was definitely looking at us.

"Are you familiar with stick fighting?" Bibi walked over to a long table holding different weapons of combat.

"I am," I said. It was an ancient way of the human world. One that had origins in Africa. And one that truly tested natural skills.

"Is it your strength?"

"I'm familiar with various techniques," I replied confidently.

"Perfect," Bibi said grabbing a hold of two long sticks that were almost as tall as I was. Back at home, we had practiced in simulated programs since we were children, and as an adult, I passed all my advanced level exams. I exercised this skill with my mom many times. I thought I was pretty good at it.

Bibi threw the stick at me and I caught it easily.

"Would you feel more comfortable with a shield?" She eyed me.

"No," I shook my head. I didn't like to hold a shield in my free hand. But I knew Bibi was really asking if I was afraid of being hit by her—I knew I wouldn't have to worry about the General intentionally doing me bodily harm.

"Perfect," she said with a smile. "I prefer the latter as

well. Sometimes I find the element of danger makes everything more exciting."

"And unpredictable," I said.

"As is the nature of life."

She stood less than ten feet away from me, when she raised her weapon and crouched low. Her shiny braids framed her face, her eyes narrowed and watched me.

"Then we dance."

I held one fist on the bottom portion of the stick and waited for her to attack. By holding the weapon at the lower end and keeping that as my base it would improve the power of impact, and my own stability. I waited for Bibi's first move to see if she would choose mid or close range combat. I knew I had to get a feel for her technique, before I mapped out my plan of attack. I bent low and moved the stick with my body to center myself and create a natural flow of energy.

I held myself on the defensive and waited.

Bibi quickly stepped forward and brought her stick down to mine. The force of the impact was strong and vibrated through my body like a memory from the past. I held myself up and deflected the strong blow, before I turned my body, lifting my weapon up at her to strike back. She easily blocked my move and hit at me again. I could tell she was testing out my strength, just as I was doing to her.

My only advantage against the General was the fact she didn't know how strong I really was. She assumed I was a weak, fragile subject from Kingdom B with no real idea how to protect myself. Bibi came at me again, slamming her stick in downward horizontal strikes, reversing the hits to keep me on the defensive and not allow me a second to look for an opening to strike. I kept my motions centered, never allowing for a wide swing, so as not to be in a position where I might lose my weapon or allow her a fatal blow.

The skills I learned as a child began to flood back through my body as cellular memory took over. I moved across the floor quickly as we both fought with all our might. If I kept up the dance, as Bibi had called our battle, I could learn her pattern and find my way in to attack. But Bibi was relentless and a worthy opponent, and she was conditioned as a soldier. I knew it would take her quite a while before she tired. My muscles quivered from exertion. Since I hadn't trained in what felt like forever, it wouldn't be long before I began to slow down.

I had to come up with a strategy quickly.

Bibi came down with another thrust, with what felt as if it were the force of twenty people. I chose that moment to use all my strength, lifting my weapon up to push her body back. For more than a few seconds, we remained at a standstill. Her arm muscles bulged, but I used everything I had, and she finally stumbled back.

I only had a few moments before she recovered.

I began to spin in circles with my stick, feeling the energy around me grow more powerful as I gained momentum. I gathered enough strength to launch myself in the air, holding my weapon high above my head and came down on Bibi with force.

She was ready.

She held her stick still and firm. When the two weapons collided, they both snapped in half. The sound of the splintering wood echoed through the arena.

I heard a few surprised gasps as I stepped back from her.

Bibi held onto the two broken pieces and gazed up at me with a newfound look of respect.

"That was fantastic," Bibi finally said. "That was really remarkable, Siren. Where did you learn those skills?"

I tossed what remained of my weapon on the ground and reached out my hand to help Bibi up. She didn't hesitate.

"I'm sorry about that," I began, hoping I hadn't gotten overly aggressive during the battle.

"Nonsense," Bibi waved my words off. "This was a mock battle. Even though it was just an exercise, we always play to win."

I nodded and looked around at the inquisitive faces staring at me unashamedly.

"But you didn't answer my question," Bibi persisted.

I shrugged.

"My mother," I stated truthfully. "She loved all forms of karate exercise. She taught me everything she knew."

"You're very lucky," Bibi said.

"I was."

"You are," Bibi's voice was forceful. "Those are your memories to cherish forever. Consider the alternative—I have none."

Funny. I had never thought of my life like that.

I looked away from Bibi and stared around at the many foreign faces. I was hit by a myriad of emotions. Some of the women looked resentful, others in awe, and I thought I even saw a few looks of respect. It could have been my imagination, but this gave me a sliver of hope.

"You continue to surprise, Siren," Bibi murmured as she stood up to her full height.

"How so?"

"These abilities of yours," she said. "They are quite unexpected."

"From Kingdom B?"

"No," Bibi shook her head. "From a woman of your nature. But then I made the mistake of making assumptions and jumping to my own conclusions, and now I know I was so very wrong."

Which meant she believed, up until now, that I was weak and helpless. I wasn't surprised by that, but I was happy to have changed her opinion.

"I can see there are many layers we have yet to uncover about you."

"I assure you this is it," I said with an uncomfortable laugh.

"Is it?" Bibi asked softly so that only I could hear. "Somehow I doubt that."

I wished I could trust her. I wished I had someone to confide in. Someone to explain my trepidation and fears. I wished more than anything I just had a friend. But I couldn't risk our entire mission over my desire for companionship— even if I had to sacrifice my own safety.

Mission First.

"I dare." A strong voice called out, interrupting my train of thought.

Both Bibi and I turned to look at the female who spoke the words. She was one of the young children who had been battling before Bibi asked them to stand down. There was a lot about her that reminded me of Kali. Her eyes, the shape of her body and most obvious, the disdain written all over her face. I wondered if they were related.

"You dare?" Bibi repeated with a stern voice as she pinned her with her gaze.

"I do, General," she replied calmly. "It would be an honor."

There was an uncomfortable silence as the females

exchanged glances. I wondered what was going on. I looked over at Bibi and waited for her to explain.

"Gaia dares," Bibi said after a long moment, pinning me with her gaze. "She dares you."

"I'm sorry," I questioned. "I don't understand what that means."

"It means she has challenged you to a battle," Bibi replied. "The same one you and I just completed. She *dares* come up against who she believes is the victor of the battle. As is the right of any Virago in the temple."

"But I didn't win," I looked over at Gaia, who had her arms crossed and brow arched. This would not be a friendly fight, I knew. She was out for blood. Or maybe something more.

"Didn't you?" Bibi chided.

"Bibi…" I began.

"If she is frightened, I bow out," Gaia called out, so the entire arena could hear. "I would not cause the Praetor's guest any fear."

I could feel my back straighten, the hairs on my arms rise as my eyes narrowed on Gaia. I knew what it was. The emotion that instantly put me on the defensive.

Ego.

It was my first taste of it. And I didn't like the feeling one bit.

"I am not frightened, child."

The words came out of my mouth before I could even stop them. But Gaia *was* a child. She couldn't have been more than twelve or thirteen years old, and here she was egging me on. I thought about the Reptilian child who attacked me. Sadly, it seemed the children born into different breeds had one thing in common—they all craved a varying degree of violence.

From the corner of my eye, I saw Bibi's half smile, but I kept my gaze on Gaia. I could not look weak to these people. If I were to assimilate quickly, I couldn't cower.

I could tell from the look on Gaia's face she wasn't happy with my response.

"Let's dance," I repeated Bibi's words as I walked up to the weapons table and threw a stick in Gaia's direction. She was barely able to catch it.

I faced her with an arched brow and waited.

This would be too easy.

Her emotions were raging and out of control. Her aura was like a rainbow surrounding her body, a tumult of colors. Her attack would be swift and foolish.

And I would be ready.

Less than a minute later, I was not disappointed. Gaia rushed me in pure rage, losing all train of thought, all sense of her emotions and just blindly attacked. She flickered into her horse Shadow, her mouth opening in fury. Her strikes were vicious but not calculated. Her anger made her clumsy and fueled her ineptness, only making it much easier for me.

I could have sparred with her forever, easily deflecting all of her blows, but for whatever reason, I chose that moment to teach her a lesson. She needed to understand the foolishness of anger. Of how it could lead her to make mistakes that could change the course of her life. She needed to control her Shadow. I cleared my mind of any feeling of empathy and stepped forward for my attack. It was systematic and bold. I moved the stick quickly, around my body like it was one of my limbs and danced around Gaia, until she was too confused or tired to even keep up with my movements. It took only minutes, before I had on her on her back, weaponless, with the sharp end of the stick facing her chest.

Gaia gasped as though she believed I would actually plunge the weapon into her body.

I pulled it back and stepped away from her.

"I hope the challenge was satisfactory," I said.

Gaia leaned up on her elbows, staring at me. "Where did you learn that?"

"In my Kingdom." I replied.

"But you're supposed to be weak..." she practically stuttered.

"Says who?"

"Everyone," Gaia practically shouted. "Everyone has said the Aliud is weak and stupid!"

"It looks like the Aliud just proved she is not weak," Bibi joined our conversation. "And from what I gather, Gaia, she is not stupid. In life, it would be wise of you to use personal experience before you cast judgment." I was grateful Bibi came to my defense. It felt good to have someone besides Aedan on my side. In another world or life, I believed she could have been my friend.

"Shall we return to the Praetor's home to freshen up before dinner?" Bibi asked me.

"I would like that."

Bibi turned and began walking out of the arena, and I followed behind.

Siren.

It was a voice. My intuition. My inner knowing.

Something I heard inside made me turn. Gaia was coming straight at me with the razor sharp stick, her Shadow completely taken over. Her human body morphed into a hybrid between the two species. The skin on her lean arms, rippled over like a domino, changing into something tough, muscled like her ancestor. Her human face shifted, eyes widening, nose and cheeks even moving subtly, where I could see the essence of a beautiful black stallion. I dodged her attack and was able to grab her arm in the process and pull the weapon away, tossing it in the air. She snarled at me and growled, but within seconds, I had the girl on her back and at my mercy.

Bibi rushed over to us.

She looked furious, but all of that anger was directed at Gaia. I looked at Gaia's pale face and saw her fear as she flickered back into her human form. She knew what she had done was wrong. And for whatever reason, I felt bad for her. She couldn't be blamed for her anger or the humiliation she felt being beaten by me. Again. I was an outsider. Feared and distrusted by most of the population of OM. She was a child and challenged me in hopes it would make me look small. And she had failed. I understood it. But I could only forgive her.

"Gaia, you have disappointed me greatly." Bibi's voice was like a rumble from the sky. "You have gone against all rules set forth in this temple. You know the consequences of your actions. You are expelled from this institution."

"Yes, General." I watched the tears stream down Gaia's face.

"Do you understand why this is your sentence?" Bibi all but screamed at the frightened girl. "For this act, on this day, you have betrayed every oath we hold sacred in Virago."

"I feel shame," Gaia whispered.

I saw her agony. This world, this temple, this training, was this child's life. And unknowingly, I had just robbed her of her happiness.

I couldn't stand by and remain silent.

"No!" I called out, pleading with the General. "Please. No."

Bibi's eyes blazed with fury.

"*You!*" She barked at me. "Do you dare speak against my ruling for the temple of Virago?"

"No," I remained calm not allowing Bibi's temper to affect me. "I wouldn't dare. I'm only an Aliud, just as you all say."

The General fought to gain control of her emotions.

"But I ask you," I went on, completely careless of the ramifications. "No. I *beg* you, to reconsider your sentence."

I heard a few gasps. And then nothing but silence.

It was as if a bolt of lightning had broken through the glass dome above us and hit only ten feet away. People were frozen still, waiting for what was about to come.

Bibi stood up to her full height, appearing almost taller than she was, her stance beyond intimidating. "And why would I *ever* consider your request?"

"You have laws," I began.

"We do," Bibi's voice was flat. "And Gaia just broke one. And before you utter another word Aliud, let me remind you our laws are in place for the safety of our people. They are to be followed and obeyed at all costs. Our lives depend on it. If one soldier makes a mistake, the rest can die. I cannot have one soldier's impetuous actions cause the demise of an entire army."

I nodded in agreement.

"I understand," I said softly. "And I'm sorry I spoke out of turn. I'm not trying to offend you. But your sentence. It is not our way…"

I spoke what I believed to be a necessary lie. But it was

the only thing I could think to say to help Gaia out of the situation she was now in.

"You have no hierarchy?"

"We do," I assured her. "But we are vocal people as I'm sure you know from your studies."

"No, Aliud. I do not know. We don't study the other kingdoms as closely as your people seem to do." Bibi's voice was cold, so different from what it had been only minutes before. I wondered if by my actions, I had just turned the General against me.

"What is it you wish to say, Aliud?" I cringed at Bibi's use of the word. Before this moment I had only been Siren. Now I was back to being a stranger.

"Her reactions were that of a child," I pled. "She didn't think…"

"If she doesn't think, she'll cause needless suffering or worse, death, to her fellow soldiers."

"Yes," I agreed quickly but continued on. "But this is different, General. I am what you all keep telling me over and over, only an Aliud. She reacted to something she's never seen in her life. Something she's never even known. I'm the first you've ever encountered. Just as you are my first *other*. Does this situation not warrant understanding? Perhaps patience, even?"

Bibi watched me for a long moment, then turned her gaze to Gaia, who was now standing and facing the General with her head slumped low in dejection. I could only hope she would see the logic.

The arena waited for the General to speak. "Though your argument is compelling, my sentence still stands," Bibi finally said then turned to Gaia. "Pack your things. You will return home and never step foot in the Virago Temple again."

I looked over at Gaia, and my heart ached for her. She looked as though she was about to burst out in tears, but she was a proud girl and controlled her emotions. Her eyes were glassy when they met mine. Even though I tried to fight for her, there was still venom directed at me.

"I'm sorry," I said to her and did not care if Bibi would chastise me later.

I could feel her pain and it saddened me. This temple had been her life. And now because of me, she was robbed of something she loved.

"Let's go!" Bibi barked out to me.

I followed her out of the deathly silent arena, and the previous excitement I had to see the city was gone. The only thought that kept running through my mind over and over was that this world was a cruel place.

No matter the Kingdom. Or the Breed. Or the people.

It was all harsh. Unwelcoming. Cold.

I knew the General was waiting to admonish me for my words or for acting out, and I wondered what the ramifications of my actions would be. Would I now be restricted to Aedan's home? My room, even?

At this moment, it didn't even matter to me.

Bibi didn't say a word, until we sat back in the pod and were alone. She waited until the pod left the temple before turning to look at me.

She was calm before she began.

"You do know that Gaia was going to kill you."

"She would never have struck," I replied.

"She *would* have struck," she replied forcefully. "Had she only been given the opportunity. Do you understand what I'm saying to you? That is all Gaia needed. One moment. One second. One weakness and she would have ended your life."

My eyes met Bibi's. It didn't matter if she spoke the truth about Gaia's intentions. I knew she would never have reached me.

"That would never have happened."

"You can choose to believe that, but it doesn't even matter," she stared at me. "It is the action that speaks for the human."

I looked at her in surprise.

"I will not have a dishonorable soldier in my army."

"She is misguided and confused. She doesn't understand me. She doesn't even know what to *think* of me."

"I am training warriors," Bibi said to me.

"Don't you want *thinking* warriors?" I replied. "How else can they learn, if they don't fail at some of their tasks? How else can they rise to the potential you see, if they never fall? It is in our darkest hours when we rise to our greatest potential. It is our errors that make us stronger. Wiser. Our mistakes have the ability to turn us into fearsome creatures."

"When we choose to learn from them," Bibi countered.

"Yes," I agreed. "And we do."

"Not all."

"What has happened to your faith, General?"

Bibi suddenly looked exhausted.

"I just don't know anymore, Siren." She closed her eyes and shook her head in sadness. "Every day the world seems to get a little darker."

CHAPTER THIRTEEN

Bibi didn't follow me inside, nor did she bother to leave the pod or even ask if I would be all right, as was customary with her. I knew she was still upset with my interference with Gaia. I hoped she would forgive her.

I walked into the Great Hall and was surprised to see the area filled with people.

Aedan's servants were busy cleaning. I stood back and watched them for a moment, feeling like more of an outsider than ever.

I felt a tug on my hand and looked down to find a young girl, who couldn't have been more than five years old, smiling up at me. She had straight black hair and blue eyes that reminded me of my own. The little girl stared at me curiously.

"What are you?" She asked in a sweet voice.

I leaned down to face her.

"I'm a girl," I returned with a smile. "What are *you*?"

She giggled and shook her head. "No. You're different," she said reaching out to touch my cheek, her action innocent.

"What's your name?" I asked her.

"Ariana," she replied. "What's yours?"

"Siren. I'm happy to meet you, Ariana."

She studied my face for a moment, like she was searching for something.

"I like you," She said. "Can we be friends?"

The pleasure I felt from hearing her words was astounding. I was overcome with emotion. I hadn't realized I was so starved for affection. This child had finally given me something I needed so badly- human warmth. And for a brief moment I allowed myself to bask in the feeling.

"I would like that very much," I could feel tears fill my eyes as I gave her a wobbly smile. "I don't have many friends here."

"Now, I'm your friend," Ariana replied innocently. "You can tell me your secrets, and I will tell you mine."

If only it was that easy.

"All right," I said kindly. "That sounds like a good start."

"Ariana!" Ariana's eyes widened as she looked behind me.

I turned quickly and saw a young woman who could only be a few years older than me, and I recognized as one of Aedan's servants, quickly walking up to us.

"I told you to stay where you were!" Her tone was sharp and admonishing.

"I'm sorry, Mama," Ariana whispered.

The woman's startled gaze met mine.

"I just made a new friend," Ariana told her mother. "Her name is Siren. We're going to tell each other our secrets."

I gave her mother a friendly smile but her expression remained impassive.

"She's very sweet," I said hoping to diffuse the situation.

"Sweet, yes," her mom replied. "But she is also *very* impulsive. Forgive the intrusion. She's a child and doesn't know you're supposed to be left alone."

"She wasn't bothering me at all," the words stumbled out. "My name is Siren."

Ariana's mother looked at me like I was holding poison. But I persisted. I kept my arm extended and waited. It took her a moment, before she finally shook my hand.

"I'm Laurel," she said.

"It's a pleasure to meet you."

Laurel nodded but didn't return the sentiment. I tried to tell myself it didn't matter. That it didn't hurt—but it did.

"Mama, Siren is an Aliud."

"Very good, my darling," Laurel gave her daughter a gentle smile. "She is. Now, you run along to the kitchen and find your grandmother. She needs help, and if you're good, she might give you another one of the sweet cookies you love so much."

Ariana's eyes lit up. She started to run away but abruptly stopped and headed right over to me. She threw her tiny arms around my waist and hugged me tight. I was so taken aback by the gesture I didn't even have a chance to reciprocate.

"I'll find you later, and we can share our secrets," she whispered to me.

"Please do," I whispered back to her. "And enjoy your cookie."

Ariana took off again, and I stood for a moment and watched her.

I felt a movement, something shift, deep within my heart. I realized I wanted OM to survive. I wanted them to find a cure for their reproductive crisis. It was not us against them, as I once believed. We all shared one binding trait— we were all human. And this was a battle we all had to fight…together.

"She has never behaved this way with a stranger before," Laurel's quiet voice broke my train of thought.

I looked over at her.

"She's usually very shy and reserved," she continued as she watched me. "I can barely even get her to talk."

I shrugged uncomfortably. What could I say? Ariana was innocent and guileless. She was a child, who saw the world with love. She would never judge. That wasn't an emotion she even understood. At least, not yet. In time, I knew everything would change.

"If my child trusts you, then so shall I."

It took me a moment to process what she was saying to me. And when her words finally settled in, I was almost brought to tears. Yet again.

It was unbelievable.

Before I had come to Earth, I had cried twice in my life. The first, was when I witnessed the slaughter of the Cetaceans through the digital programs. The second, was when my mother had closed her eyes for the last time.

"Are you all right?" Laurel asked in concern.

I blinked back the tears that threatened to spill over and nodded my head.

"I'm fine. Thank you."

"Can I bring you anything?" She asked, gratefully changing the subject.

"No. Nothing," I shook my head.

"Then if you'll excuse me, I must see to the arrangements for dinner."

As Laurel walked back toward the other women, they rushed over, closing the distance and whispered to her furiously. I knew they were asking about me. Laurel quickly glanced at me before leaving the room with them.

I turned away from the scene, not wanting to think about the conversation or the feelings it evoked inside. So much had happened already today, I just craved the solitude of my room.

"And here you are," a cold voice sneered at me. "The Aliud I wished to find."

Milo appeared out of the darkness, his stance

intimidating. His gaze flickered over me with hatred. I was surprised to see him in the Praetor's home. It was a bold move on his part, considering the animosity he and Aedan mutually shared.

I stared at him coldly. I would not let him intimidate me.

"I see and hear the shy, timid girl we met in the Assembly has disappeared," Milo said, his eyes glinting. "News of your exploits in the Virago Temple traveled fast.".

"My exploits?" I asked meeting his gaze.

"You're a warrior," he said with a look of icy displeasure. "Fully capable of battle."

"I am capable of many things," I replied evenly.

"Oh, I have no doubt," Milo said as he cocked a brow. "You are an unknown anomaly who has yet to show her true colors."

He advanced upon me slowly, his stance menacing.

"I don't know what you're talking about," I returned standing my ground.

"Don't you?" He whispered softly leering down at me.

"What are you doing here?" I asked him harshly.

"This is *my* Kingdom, Aliud," his voice was laced with the power of his ancestor. "I do as I please here. I am OM. And you are nothing."

His aura darkened and swirled around his body.

"If I am nothing, then why seek me out?" I replied, my voice emotionless.

I stared up at him and waited, allowing him to see the disdain I had for him. I knew it was there in my eyes. He reacted swiftly, his rage taking over, grabbing my long hair in his hand and jerking my head back roughly, so he could leer down in my face. His face slowly changed into his Shadow. And he smiled when I flinched in reaction.

"I think you're a danger," he said slowly, his hot breath hitting my face. "An abomination. Your kind and the rest of them. OM is the only Breed that should walk this Earth. The rest of you are weak, a waste of the planet's resources."

"Then we should count ourselves lucky that you're not Praetor," I returned coldly, remaining still. "You lost that competition…so I hear."

I knew I was egging him on, but I couldn't stop myself. Milo's eyes flashed in anger as he tugged harshly on my hair. "Some reigns are short-lived," his voice rumbled.

"You threaten your own Praetor's life?" I asked in disbelief.

Milo's smile was slow, sure.

"War is coming."

He held my gaze for a minute longer before letting me go and flickering back to his human self.

"And when it does, you will be the first Aliud to feel my sword."

Chapter Fourteen

KINGDOM: Animilia
BREED: Human Reptilian Hybrid
NAME: Niall
SEX: Male
AGE: 3
CLASS: The First

Physical Features:

Niall has extremely oily skin, and we are forced to always put a special lotion on his face. His skin is very tan because of the long hours he likes to spend in the sun. His eyes are pale green, and even at his young age, he needs glasses. After many tests, we realize his sight might get even worse because of his need to be in the sun with absolutely no barriers.

Personality Traits:

In simulated games, Niall is known to plan an attack for months. He is a master in the art of patience. He also has an appetite for the best and understands in order to get it, he must be calculating and methodical. His IQ is above average, and he processes things in a Machiavellian way.

Habitat:

When shown different habitats, Niall chooses areas

where there is much sun year-round.

I spent the evening looking through Dr. Hedy's video logs, needing a distraction from my encounter with Milo.

After he left me, I went to my room and stayed there through the night. I hadn't wanted to face Aedan or any of the others. I also made the decision not to tell Aedan about Milo's threats. My presence in OM was causing him enough hardship, and to be fair, Milo wasn't the only menace I faced. The list seemed to be growing by the minute. Aedan couldn't protect me from every danger I confronted here, and the only thing I wanted him to focus on was getting me to Kingdom B. That was the best way he could help me.

After experiencing Dr. Novak's first experiment, I barely slept and even kept one of the knives from dinner under my pillow. After a long while of staring around my dark room with anxiety, I remembered Aedan was right next door, and if something happened, if I had another unexpected visitor, he would reach me quickly.

When morning came, I wasn't even fearful about meeting with Dr. Novak. I was resigned to it. I would allow the doctor his experiments, play the meek Aliud, all while searching for my own way out. The storm weakened, which gave me hope. Once it was safe, I knew Aedan would be true to his word and help me find a way to Kingdom B, and if he didn't, I would somehow find my own. As long as he stayed on my side, believing me, I'd be able to keep my freedom.

It was early in the morning, and the General brought me to another wing of the Praetor's Observatory Lab to meet with Dr. Novak. The square room was fairly large, lined with a dozen or so microscopes and a table that ran down the center that spanned almost the full length of the room.

"Welcome, Siren." Sara's robotic voice said in greeting.

Until she spoke, I had forgotten all about her.

"I apologize if I make you uncomfortable," Sara said.

"You do not," I replied.

"You speak an untruth," Sara said. "Your vitals spiked the moment you heard my voice."

"Do you monitor all vital signs of everyone who works in the lab?" I asked as I crossed my arms.

I *was* wary of Sara. Not only because of everything we were taught, but because of my first encounter with her. She- a computer- warned me against her master and had as far as I knew, kept silent. Which only posed the question, to what or who was she loyal to?

"I am trained to alert Dr. Novak if a citizen who crosses the barrier into the Praetor's home has a dangerous health issue. If vitals are unusual, I am permitted to scan the body. This is not an invasion of privacy, it is a safety and health issue."

"Then I can assume you found nothing that would cause alarm?" I said.

"I did not," Sara replied. "But I will continue to monitor your organs."

"Why?" My voice was sharp.

"Dr. Novak specifically asked I study your vitals, while you move about in the lab. You are a Cetacean. An unknown anomaly."

"Wonderful," I muttered.

"I detect sarcasm in your voice." Sara stated matter of factly.

"Yes, you are correct in your observation," I told the computer.

"My studies will not be intrusive."

"The very nature of your study is intrusive. It's an invasion of my privacy."

"As you are invading the privacy in Kingdom OM." She returned.

It was unnerving, talking to a computer with the same cognitive ability as a human.

And much more powerful, if given the opportunity.

"You have nothing to fear from me." The tone in Sara's voice changed, like she sensed my mood.

"No?" I said with a cold laugh. "You forget, I have just experienced one of Dr. Novak's experiments."

"They are his design."

"And that's supposed to make me feel better?"

"It is exactly as I say," she returned.

"Dr. Novak told me you only make yourself known to him," I continued. "That you offer your advice to him."

"He has changed the law and extended my freedom to you."

She was to gather more information for the doctor.

"How old are you?" I asked.

"I came into full cognitive existence thirty-five years ago."

Her program was not ancient and seemed to be comprised of modern knowledge. Although, I was not entirely sure her intelligence wasn't greater than she let on because it would be wise of her to hide what she knew, in case Dr. Novak had a change of mind.

I made my way to a large wall covered with various scientific studies and equations. I could only assume this was Dr. Novak's work.

Everything I saw had to do with human reproduction.

"The human species is in danger of extinction," Dr.

Novak said as he walked into the room. I watched him motion toward the wall, his look serious.

Just being in his company filled me with rage.

Dr. Novak gave me a sympathetic smile. "Are you angry with me?"

"What do you think?" I returned.

"Yesterday's experiment," he said. "It was a rather dramatic taste of what's to come. But after I left you in the library, I thought why not? What better time than now?"

"It must be nice standing where you are," I couldn't help but say, even though I had planned to be amiable.

"Holding all the power?" Dr. Novak said smiling. "I'll tell you something, Siren—it is."

"What did you do with her?" I asked.

"She is safely hidden away, back in her little cage."

"How many more are there?" I asked in horror. "How many more children?"

"Unfortunately, she is my last, and I don't know how much longer she can withstand my tests," Dr. Novak said. "But I'll get more."

He was giddy with joy as he clapped his hands together.

"Now back to the problem at hand," Dr. Novak said, dismissing the child's life as if it meant nothing. "In OM, our women are spontaneously miscarrying their fetuses. That is, *even* if they are lucky enough to become pregnant."

He stood next to me as we both stared up at the various equations.

"And we cannot seem to understand how or why."

I waited for Dr. Novak to continue.

"How do Cetaceans procreate?" He asked as he turned to look at me.

"The same way as our ancestors," I told him. Delphine

was the last Cetacean birth and that had been seventeen years ago. She was five months younger than me.

"Where did you come from?" Dr. Novak asked.

"Akasha," I told him truthfully. "A planet far from Earth."

"I'm assuming your ancestors left Earth on a spacecraft?"

"Yes," I said. "A research pod."

"How many of your people escaped the massacre?"

"Not enough," I replied harshly.

"Why have you returned?" He continued his cross-examination.

"To study the planet," I lied easily.

"Come Siren," he said with a small smile. "I was hoping we could start by being honest with one another. You know what I intend. I would like to know what you planned to gain by coming back here?"

"I told you," I said forcefully. "I was sent here to study the people."

"To what end?"

I looked away from him and shrugged.

"To come back to Earth and take back what was stolen?" Dr. Novak asked curiously as his eyes narrowed.

His response made me laugh.

"There are eleven Cetaceans left in the universe," I only told him because I wanted him to know what OM had done to my people. "I can assure you there is no war coming."

Dr. Novak stared at me for a long moment.

"Sara?"

"Her vitals have not spiked," the robot answered his command. "She speaks the truth."

So now I would have Sara, the lie detector, reading my

every thought.

"Excellent," Dr. Novak finally said as he made his way to a metallic panel and placed his hand on the silver knob. "Follow me."

A secret panel slid open to reveal a small chamber. Dr. Novak stepped inside, while I watched him warily.

"Come, Siren," he said with an excited smile. "We only have five hours a day together, and I want to use every second of our time."

Five hours. It seemed like an eternity.

Once I stepped inside the chamber, the doors closed, and we began our descent.

"I built this laboratory years ago," Dr. Novak told me in an excited whisper. "It's where I conduct experiments that are better left in the dark."

My heart fluttered in fear as the doors opened, and Dr. Novak led me out.

I stared at the room.

It was similar to his office but filled with many more stations stacked with various scientific devices. My gaze flickered over the small pool that was in the center of the room. Dr. Novak rushed forward as he continued to speak candidly.

"I've petitioned the Assembly many times to reach out to the other Kingdoms, to all the great scientists—to have us all come together in a conference of sorts. I wanted to pool our resources together in hopes we could find a cure."

"A cure?"

"I am convinced it is a disease," he explained. "It is a virus that infects and prevents reproduction."

"And has the Assembly agreed to your requests?"

He shook his head.

"Sadly, no. Our Praetor agrees with me, he understands the need. But the Assembly is ruled by archaic laws," Dr. Novak's face twisted in anger. "They are afraid to open any discussions. And unfortunately, the Praetor will not fight them."

"Why are they afraid?"

"They believe we would be inviting danger," he said. "Possibly another genocide as was the case with your people, the Cetaceans."

I tried to remain impassive when he mentioned the massacre.

"By the way, how do you do that?" His voice was curious.

"Do what?"

"Control your Shadow the way you do," Dr. Novak smiled when he saw the look on my face. "You know I'll eventually get it out of you. Just as I will inevitably get you to flicker."

"How do *I* fit into your research?" I asked him bluntly, ignoring his threats. I had no doubt he'd do everything in his power to break me. "Besides testing my capacity for empathy?"

Dr. Novak gave me a look that made the hairs on my neck stand.

"Up until six months ago, I believed I would never find a cure," he explained. "And then everything changed."

He walked over to a panel against the wall that lit up to reveal a keyboard. He quickly typed a code into the display. Two sheets of metal slid open, exposing a heavy door with one large knob that you could twist to open.

"What's in there?" I asked him suspiciously.

"A tunnel," he said with pride. "An ancient tunnel that

was safely hidden for years, until I discovered it. It's three miles long and leads out of the city of Larsa. Past the wall and beyond the watchful eyes of the guards."

My gaze flickered over to him in surprise.

"I needed to collect samples of the land," he told me with a shrug. "Data research. This way I could do it away from prying eyes. I believed my secret was safe."

"You believed?" I repeated.

Dr. Novak typed in the code again, and the doors slid shut. He turned to me and crossed his arms. "On one of my many expeditions, I was tracked," he said.

"By who?" I asked as I tried to process everything.

"Milo," he said quietly. "Milo had been watching me for some time."

My stomach sunk in dread.

"You can imagine my surprise," Dr. Novak said slyly. "But luckily, the situation wasn't as dire as I believed. We made a pact, he and I—he could use my tunnel when he pleased and he would keep my secret safe."

"Why would he want to use your tunnel?" I asked in mounting fear.

"Why would any ambitious soldier see the need for such a hidden treasure?" Dr. Novak asked with a dismissive shrug.

My breath hitched.

"To devise a plan to overthrow the existing ruler, so he could take his place."

Dr. Novak confirmed what Milo had said to me the day before...*war was coming.*

"You would help Milo?" I asked in disbelief. "Your daughter is the Praetor's intended mate—"

"She is young and foolish," Dr. Novak said with a

dismissive shrug.

"She loves him," I said forcefully.

"Love?" Dr. Novak scoffed. "In the world we live in, there is no room for such an emotion. Survival trumps everything. And Milo's nature better serves OM's needs. For now, that is."

I let his words sink in. The doctor was more of a danger than I had imagined. He was part of a plan more sinister than I could have ever thought.

"You must know, his ambition wasn't the only reason why we made our pact," Dr. Novak went on to my horror. "I am a scientist, after all, and his gift to me was what swayed me more than his desire to rule."

"Gift?" I whispered.

"You can turn the holographic image off now, Sara," Dr. Novak called out to the room. "It's time for Siren to see our guest."

I watched in fascination as the area past the pool flickered, and what I believed to be rows of tables with microscopes faded away and what was really there took shape.

It was a giant cage.

Inside were two beds and a vanity where someone could take care of personal needs. A tall man leaned against the cage, gripping the metal, his gaze fixed on Dr. Novak in rage. He was young. He couldn't have been older than I was. He had inky black hair and turquoise eyes that seemed to beam out of his face.

"Milo was given a gift from some friends of his to dispose of," he told me. "And I wanted a test subject. One I had dreamt of for so long. And so I agreed to take this treasure off his hands."

"What is he?" I asked in dread as I stared over at the young man.

"A *Reptile*."

CHAPTER FIFTEEN

"Reptile?" I repeated in panic.

"Yes," Dr. Novak said in excitement. "And from the line of The First."

A descendant of Niall, the first embryo injected with the Soul Particle.

"How?" I whispered in disbelief.

"How is irrelevant," Dr. Novak said with a shrug. "All I care about is that he's mine now. To do with as I please."

The Reptile hissed in anger as he rattled the cage.

"I see that temper of yours is about to rear its ugly head," Dr. Novak said with a laugh as he looked over at the Reptile. "I would hate to have to trigger the collar."

The man gripped the metallic collar around his neck in fury.

"Of course I had to make sure he could never attack me," Dr. Novak explained. "The collar insures he'll remain obedient. You do remember the child was wearing one as well—"

"Was she also a gift from Milo?" I whispered.

"Yes, she was," Dr. Novak said. "She's an aggressive little Reptile, who has to be reprimanded quite often."

I was going to be sick.

"But you won't have anything to worry about when I leave the two of you alone together."

Dr. Novak took in the look of disgust on my face.

"Testing the other breeds and using their samples is the only choice left for us," he said almost defensively as though he was trying to justify his actions.

"This is wrong," I said in horror. "It is immoral."

"I have learned that morality and science cannot coexist."

Before I could respond, Sara's voice rang through the room.

"Emergency," She stated ominously. "Emergency."

Dr. Novak's eyes widened in alarm, before he quickly made his way over to the chamber that had led us down to the lab.

"What's going on?" I asked Dr. Novak as the lights in the room flickered twice.

"You will remain here," Dr. Novak commanded. I chased after him, but before I could reach his side, the doors to the chamber closed.

Leaving me alone with the Reptile.

The only sound in the room was my labored breaths.

Though the Reptile was in a cage, I was still frightened. I turned to stare at him. He looked nothing like the Reptile who assaulted me—or even the child. He was quite human looking. In fact, one could say he was handsome. He was almost as tall as Aedan, and his features were angular, well defined. His body was lean and muscled, like he was primed for battle.

"We come in all shapes and sizes," his voice was strong, authoritative. Clearly, he read the surprise on my face.

I nodded in embarrassment.

His gaze flickered over me knowingly.

"You're not OM."

"I'm not," I shook my head.

"Welcome to the party," he snickered. "I see your circumstance is better than mine. But you're still a prisoner —just like me. The dangerous Reptile."

I eyed him warily.

He slammed his hands against the cage and stared at me in rage, his turquoise eyes beginning to glow.

"I *will* kill him."

I did not blame him for the sentiment.

"For six months I've suffered from his hands," the Reptile went on in a frenzied madness. "His delusional speeches of saving his people from extinction. His experiments—"

The Reptile closed his eyes, and I could see the agony he was in.

My heart softened. I tried to not focus on my fear of his kind, of what I had experienced firsthand, but instead to see him for what he was. A young man—trapped. Prisoner of a mad scientist. And to what end? I could only imagine.

"I'm so sorry," I said to him, hoping he could see that I meant my words.

His turquoise eyes met mine, and I watched them round in surprise. Kindness. He hadn't expected it.

"What's your name?" He asked softly.

"Siren," I told him.

"Siren," he said with a cold smile, looking me over. "I can tell why he's excited to have you join this little cabal of his."

His words unnerved me, striking fear within my soul. But before I could answer him, the doors to the chamber swished opened again and Sara's voice commanded me.

"You will enter the chamber now."

My eyes met the Reptile's and an understanding passed between us. We were both the same. Aliuds. To be used against our will. And that bond united us no matter the danger he posed. I stepped inside the chamber, and the doors closed quickly as my mind tried to process everything I had just seen. A Reptile—a descendant of The First. A prisoner of Dr. Novak and Milo. Alive in OM.

It was then I remembered the emergency situation that called Dr. Novak away.

"What's happening?" I asked Sara.

In a second the lights were dimmed, and a three dimensional hologram flashed before me.

I saw Bibi and Cyrus following Aedan into the Praetor's Observatory Lab. A few soldiers were behind them but stopped when the three walked into a room with a med scan, similar to the one I had been in before. Aedan was cradling a young girl in his arms. Her limp body was soaking wet—and parts of her body had flickered into her Shadow—a young stallion.

"Gaia. Grandchild of Eadric." Sara said as I watched them.

Gaia. The young girl who challenged me only a day before.

"What happened?" I asked.

The scene changed and Sara played back video that was filmed. I saw Gaia running outside through the storm, tears streaming down her face, looking as though she was being chased by monsters. I felt a pang in my heart, because I knew why she was so upset. I watched her stumble through the rain, holding her hands to her face and sobbing before flickering into her Shadow and starting to run.

A giant light flashed before us as lightning struck her from the sky. Her body rattled and sizzled as she fell to the ground.

She had to be dead, I thought in horror.

And it was my fault.

"Immediate medical attention required," Sara said.

"How bad?" I asked as the doors to the chamber opened.

"Her heart has now stopped beating for four minutes." Sara said. "The child has a two percent chance of survival."

"Maybe I can help her!" I called out. "Please, Sara... let me try!"

Sara took a moment before she responded.

"The doors will open, leading you to them." She finally said.

I took off running through the room, forgetting Dr. Novak's prisoner and blindly followed every door that opened through the hall. I entered the med scan room and took in the somber expressions. Bibi glanced at me, and I saw the pain in her eyes. I understood why. She blamed herself. I shook my head at her, but she looked away.

Aedan and Cyrus were soaking wet. They all stared down at Gaia's lifeless body, the grief etched on their faces.

Dr. Novak was with them, in front of the young girl. I stood behind, giving them space. The door slid open behind me, and another man ran in. He was almost as tall as Cyrus and Aedan but not as physically built. He was dark skinned with curly black hair and dark brown eyes and was wearing a white coat.

"Justus," Aedan's voice was somber as he looked at the man. "The med scan shut down."

"Her heart stopped," Justus said somberly. "The med scan will only work if it senses heart function."

Bibi let out a cry. I wanted to comfort her, but I was afraid to intervene in the scene before me. Justus reached the child and pulled out a long, thin, metallic object, put the point over Gaia's heart and shocked her. The room was deathly silent except for the noises coming from Dr. Novak and Justus as they tried to get Gaia's heart to start pumping.

Maybe only a minute went by, but it felt like an eternity. Her face was pale and lifeless, her lips almost blue. I could see her aura fading around her body. She was leaving. Her soul was crossing to the other side, and they could not bring her back.

They stepped back.

"It is done," Justus's voice was sad. "There is nothing more we can do."

Dr. Novak's head was bent over in grief.

"No!" Bibi cried out as she tried to reach the girl. Cyrus grabbed hold of her.

"She's gone, Bibi," Cyrus's voice was gentle.

"It is not your fault." Aedan's voice was soft as he closed his eyes. The pain on his face was unmistakable. I wanted to reach out to him, to Bibi, but I was afraid.

At that moment, I looked over and stared at Gaia's ashen face. It was devastating. Only a day before, this child had been alive. And now, because of me, she was gone. I slowly made my way toward Gaia's body, everyone in the room immersed in their own grief.

"We must inform her grandmother," I heard Dr. Novak whisper to the others.

"This will kill Eadric," Aedan said.

Their voices began to disappear around me as I focused only on Gaia. I felt as though I was walking in a tunnel of energetic light, where only the girl and I existed together. Everyone else faded away. I reached her side and placed one hand on her head and took hold of her hand with my other. I closed my eyes and used my heightened sensory skills to see beyond the dimension we were in. I knew there was still time to reach out to her. Her organs were still able. She could still live.

Gaia, I called out into the darkness before me.

I know you're still here. I can feel your energy. You haven't crossed over.

At first there was nothing. Only silence. And then I felt a jolt. I saw space, white luminous stars zipping past me, traveling through different dimensions, experiencing the wonder Gaia was seeing.

Come back, I said to her. *It is not your time.*

Why are you here? Gaia asked me. *I was so cruel.*

Because I want you to live, I told her. *Come back to your body. Your people need you. Your grandmother needs you.*

A long silence greeted me and then I felt her hand squeeze mine. I opened my eyes and stared into her bright gaze. There was an understanding between us. An acknowledgement of sorts. She smiled up at me, and I leaned down and kissed her on the cheek.

"Welcome back," I whispered into her ear.

The room around us was deathly silent.

I was almost afraid to turn. The realization of what I had just done—in front of strangers I was trying to gain the trust of- hit me hard.

The med scan came to life, and I jumped back from the table as it moved over Gaia's body. The crackle and hiss of the machine echoed through the room, the glare of the light forcing me to turn around. Aedan, Cyrus, Dr. Novak, Bibi, and Justus were lined up staring at me, like I was some freak of nature. There was a combination of awe, shock, and incredulity.

"Body scan complete."

Before anyone could speak, the door slid open, and a sobbing Eadric ran in and straight over to Gaia. I saw a glimpse of her Shadow, an older regal white wolf.

"My baby girl!" she screamed out in horror and sadness.

"I'm all right, grandmother," she said from behind me. I could hear her struggling to rise.

"But they said..." her voice trembled.

"I'm fine," she assured her. "I'm here."

My eyes filled up with tears from the crashing waves of emotion coming off Eadric. I felt like I was intruding on something private. "If you'll excuse me," I pushed my way past everyone and walked out the door.

"How do I get out of here, Sara?" I asked, knowing she was following my every move.

"I will light the way until you reach your room," she told me.

I was happy I didn't have to wait for anyone to show me back, and for once, I was thankful for Sara.

"Is there a private way?" I asked. "Where I won't have to see anyone."

"Yes," Sarah said. "Follow the light."

I went through twists and turns, and somehow Sara was able to get me back to my room without seeing a single soul. Once inside, I quickly shut the door and fell to my knees with relief. Thankfully, no one followed me. With this one act, I may have revealed too much about myself. Who knew what would happen now.

But I didn't care. Saving her life was worth it. And I would do it again.

"Are you well?" Sara asked in concern.

"I am."

"You brought the child back."

Somehow her robotic voice suddenly sounded more human.

"I did," I whispered.

"The Elder is here," Sara warned me.

Just as Sara finished saying the words there was knock on the door then it opened. Eadric stood there, her face now dry from the tears she had just shed. The stress of her experience still covered her face.

I stood up and faced her.

"You are an Aliud." Eadric's voice was soft as she stepped in the room. "I have not made your stay easy. And yet, you have given me the greatest miracle I could have ever asked for."

I waited for her to continue. To accuse me of lying to her about who I was.

"I believe we have much to learn from each other," Eadric's voice was filled with emotion. "What you did for me, for my grandchild, I do not understand it. I do not understand how or why you did what you did, but nevertheless, I owe you my life for it."

"You owe me nothing," I rushed to tell her, overwhelmed by her reaction. "I did what anyone would have done in my place."

"You overestimate the good in humanity," Eadric gave me a gentle smile. "And underestimate the light in your soul."

"You flatter me."

"I speak only the truth."

Eadric took a step closer to me, reached out and took my hands in hers.

I did not know how to respond to the gesture.

"I give you my word, here and now, I will do everything in my power to see you get home safely," Eadric's voice was solemn. "When the storm passes, your return will be our first priority."

"Thank you," I replied.

"And there is another thing," she continued. "I want you to know there is nothing for you to ever fear in our land. You will always be welcome. You are allowed any and all freedom. By saving my granddaughter's life, you have proven to be more than just an Aliud."

Our eyes met.

"You are like us," she said with a smile. "You are like OM. We are one."

And just like that, I suddenly felt like I belonged.

CHAPTER SIXTEEN

After Eadric left me, I took a long bath. I needed to go underwater, have a moment of pure silence, and come to terms with my actions. I was at a loss. My entire life had been spent leading up to this moment here on Earth. Though Eadric had reassured my safety, I still didn't know how the others would feel.

I exhibited a skill the people of OM had no basis to judge. And now, I didn't know what they'd think of me.

And then there was Dr. Novak's lab and everything he had shown me. His Reptile prisoner. And foolishly on his part, a way out of OM. I had memorized the sounds from the keyboard for the code to the tunnel. What Dr. Novak didn't know was each number and letter he typed emitted a tone faint enough for me to pick up with my sensory skills. The only problem I faced was accessing the code without him there. I would have to find a way to get Dr. Novak leave me alone in the lab. But most importantly, I needed to find a way to make sure Sara wasn't watching, which seemed like the most impossible part of all. But there had to be a way.

After my brief reprieve, I made my way back down to the hall.

The last thing I wanted to do was return to Dr. Novak's lab, but it was the only way I could find an escape. The more time I spent down there, studying the environment, the faster I could set my plan in motion.

"Siren." I glanced over my shoulder and saw the General waiting for me at the stairs.

"I was afraid you'd stay in your room for the rest of the day," she said to me.

"I thought I'd go back to Dr. Novak's lab," I admitted trying to gauge what she was thinking.

"There's something I want to say to you," Bibi's said slowly. "What you did today—beyond witnessing what I still cannot seem to wrap my head around or comprehend, there is something else you changed for me today."

"Bibi…"

"Let me finish, Aliud," Bibi's tone was strong, but she was smiling. "I'm not used to speaking like this with anyone. Aedan and Cyrus are the only ones who hear my thoughts."

I nodded in surprise and waited for her to continue.

"I feel compelled to tell you that what you did—*what I saw*—by saving Gaia…you saved a piece of me."

"I don't understand."

"I believe now. Your actions today changed everything for me," she explained softly. "I know now. There *is* good. There *are* miracles. And there *is* hope for us."

I was overcome by Bibi's admission. Selfishly, it made me feel good. I was happy I had somehow helped the General believe again.

"I think if Gaia had died, a large piece of my soul would have gone with her," Bibi went on. "Do you understand me now, Siren?"

"Yes, I think I do," I was grateful for her words.

"There's one more thing," she said. "If there is anything I can do for you—"

"Allow Gaia back into the Virago Temple," the words came out before Bibi could even finish her sentence. "It is her whole life."

"I've already forgiven her," the General assured me. "You see, I'm a step ahead of you."

We shared a smile. And it hit me. Bibi was becoming my

friend. And even for me, someone who had never had one before, I knew it was an honor.

"I won't keep you anymore," Bibi finally said.

Her entire demeanor softened, and I couldn't stop the pleasure I felt from it. It was dangerous to get too close to Aedan, but I would allow myself freedom with Bibi. These would be memories I would cherish.

I would miss her.

I left the General and continued on my way to Dr. Novak's lab. Servants were still busy with daily tasks. I felt my gaze linger on a few unfamiliar faces before looking away.

Something was different.

The looks I received weren't filled with immense dislike as they were before. Not even mistrust. These glances were ones of curiosity and even gratitude.

Something had definitely shifted.

"Siren." My heart sped up at the sound of his voice.

Everything around me suddenly vanished. And all I saw was *him*.

Aedan.

It looked like he'd just taken a bath. His hair was wet and slicked back. His eyes were glowing from his tanned, sculpted face.

He held out his hand.

"Come with me?"

I knew he wanted to talk about the earlier events, what happened with Gaia.

When my hand touched Aedan's, I felt an electric shock race through my body. It was as if, like Gaia, I too had been struck by lightening. The way his hand squeezed mine led me to believe he felt the same thing. I allowed Aedan to guide me through the side of the hall that was practically hidden in the shadows. He led me into a room I assumed by the décor was his office.

Once inside, he let go of my hand and shut the door.

We were now alone.

Aedan faced me. "You know why I brought you here."

"Yes, I do." I said.

"How did you bring her back?"

I was expecting the question.

"It's a sensory skill we have," I explained to him, choosing to tell the truth about my own people and not those of Kingdom B.

"All of your Breed?"

"Some," I replied evenly.

"Explain it to me," he demanded.

"I don't know how to explain it, really," I told him with a shrug. And I was being honest, because it was a skill that was hard to put into words. It was just there.

"Try."

"I could just sense she wasn't gone yet. Her soul lingered. There was still life in her organs. She was still there. And I could still reach out to her."

"And then what?" he asked. "You could bring her back? Make her heart start again? Help me comprehend it, Siren."

"I just did."

"What I saw," he said forcefully. "That was not a human skill."

"You're wrong," I told him. "I can assure you, I'm just as human as you are."

He crossed his arms and stared at me, his look unsure.

"Why are you doubting me now?" I asked defensively. "I saved her life. Shouldn't that make you happy? Shouldn't that be enough?"

"It makes me happy," he agreed. "And I thank you for it. But your explanation isn't satisfactory. What I saw happen—it only leads to more questions about who and what you really are."

"I'm sorry to hear that." I wasn't surprised. The others had thanked me and seen what happened as some sort of miracle, but for Aedan, it wasn't so simple.

"You're not making this easy," he went on slowly. "I'm trying to understand and make sense of everything I saw."

"I don't know how to make it easier for you. And I don't know what you would like me to say." I told him.

"The truth."

I met his amber gaze. "You have it."

"Do I?" he arched a brow.

I looked away and waited for Aedan to continue his cross-examination. It didn't come.

There was an uncomfortable silence between us.

"If that's all, then I'd like to get back to Dr. Novak's lab," I said, wanting to escape his company and the forbidden feelings he evoked.

Aedan continued to stare at me.

"I might as well get in as much time with him before I leave," I blurted out desperately needing space.

"Leave?" He said, his expression inscrutable.

"When you take me back to Kingdom B."

There was a finality to my words. The truth in them darkened my own mood considerably. I would leave OM one way or another. I would never see Aedan or anyone else from this Kingdom again.

I waited for him to excuse me, and when he continued to stare at me in a way that made my toes curl and heart race even more, I knew I had to get away from him. The look in his eyes had softened, reminding me of the Aedan I first met in the forest of OM.

"Is that all you wanted to discuss with me?" I wished I didn't sound so nervous.

"No," he shook his head and took a step toward me.

"What then?" I whispered.

I didn't know how close I was to the door. When the wooden frame touched my back, I realized I'd been slowly backing away from Aedan, as he had been slowly making his way toward me.

Almost as if he were stalking me.

I had to crick my neck back to look up at him. He leaned down toward my neck and took in a deep breath. His proximity evoked foreign emotions in my body. I was sure he could hear the erratic beat of my heart.

"What are you doing?" My voice was faint.

"Just taking you in," he whispered back to me.

It was wrong. I knew it. Whatever this was, couldn't be right. Kali was probably outside looking for him and here we were. Alone. Sharing an intimacy that was forbidden.

"Aedan…" I started.

"Shhh," he said softly. "Just another minute."

He rubbed his cheek against my neck, his skin causing goose bumps to race all over my body. I did not understand this reaction I had to him. Why I longed for it.

His proximity.

His touch.

"I've dreamt about this," he whispered to me as he moved his lips up against mine. Almost kissing me.

"Every night, Siren," he told me. "I've thought about you."

My legs practically gave out beneath me as he spoke the words I didn't realize I longed to hear until that moment. His arm wrapped around my waist to hold me close.

"Every. Single. Night," his voice was like a caress against my lips.

And just as soon as it became something I needed, I was robbed of it.

Just like that.

He moved away, like he had been burned by the sun. He turned his back to me, and I stood there staring at his imposing figure, longing for him to come back.

What was happening to me?

"You can go." His voice was gruff.

I could see his internal struggle, like he was fighting for control.

Just as I was.

"Aedan?"

He turned his head to the side, showing me his strong profile.

"Siren. Just go to Dr. Novak."

Dr. Novak. I thought about what Dr. Novak had revealed to me—Milo's plans for Aedan. There was no way I would leave OM without warning him of the danger he faced from Milo and the doctor.

The thought of anything happening to him made me sick.

I watched him for a second longer, before I all but ran out of the room, shutting the door and moving through the corridor quickly, as if something was chasing me.

And there was. It was trying to overpower me. Trying to get in the way of my entire purpose here on Earth.

Aedan.

I couldn't deny my emotional connection to him. It was there. And even in all my ignorance, I knew he felt something too. I moved blindly ahead so unnerved by our encounter that I didn't see the man standing next to the entryway leading to the Praetor's Observatory Lab.

His hand reached out and gripped my arm.

It was Milo.

"In a hurry?" His voice was cold.

"Let go of me," I said as I pulled my arm out of his grasp.

I tried to move past him. "Let me by."

"Not until we discuss that little miracle you performed."

"I'm sorry?"

"Word has spread across the Kingdom of your magical healing abilities. The city is buzzing with the news. The Aliud who saved a child of OM," he told me.

"There is no magic," I replied as I moved as far away from him as I could. Everything about his stance was meant to intimidate.

I could feel the hairs on the back of my neck stand.

This man wouldn't hesitate to hurt me. To kill me. Just as he insinuated the day before.

"Really?" He shook his head from side to side as if he were admonishing me. "What would *you* call it?"

"A gift," I said with a shrug. "Just as your people possess different skill sets so do mine."

He took a step back from me and began to clap. It was slow, methodical. And loud enough to draw the attention of anyone who was close enough to hear.

"We are indebted to the Aliud," Milo called out.

There was a silence that descended upon the room as I stared out at the servants who stopped to listen.

"As I'm sure you all know by now, she saved our precious Gaia's life today. A citizen of OM. A Breed different from her own," Milo told the people. "What a wondrous gift she possesses, *the power to bring back the dead.*"

I could hear a few whispers in the crowd, but I kept my gaze locked on Milo.

"I have no such power," I said.

"Then what would you like to call it?" Milo's laugh was cold. "I looked over the report from today. The med scan found no heartbeat, no signs of life from the girl. She was gone. And yet, there you were, an Aliud, bringing her back from the dead for us."

"She was not dead," my voice was forceful. "Your med scan was wrong."

I heard a few gasps.

"Wrong?" Milo countered. "Our med scan doesn't make mistakes."

"This time it did," I replied.

"So you say."

Milo looked back at the crowd of people that was forming.

"I'm sure you are all wondering why I would even question this miracle," Milo continued. "And I can explain it to you very simply. Imagine this, my friends. Imagine this Aliud being one of a thousand from her Kingdom armed with this *gift*. This power to possess in a war. In battle. To continuously be able to bring back soldiers, no matter how many times they're taken down. Every time you think the enemy is dead, they come back. They get back up and fight."

"We are not at war," I said forcefully.

"Not yet," Milo agreed. "But such a power, such a gift

you have would only put the opposing side at a disadvantage, wouldn't you think?"

"You misunderstand the ability," I told him shaking my head. "It is not as you say."

"I don't think so," he shook his head. "I think I have it *exactly* right."

I looked over at the crowd of people, inching their way towards me. I saw a flash of a picture I'd seen from my childhood. One my mother had shown us from a time on Earth, when mobs were easily incited. When one man's words could turn a crowd and create hell on Earth.

This was the way it had always begun.

"Milo!" Aedan's voice barked out across the hall. "What is the meaning of this?"

I looked over at Aedan, who was standing at the opposite end of the room. His face was filled with fury, his body tense, and his hands in fists at his side. I could tell he was on the verge of flickering into his Shadow.

"I was thanking the Aliud," Milo's voice sounded innocent enough.

"Her name is Siren," Cyrus stated coldly.

He'd come up to stand beside me, appearing out of thin air, protecting me from Milo's ruthless hatred.

"Cyrus," Milo seemed surprised. "You're usually more discerning than Aedan. I would have expected more from you."

"Sorry to disappoint you," Cyrus's voice was like ice.

"I merely point out the obvious," Milo said. "I'm sure I'm only voicing what you might have considered yourself. What the others might even be considering now. I think it's only fair for me to voice my concerns—I'm sure I speak for many others in the room."

"There is nothing for you or anyone to consider," Aedan's voice rung with authority through the hall as his people turned to stare at him. "Siren *is* an Aliud. But she is now our guest. The Assembly voted on it. Eadric, our Elder, has personally offered her protection. She saved one of our people's lives. A child of OM. One that will grow to give birth to more children of OM. We must be indebted to her for this act of kindness. There is *nothing* for anyone to fear."

"So *you* say," Milo said with wide eyes. "Just as *you* thought there was nothing to fear from Kingdom R."

I watched Aedan's face turn to ice, and then I felt my blood run cold. The last time I saw this look was when the Reptile had attacked me. And I knew how that had ended.

"Do you challenge me?" His voice like a slow rumble of thunder.

"Never," Milo smiled coldly.

There was a terrible silence between the two men. I could feel the tension radiating from Cyrus. I saw Milo glance at something over my shoulder, before he started to laugh.

"Enough!" Aedan bellowed out before rushing across the room toward his nemesis. He flickered into his Shadow, pouncing like a lion about to attack.

I tried to step forward and stop him, but Cyrus put a hand on my shoulder.

"No."

Milo flickered into his Shadow, pounding his chest before he turned, ready to meet Aedan, who brutally shoved his body into Milo's. He pushed back, howling in anger. Milo wasn't prepared for Aedan's wrath or strength, but he was still a force to be reckoned with.

They were two alphas, each trying to prove his power.

Milo grabbed hold of Aedan's head, pulling his hair back and punching him deftly in the gut with the arm of a silverback gorilla. If it had been any other man, he would have fallen over in pain. But not Aedan. He actually smiled, like he enjoyed the effort, before taking Milo's muscled arm and twisting it behind his back so he could take a jab at his side with his free fist.

Milo doubled over from the blow.

Aedan spun him around, grabbed him by the shoulders, and shoved him up against one of the walls. He growled low in his throat and forcefully pushed Milo into the stone.

His brute strength was a sight to behold.

Milo's eyes took on an eerie glow, anger radiating from his core.

It was a testament of Aedan's power.

Of his right as Praetor, as Alpha, even in *his* Kingdom. In a land filled with men who had been conditioned to be warriors from a young age, Aedan stood above them. And Milo could only bow his head in obedience. Aedan held him like that for a minute longer, lifting him up high against the wall, so the room could see Milo's submission and then threw him down on the floor, as if he weighed nothing.

Aedan's eyes were like liquid gold, alight with fury and animalistic instinct.

He stared around the room, at his people, who all bowed their heads at the sight of his awesome strength. He threw his head back and roared with the power of the king of the jungle.

No one would dare question him again.

Aedan met my gaze, his eyes alight with strength.

I wanted to say something, to thank him for protecting me yet again, but Kali appeared, running over and wrapping her arms around his waist. It took him a moment, before he responded to her touch. And when he did, I had to look away. I felt as though I had been hit in the gut.

"If you'll excuse me," I said to Cyrus. "I was on my way to see Dr. Novak."

Cyrus's bright gaze held mine for a long moment before nodding, understanding reflected in his eyes. "Will we see you for dinner?" He asked.

"I don't know yet," I said with a shrug. "I guess it depends on how late we work today."

"There is a full moon tonight," he told me.

"How would we even be able to see the moon with this weather?" I laughed.

"Have you looked outside recently?"

I glanced over at the large windows, and sure enough, the rain had stopped. Even the wind slowed down considerably. I'd been so distracted by Aedan, then Milo, I hadn't even noticed.

"The clouds have cleared. You can even see the stars. I feel like it's been a lifetime, since I could gaze up at the sky," Cyrus sounded pleased. "But then, that's the beauty of such an unpredictable land and climate. Everything can change in a second. I guess that goes for all of life?"

"It does," I agreed.

"Don't let Milo's words hurt you," Cyrus said as he stared down at me.

"They didn't," I tried to assure him. I wished Milo was the reason I wanted to flee.

"He's after the Praetor," Cyrus continued on. "He's jealous of him. He always has been."

It is much more devious than that, I thought.

"It's not that, Cyrus," my voice was strong. "I promise

you I don't need the reassurance."

"You look sad," Cyrus's voice was gentle. The sensitivity behind his words startled me, even if his observation was correct.

"I'm…" I tried to smile and then chose to admit the truth. It was easier than always speaking lies. "Maybe a little. I just miss home. That's all."

"I don't blame you," Cyrus was sympathetic. "It can't be easy. None of it. But rest assured, what you did today was a miracle. And I for one will make sure you're protected, while you stay here. You don't have to fear Milo or his words. I promise you."

"I don't fear him," and I meant what I said. "But offering your protection means so much to me, considering what I am. I just hope I'll never have to ask for it."

"What you are?" Cyrus repeated my words and shook his head. "Without a doubt there are differences in our genetic makeup and habits, but we're still the same. We all have souls. We all come into the world the same way, and at some point in our lives, we all die. So, I'll tell you what you really are. You're human, Siren. Just like us."

øøø

"I'm glad you returned," Dr. Novak said as we exited the chamber and entered his secret lab. "I thought you might use that miracle you performed with Gaia as an excuse to stay away, at least for another day."

I glanced over at the Reptile, who was sitting on the bed watching our every move.

"I thought I didn't have a choice," I returned evenly.

"An astute observation," Dr. Novak replied, sounding pleased. "And how did you perform that little miracle by the way?"

I watched Dr. Novak in silence, refusing to answer.

"It doesn't matter," he shook his head. "I'll get the truth out of you one way or another."

He walked over to the cage housing the Reptile, and I watched as he hit another code into the keyboard that would unlock the doors.

I memorized the sounds again.

"Does Milo know about me?" I asked him quietly.

"For now he believes you're from Kingdom B," he said to my relief. "If you haven't noticed his temper is quite explosive, and considering his xenophobic philosophies, I can't be certain how he'll feel about a Cetacean in our midst. He can be quite impulsive."

Dr. Novak turned to me as the door to the cage slid open. "I can't have anything happen to you just yet," he said with a wink.

The Reptile rose to his full height as Dr. Novak motioned for me to come closer.

"Come, Siren," he said with a devilish smile. "He won't bite."

Even though I knew Dr. Novak was correct, I was still afraid. Everything I knew about their Breed made me want to run in the opposite direction. And I knew it was unfair to judge him. I made my way toward the cage, until I stood just outside next to Dr. Novak.

"Test subject R meet subject C," Dr. Novak said as though he was introducing us at a party. "Now step inside, Siren and meet your temporary cellmate."

"Inside?" I turned to him in surprise.

"Yes," he nodded. "I'd like to monitor your bodily functions, while you remain enclosed together. Observe your interaction. For hundreds of years, our breeds have remained separated with virtually no contact. You're taking part in research that can pave the way for the future. You should consider yourself lucky, just as I am, to be the father of such groundbreaking trials."

Father? Dr. Novak was clearly delusional enough to compare himself to Dr. Hedy.

"It will only be for a few hours," he went on. "This should be painless enough."

"Hours?" I whispered. I could feel the heat in my body rise at the thought of being trapped with the Reptile.

"Sara will be watching closely," he sighed in annoyance. "I told you, no harm will come as long as that collar remains wrapped safely around his neck."

I looked over at the Reptile, subject R, as Dr. Novak introduced us, and met his gaze. It was filled with hate, his aura ominously dark—but he kept his Shadow at bay. Panic washed over me at the thought of being in an enclosed space with him. What if he attacked me? What if he was as hungry as the child and tried to eat me? This could be another of Dr. Novak's tricks—to see how long I could fend him off.

"But before you get inside—" Dr. Novak said, grabbing my upper arm and punching a needle into my skin as my thoughts raged. I yelped out in pain. The Reptile hissed in anger, stepping menacingly toward the doctor, his eyes changing color. A surge of electricity crackled in the air, zapping him around the neck. He cried out in agony, half of his body flickering into his Shadow—a crocodile—before falling back on the bed.

I screamed in outrage, trying to move toward him, but Dr. Novak held his grip. "You know what happens when you disobey me," he warned the Reptile as he held onto my arm.

I couldn't control myself a second longer, it was like my

Shadow needed to escape the confines of its self-inflicted prison. And it didn't matter because he knew what I was. I flickered into my dolphin Shadow, right when he turned to face me. I watched his eyes move over my face in fascination. I knew what he saw.

My skin changed into something silvery grey and smooth as silk. My eyes grew, shifting to the side, my entire face resembling something almost ethereal from the sea.

"There you are," he smiled in pleasure, unable to hide his awe. "Simply magnificent."

I stared at my tormentor in fury, biting down on my lip, fighting against the pain, until the extraction was complete.

"It will get easier with time." He pulled the needle out and patted my arm.

I hated him. Everything he stood for. Everything he was. I hated.

"Now, be a good girl and step inside."

"You will pay for these crimes," I told him, my voice trembling.

"I think you're wrong," he whispered into my ear.

I walked into the cage and made my way to the bed, opposite to where the Reptile had fallen over. He was breathing heavily now, his pain slowly subsiding. Dr. Novak locked the doors and stared at both of us with glee.

"I'll be upstairs," he said to us. "This room is quite sterile, and as you can imagine, I'd prefer to monitor you from the comfort of my office. And now I have this vial of blood, I cannot wait to get a closer look at. Do remember, Sara will be recording everything."

Then he left us.

Alone.

A Reptile and a Cetacean locked in a cage together.

I looked over at the Reptile as he fought to steady his breath.

"Are you in pain?" I asked him in concern.

"Nothing I'm not used to."

My body shook with fury over the cruelty he had endured at my account. It was not fair. None of this was.

"I'm all right," he told me as if he could read my thoughts. "Really."

I nodded in acknowledgement as I tried to swallow my anger.

"Siren, are you..." He broke the silence between us, his gaze bright as he studied my features.

"I am a Cetacean," I affirmed meeting his gaze dead on.

"How is that possible?" He stared at me in disbelief.

"Does it really matter?" I said with a sigh as I looked around our prison.

"I guess it doesn't matter for now," he finally said. "How did you end up in OM?"

"An accident," I told him truthfully.

"Unfortunate," the Reptile said sympathetically. "This accident might cost you your life."

His words were true.

"So what's your real name?" I asked him.

"Michael."

My eyes flashed in surprise. It was an ancient name, given to humans without the Soul Particle injection, uncommon among the breeds in our time.

"My mother said I was born in a dark time in my Kingdom," he explained. "An angel of light given to her from the gods. Michael was a savior for our non-hybrid human ancestors. I think she hoped I would be for my people."

"You're of The First," I said remembering what Dr. Novak had told me.

"My father rules Kingdom R. I am his heir."

I stared at Michael in shock.

"How—"

"Did I end up here?" He finished with a bitter smile. "I was betrayed."

"Betrayed?"

"Let's just say my philosophies aren't shared by some of the people in my father's cabinet."

"Your own people did this?" I couldn't believe what I was hearing.

"Yes," he said in fury. "I was drugged, taken out of Kingdom R and given to Milo..."

To dispose of, as Dr. Novak had told me.

"Milo is in contact with members of your government?" I continued on in disbelief.

"Yes. With a few plotting to overthrow my line," Michael said with disgust. "From what little information I can piece together, they've been conspiring for a long while now."

"For what?"

"I don't know yet," he said as he looked across the room. "But I intend to find out."

As did I. But I chose to keep silent.

"And what about the little girl I saw?" I whispered.

Michael painfully closed his eyes.

"Another Reptile given to Milo by my people. He keeps her hidden away from me in another cell," he said softly. "I fear her time on Earth is coming to an end."

CHAPTER SEVENTEEN

I tossed and turned all night, wondering how I would ever complete my mission as a Cetacean.

As Elora's last living descendant.

After everything I now knew about OM and Kingdom R, the future seemed bleak. There were only two possible positive outcomes. Either Aedan and the Assembly would help me get out of OM, or I'd find a way to use Dr. Novak's tunnel to escape. No matter the option, I couldn't leave without warning Aedan about Milo and now, without helping Michael as well. I could not...I *would not* leave him to Dr. Novak or Milo's mercy.

It didn't matter that he was a Reptile. He was an innocent pawn, used in a game of war.

Unknown to Michael, he was now a part of my escape plan. But I couldn't risk saying my thoughts out loud to him, in fear of Sara hearing and reporting back to Dr. Novak, so I was completely on my own. Since I didn't know where the doctor held the child, I couldn't try and help her escape as well. I could only hope her life would not end in suffering.

I woke up early in the morning and stared out at the clear sky from my windows.

It was hard to believe that less than twelve hours before a wild and unpredictable storm had raged through the land. Now that the threat of bad weather was gone, Aedan and the Assembly would begin to put the plan to take me back to Kingdom B into motion.

Or so I hoped.

I was told by Sara to meet Dr. Novak later in the afternoon, giving me the morning to myself. I dressed quickly, grabbed Dr. Hedy's journal, and found my way outside. The weather had drastically changed for the better, which proved to lighten my mood. I walked the perimeter of the Praetor's home, enjoying the fresh air. The sun was bright and felt good on my skin.

I found myself wandering aimlessly, until I came across an open area with large benches and tables overlooking the vast plains. I sat down on one of the tabletops and stared out. The view stretched out for miles. And then, I saw it, and my heart cried out in joy.

The ocean.

I could actually look upon the beautiful sea from where I sat. And it was so close.

I felt something pulse through my body.

A calling.

Like I was being summoned to the dark blue waters that seemed to stretch out into oblivion. Those currents made me want. Made me desire to get closer. On my home planet we had a lake we'd swim in. But it was *nothing* like this. This was like a sweet dream.

I could feel my body tingle as heat enveloped me, starting in my forehead. I was consumed with a deep craving. A need. My Shadow cried out in joy after being deprived of its natural right for over two hundred years. Something inside my soul found peace. I was almost home.

I looked down at Dr. Hedy's journal, the more knowledge I could gain from him on the other breeds would only serve my mission.

I pressed the gold chip at the top of the tablet.

KINGDOM: Animilia
BREED: Human Bird Hybrid
NAME: Daniella
SEX: Female
AGE: 3
CLASS: The First

Physical Traits:

Daniella has wide beautiful eyes and graceful arms. She prefers to keep her hair long. She is slender and able to regulate her body temperature, never being either too hot or cold. She adapts easily, in that she can be vegetarian, pescatarian, or carnivore with no effect on her mental or physical state. She has large teeth, which seem to evolve depending on what she consumes for food. I have watched her jump from great heights, her long arms allowing her to almost glide. When tested, Daniella has also shown to have a rare immunity to super viruses known to kill others.

Personality Traits:

Daniella prefers to keep to herself. She gets along peacefully with the others but doesn't really socialize with them. When taken outside, she climbs trees and can be found to stay up there for hours, using a hand glide we had made for her in fear she'll hurt herself. She is skittish in nature and doesn't like to be still. She exhibits levels of cognition as complex as primates and is extremely intelligent.

Habitat:

When shown different habitats she prefers a forest, with a home high up in the sky.

KINGDOM: Animilia
BREED: Human Amphibian Hybrid
NAME: Sylvia
SEX: Female
AGE: 3
CLASS: The First Injected Embryo

Physical Features:

Her skin color is light, but when exposed to sun, she tans quickly. Her skin also peels quite easily. Her body is lean in the legs and arms but with a distended belly. Her eyes are nonhuman. They can regenerate damage to their cells, and through our genetic testing, we believe this will enhance as she gets older. Her hearing is average, but as is the case with her Breed ancestors, we believe the male Amphibians will have superior hearing. As this Breed aged in the wild this characteristic became more predominant, especially in the males, which proved to enhance their survival instincts. We believe this will be the case with Sylvia and the other females. She is an incredible swimmer, not as superior as the Cetaceans but can hold her own. She also has the ability to leap from extraordinary heights.

Personality Traits:

Sylvia possesses a pleasant enough sensibility but prefers to keep to herself. On the whole, she is elusive but will surprise us with a sudden outburst of humor and intelligence.

Habitat:

When shown different habitats, she always chooses a land with everglades.

"Siren?"

I was so immersed, I didn't even hear Gaia approach. She stood next to the table, patiently waiting for me to acknowledge her presence. I hit the button on the tablet, the visual scene cutting out and gave her my full attention.

"I'm happy to see you're feeling better," I said in genuine pleasure. It was hard to believe this was the same girl who had been so close to death just the day before.

"All because of you," she said. "Thank you for saving my life."

"I'm happy to have helped," I told her.

"Even though I was so awful to you?" Gaia had to look away from me, and I could see the shame in her eyes. "I'm sorry I was cruel. I'm so sorry I attacked you the way I did."

"Gaia…" I began.

"No," she shook her head. "It wasn't right what I did. The anger I had for you was completely unjustified. I'm so sorry."

"There is no need to apologize," I said. "I promise you, I haven't lived my life perfectly, far from it in fact, and I'm sure I'll make plenty more mistakes in the future."

"Like mine?" Gaia asked solemnly.

"You never know," I shrugged and patted the seat next to me. "Join me, if you'd like."

I could sense there was more she wanted to talk about. Gaia made her way over and sat down. We both quietly stared out at the magnificent view.

"Is it far?" I asked her, breaking the silence.

"What?"

"The ocean." I knew she could hear the longing in my voice.

"No," Gaia shook her head. "Not that far. Maybe five or six miles."

I let out a breath of excitement. It was near enough to actually go and see it up close, swim in it, sink my feet into the sand, and breathe in what I knew would be salty air.

"You've never been?" Gaia asked curiously.

"No," I smiled ruefully. "I've only seen it from a distance but never up close."

"I'm sure the Praetor can arrange for you to go while the weather permits," she said.

I could only hope.

"Perhaps," I said with a wistful smile. "But until then, I guess this will have to do."

Gaia was silent as I turned my gaze back toward the ocean. I could stare at it forever and imagine history unfolding. If only the sea could speak of the tales it had seen.

"There's something else," I told her knowingly. "You didn't just come here to thank me."

"No," Gaia's body tensed. "I didn't."

"Tell me, then." I urged. "I promise whatever you talk about will remain between us."

"I know," she sighed. "It's just—it's just hard to articulate."

I waited.

"I remember everything," she finally whispered.

I saw the uncertainty in her eyes. I knew there was a high probability she'd recall what she'd seen and even heard on the other side, but I hadn't been one hundred percent sure.

"I heard your voice," she went on. "I remember our conversation. And I saw—I saw this beautiful light. This energy. Filled with love—and the universe, I saw it all in its entirety. What we are. What we're made of. I remember all of it."

"You're so lucky," I told her. And I meant it.

"Am I?" Gaia's smile was sad. "To see that and have to come back to this world—I don't know if that really makes me lucky. And also…everything is different now, because *I'm different*. There are so many questions racing through my mind."

"Like what?"

"Why do we train for a war that may or may not come? It makes no sense."

"What do you mean, Gaia?" I asked, confused.

"Why should there even be a *possible* war?" She sounded older than she was. "Why must we try and destroy each other?"

"It's the way of the world you live in, and at the end of the day, you have to protect yourself," I told her simply. "And now you know there's something greater awaiting us —and I think you came back for a reason."

"Came back?"

I held her gaze and smiled softly. "I don't think you were done living just yet."

She was quiet and broke my gaze, looking away. "There's one more thing," she said.

"Yes?"

Gaia looked back at me. Again I was struck by how different she now was. An ethereal light surrounded her, a maturity, like she could see into your soul.

"I saw you," her voice was low.

"I know," my voice faltered. "I saw you too."

"No," she shook her head. "I *saw* you, Siren. I know what you are."

Of course.

Foolishly, I hadn't even thought about that possibility. Gaia had seen the essence of my soul. The human *and* Cetacean in me. She had seen the truth on the other side. But for whatever reason, I wasn't afraid. If the girl wanted to expose me, she was now armed with the knowledge and tool to do so. And there was really nothing I could do to prevent her from doing it.

"I won't tell them," Gaia said solemnly. "It is our secret. Actually, it's *yours* to tell or not."

"Thank you," I whispered. She reached out and took my hand in hers.

"You're not alone anymore." Her innocent words were almost my undoing. I had to look away, afraid I might shed tears yet again—the one human emotion I seemed to be developing an affinity for.

We sat like that in silence, gazing out at the sea together, both of us grappling with our own thoughts. I felt relieved someone who wasn't afraid or wanting to use it for an advantage, like Dr. Novak, finally knew the truth.

There was one person in OM who knew what I was and didn't despise me for it.

A horn sounded and interrupted our moment of solitude. Gaia jumped up and looked over toward the Praetor's compound in worry.

"Is something wrong?" I asked standing and grabbing hold of the diary.

"I don't think so," Gaia said but looked concerned. "We have to go back now."

I followed behind her but had to stop and give the ocean one last look. I would have to ask Bibi to take me to see it as soon as she could. I hoped she'd grant my request.

We reached the compound in no time and entered Great Hall. Aedan was there with Bibi, Cyrus, Kali, and what looked to be over fifty male and female warriors.

It was an incredible sight to behold. They were lined up before Aedan in perfect symmetry, armed and lethal, awaiting his command.

"For now, the storm has cleared," Aedan's voice boomed out. "But there is a more ominous threat than the weather. One that could very well be raping and pillaging our land even now, as we stand in this hall. On my last scout, only a few days ago, I came across Reptiles on our land."

The soldiers stood utterly still as they listened to Aedan's words.

"You all know the atrocities Kingdom R has only recently brought to our border. You all know what they are capable of. What they've been doing to those poor citizens they find."

Gaia's grip on my hand tightened, and I gave her a reassuring squeeze back. The soldiers who'd come from Kingdom R had made one thing clear, they had become the monsters of the world. I wondered if Michael knew what his people were up to. It was a question I'd ask as soon as we were alone again.

"We must find these serpents if they remain in Kingdom

OM and destroy them. If found on our land, they die. If they place a foot on our soil, they die. There is no mercy. Only justice for the lives we've lost. My brothers and sisters, the world is changing around us," Aedan continued on. "You are my best warriors. The Kingdom's Praetorian Guard, and I now call upon you to join me for the future of OM."

The warriors began to pound their chest in unison.

"We go hunting!" Aedan roared out as the soldiers continued to beat their chests. Some flickered into their Shadow in the adrenaline fueled moment, but most remained as they were.

I feared for them.

But mostly, I was afraid for Bibi and Aedan. I knew what could happen out there. In life, no matter how fierce one was, there was always a chance for things to go wrong.

The Reptiles who were on OM land were dangerous and ruthless. They had no morals or respect for human life, and it was clear they would do anything to achieve their ultimate goal, which still remained to be revealed. And now these young men and women would battle them.

I met Bibi's gaze across the sea of soldiers. She left Aedan's side and walked over to where Gaia and I stood. "It is time for you to return to Virago," Bibi turned to Gaia.

"Yes, General," Gaia responded obediently. She let go of my hand and faced me.

"I will seek you out again," she promised before disappearing out the door.

I was sad to see her go.

"You are friends now?" Bibi asked curiously.

"Yes," I said confidently. "We are."

"I'm glad," Bibi replied.

"When do you leave?" I asked.

"We leave in an hour's time."

"An hour?" I practically shouted it.

They would all go? And I would be left alone. With Dr. Novak.

"Yes," Bibi said. "I think that's plenty of time for you."

"Me?" I asked in surprise.

"You are coming with us," Bibi replied.

"What?" I was shocked. "Why?"

"Because I command it," Aedan said as he came up next to us.

He had a way of doing that, sneaking up and catching me off guard.

"But why?" I asked again.

"If there is no threat," he explained in a low voice that only we could hear. "There might be a way we can safely take you back to Kingdom B."

My mind reeled from the possibility.

"Dr. Novak?" I asked, thinking about Michael. I could not leave him trapped, now that I knew what would become of him.

"The others don't know my plan," he said as his eyes met mine.

I was sure he saw my surprise.

"I don't know when the next opportunity will come," he said to me in a pointed voice. "There are too many factors here that might change your circumstance. And no matter how hard I try, it's not safe for you."

I appreciated his honesty.

And he was right. With Milo, Dr. Novak, and the Assembly, who knew what or who would come for me? I would tell him what I knew once I was safely at the border. Aedan was a good man. I knew it with every ounce of my soul. I had to think about the others. My Breed. My mission. He would do the right thing. I could only hope he'd be able to change Michael and the child's fate.

"I'll get ready," I finally said in agreement.

øøø

Our journey out of the city walls was entirely different from when I first arrived in OM with Aedan. We marched over the bridge toward the gates that led out of the protection of the city walls to the sound of people cheering the guard on. I was flanked by four different male guards. They stood around me and were careful to avoid eye contact. They did not speak or even acknowledge my existence, but they moved in sync with me, there to protect me.

I could see Kali up ahead, walking next to Aedan. Luckily she had avoided me since our last interaction. I knew she hadn't been very happy about me joining them on their expedition. In fact, I was sure she had voiced her complaints about it, because there was a frostiness between her and Aedan that hadn't been there before.

It wasn't my problem, I told myself. I decided to just enjoy the journey back through OM land. This time, I was able to truly soak in the sights and sounds the trees made when the wind would rustle. I found myself gazing up at the sky's pale blue canvas for what felt like hours.

We traveled at a quick pace, and for the entire duration, I was kept in the middle, cocooned between the line of soldiers. I knew there were scouts out ahead of us, leading the way. I didn't ask any questions, just remained silent and waited. I didn't want to burden anyone, especially considering they were concentrating on finding the Reptiles.

Lunchtime came and went, and still no one spoke a word to me. I ate alone, sitting up against a tree as the others saw to their business and spoke to one another. Neither Bibi nor Aedan came to check in on me.

I should have been comfortable with the silence since I had spent so much time alone in my life, but now, because I knew what it was like to have human companionship, to actually speak to different people, everything was different. Life would never be the same for me.

Our group stopped on a knoll overlooking the valley that had a decided vantage point.

"We will camp here for the night," a soldier finally acknowledged me. "The perimeter is safe. You may have freedom and see to your personal business."

"Thank you," I replied politely. He barely gave me a nod in return so I continued. "And your name?"

The young soldier's brown eyes flickered up at me in surprise. He recovered quickly before he looked away. "Dar."

"It's a pleasure to formally meet you after *all* these hours, Dar," I said pointedly. He had ignored my existence the entire day, and I wanted to show him the difference. "I thank you for your protection."

Dar lowered his head. "It is our duty."

But it wasn't.

In no way was he obligated to sacrifice his life for me or anyone else for that matter. And yet here he was doing just that. Protecting me at all costs.

"If you'll excuse me now," I said as I glanced at the would-be campsite that was already buzzing with lots of activity.

"Of course."

I walked past Dar, past the women and men who were setting up tents and others who were already preparing dinner. I walked past them all and moved within the forest, getting as far away as I could. I took in deep breaths, smelling that sweet smell of pine again—that scent I loved and knew as well as my name. I had burned it into my soul, and now it moved through my body to calm my frayed nerves.

"Are you all right?" Cyrus asked from behind me.

Again, asking me how I was doing. Asking me if I would be okay. I realized he and I were on the same tormenting path of destiny. Both of us would long for what we could never have.

"Were you told to follow me?" I asked almost annoyed.

"Yes," he replied honestly. "I was. But you knew that already."

"I did," I sighed. "You keep asking me if I'm okay. Do I look like I'm about to fall apart?"

"Maybe," Cyrus shrugged as he crossed his thick arms. "I don't know your kind—how you adapt to stressful circumstance, if you are prone to nervous breakdowns—"

I laughed.

"What?" Cyrus looked wide-eyed. "It's entirely possible."

"Is that what you think?"

"We've heard that Breed B can have frenetic energy and nervousness."

"No," I shook my head. "Thankfully, you don't have to worry about any of that with me."

I tried not to laugh as I walked up to a large tree trunk and leaned down to pick up a few shards of pine needles. I held them up to my nose and took in a satisfying breath.

"I promise you I'm not about to fall apart," I said.

Cyrus smiled at me.

"Not yet," I whispered softly enough, so he couldn't hear.

"This must be a treat for you," Cyrus said. "Experiencing the terrain without the storm. Especially considering what you do."

"Yes, it really is." I faced him and watched him cover a yawn. "We can go back now. You must be tired."

"Not in the least," Cyrus shook his head. "Only if you're ready."

"I am," I lied and headed back the way we came with Cyrus walking next to me.

We reached the campsite, and I was impressed to see the tents had already been set up. There were two small fires going and the scents of freshly warmed bread and synthetic meats filled the air.

I saw Aedan sitting with Bibi in deep conversation.

"I can show you to your tent?" Cyrus offered politely.

"Please," I said.

He led me to a small brown canvas tent that was placed beside a tree, almost hidden away from the other tents. If someone were to attack, it would be hard to see.

"This is yours," he told me. "You're well protected here so you can rest easy."

"I wasn't too worried," I said.

"Food should be ready shortly," Cyrus went on. "You can rest for a bit and then I'll come for you."

"Thank you," I said before I entered my tent.

I closed the flap behind me and sat down in the small space. Someone had laid down blankets and a pillow for me. The small bag filled with fresh clothes and toiletries Aedan's servants had packed for me was placed in the tent as well. I laid down on the blankets and placed my hands on the thick black belt I had worn from the moment I crashed in OM.

I closed my eyes and tried to clear my mind.

Before I knew it I was overcome with exhaustion.

øøø

I felt someone harshly nudge my side with their boot before I shot up.

My gaze was slow to focus on Kali's cold face. She leaned down at my side.

"Feeling relaxed?"

I pushed back away from her, putting as much space between us as I could.

"What are you doing in here?" I demanded.

"I volunteered myself to wake you up," she said as she looked down at her nails. "I thought it was quite magnanimous of me."

"I'm awake," I told her. "So you can go now."

"Can I?" she said pointedly. "I don't recall needing *your* permission."

I pulled my knees up to my chest and stared at her.

"What are you doing in here?" I was tired of her anger. "We both know you didn't come to wake me. If this is another one of your warnings about Aedan…"

"Aedan?" Kali hissed, her eyes glowing and voice changing. "*Aedan?!* He is Praetor to *you*! I am done with your act. You think because you saved Gaia things will be different for you?"

"No, actually I don't." My voice was cold. "What is it about me you hate so much? What have I ever done to you?"

Kali's eyes narrowed at my words. "Your very existence bothers me," she said. "And that Aedan fails to see you for what you are."

"If you're so worried about the Praetor, maybe you

should seriously consider reevaluating your relationship."

"How dare you!'"

"I dare," I replied.

Something snapped inside.

I caught Kali off guard, tipping her up on her back, and moved too fast for her to even react. I grabbed her by the neck, straddled her body, and cut off her ability to move, by using an ancient technique I had learned. By hitting specific pressure points, one could target different motor skills and render an enemy almost useless. The hardest part was always the ability to catch someone off guard and be able to get to them. The rest was easy enough.

Kali's eyes were wide, and the look of surprise on her face was worth losing my temper.

"I'm tired of seeing your angry face every time I turn around," I whispered down to her. "I am not trying to steal your Praetor. Regardless of what you think, I didn't even want to come on this hunting trip of yours. I was ordered to."

I held on to her neck for a second longer, before I let go.

She came up gasping for air, her hands circled her neck as she looked at me with incredulous eyes.

"How did you do that?" She croaked out. "Show me."

"Why would I ever tell you when you have been nothing but cruel to me?" Was she mad?

Kali's eyes flickered away from me. "You're right," she whispered.

At first I didn't think I heard her correctly. I was convinced it had been my imagination, or wishful thinking even. But then, Kali met my gaze again, and I saw the uncertainty. The ice was still there, but maybe there was a chance some of it could thaw.

"I don't want to fight with you," I allowed myself to

speak the truth, to override any other feeling I might have for her. "I know you don't trust me," I continued on. "But let's try and figure out a way to coexist, while I'm here."

Kali didn't answer me. Instead, she rose and made her way to the flap of my tent. I watched her carefully, not knowing what to expect. For all I knew, she could turn around and try to pounce on me in retaliation of my attack on her.

I felt guilty I had allowed my emotions to get the better of me, yet again. It seemed the more time I spent on Earth among other humans, the more volatile I became. I was slowly losing all sense of who I had been on Akasha. I could no longer see the line between right and wrong. I was reacting without a thought of what consequences my actions could bring.

Somehow everything I had feared was becoming my reality.

"He doesn't look at me."

Kali spoke the words so softly I was barely able to make them out. She opened the flap and stared outside, the light from the moon illuminated her face.

If possible, she looked even more exotically beautiful than before.

"I don't understand," I said.

"Aedan," Kali's gaze met mine head-on. "He's never looked at me the way he looks at you."

CHAPTER EIGHTEEN

The moon lit up the entire sky with an ominous glow.

The warriors not standing guard against the Reptiles had gathered in a circle around the campfire, either eating or speaking amongst each other.

I sat in silence next to Bibi, occasionally casting glances across the circle at Kali or Aedan, who sat to her right. He seemed to be in good spirits, laughing and joking among his men. Kali, however, was lost in thought.

Our eyes clashed a few times, and she had been the one to look away.

He's never looked at me the way he looks at you.

I was filled with a profound sense of guilt from Kali's words. Our encounter had left me drained and unsure. After all, she was right. Aedan and I *had* shared intimate moments.

If she could sense them, it would be devastating for her. I didn't try and trick myself into believing otherwise.

"Your energy feels as though you have the weight of the worlds on your shoulders," Bibi said as she looked over at me.

"I'm just lost in thought," I returned as I glanced around the campfire.

"I saw Kali leave your tent," Bibi said. "I don't think I've ever seen a look of such confusion on her face before. What happened?"

"I set her straight," I told the General with a shrug.

"It was time," Bibi agreed. "You should feel pleasure."

"Making someone feel small doesn't bring me any joy," I replied.

"Perhaps she deserved it," Bibi returned.

"Did she?" I whispered and looked over at Bibi's face. There was an unspoken message that passed between us. Bibi slowly acknowledged my comment with a nod.

"Regardless," she said with a sigh. "There was no need for her attitude. Kali's pride needed to be checked. And I, for one, am happy you stood your ground."

"That makes one of us," I muttered under my breath.

Bibi burst out laughing.

"What's so funny?" I asked.

"Your temper," she replied with a grin. "Up until this moment, I didn't think it was possible for you to ever have a dark mood. You're always so pleasant. It pleases me to know you're just as human as the rest of us."

"I am human," I muttered.

"Are you trying to convince me?" Bibi raised a brow.

"At times I've felt the general consensus is that I might not be," I said.

"No," Bibi shook her head. "That's where you're wrong. It is not your humanity we question, but the Breed which you hail from."

"May I ask you something?" My voice was harsh.

"By all means," Bibi sounded pleased. "I feel like I'm finally getting the real Siren."

"What difference does it make?" I ignored her last comment.

"What do you mean?"

"My Breed," I said pointedly. "Kingdom B, Kingdom A, even Kingdom R. What difference does it make to you or anyone here? Shouldn't you place the value of my character above the value of my Shadow?"

"A Shadow I'm dying to see." Bibi returned with a smile. "But it's a noble thought. Unfortunately, reality doesn't seem to ever work that way."

I took a moment to answer.

"Then we should strive to be noble."

Before Bibi could respond, a member of the Praetorian Guard rose from the semicircle commanding attention. He walked to the center, stood next to the small fire, and stared out on the group. The warrior looked younger than the rest of the soldiers but just as formidable.

"Give us a story, Rex!" one of the female warriors shouted out to him.

"What kind would you like?" He said as he rubbed his palms together.

"Tell us!" Another called out.

"A tale of love and honor? Or a tale of heroes falling but ultimately victorious in battle?" He asked.

"Both!"

"You're in for a treat. This will be quite special," Bibi whispered to me. "Rex is a member of the *Goliard*. He is a gifted storyteller."

"Armies stand and fall with their general!" Rex called out to the soldiers listening. The group cheered him on. "By the command of their leader, they rise to greatness and achieve ultimate victory or tumble into darkness, where no man or woman will live to tell their tale. And in human history, there was no greater leader to ever walk this Earth than the Carthage General, Hannibal."

The warriors gave shouts of pleasure as he spoke with great gusto. He moved about the campfire, changing the tone of his voice, enrapturing all that listened.

"And what makes you a great leader, you wonder as you wait for my tale?" he asked the group of people. "Greatness is a culmination of actions that achieve a moment that will change the world. For the better or possibly the worse, depending on which side you are on."

"It was a day like any other," Rex continued on in a somber tone. "The sun burned the land, and the beasts themselves called out to the great Mother Earth, knowing history was about to be made. The year, 216 BC—"

I knew the battle well. Hannibal had been an excellent strategist, revered among men for thousands of years after his existence. My gaze moved across the group until settling on Aedan, who happened to be watching me.

He reminded me of Hannibal.

When I was younger, I had seen the written logs of the great General Hannibal. Aedan had the same drive and purpose: the ideal, the gravitas, to shine through the mundane and ultimately change the world.

This was Aedan's gift as well.

He would be a history maker.

"I'm tired," I whispered to Bibi. I needed to leave the encampment and escape to the solitude of my tent.

"Sleep well," she said not putting up her usual argument for me to stay. "I'll see you in the morning."

I leaned down and quietly made my way away from the campfire to not disturb any of the other soldiers.

I thought I had left unnoticed.

But I shouldn't have been surprised. I felt him before he even spoke.

Aedan.

He was standing maybe ten or so feet behind me, watching my every move. I stood at the flap of the tent, pausing before I stepped inside.

"Aedan," I couldn't look at him just yet.

"I came to see how you were doing," he explained

quietly. "You left in such a hurry. I was worried."

"I'm fine," I replied, touched he was concerned. I turned to look at him. He was standing closer now with his arms crossed, watching me intently.

"You didn't enjoy the story?" He asked. "He is a famous Goliard…"

"Yes, I know. Bibi told me. I've heard the story before though," I told him with a small smile. "Great warrior defeats the enemy…the only thing that seems to change in each tale is the name of the hero."

"Fair enough," he agreed.

We were both quiet.

"I promise I'll take you back to your Kingdom," Aedan said to my surprise. "You have nothing to fear. I will keep my word."

"I'm not afraid you won't keep your word, Aedan," I told him the truth. I was more frightened of my emotional connection to him, and how I would feel when he was gone from my life forever. And now crushing guilt washed over me as I remembered Kali's honesty.

"Then what is this mood of yours about?" He frowned at me. "I can feel your anxiety."

"My anxiety has to do with my circumstance," I said.

"No," he shook his head. "I know it's not that. There is something else."

Here we were.

Dancing around emotions neither of us wanted to acknowledge, feelings we both knew were dangerous.

"Aedan," my voice was soft. "What are you doing here?"

"I told you…"

"No," I shook my head, overwhelmed by it all. "What

are you *really* doing here?"

He watched me in silence, his eyes glowing.

I hadn't expected him to answer me, so I turned away from him and opened the flap of the tent. The safest way forward for Aedan and I was to ignore any feeling we might have for one another.

"It's wrong," his voice was quiet but strong.

My heart sped up, and I remained utterly still as he spoke.

"This," he continued in a low voice. "Whatever it is between us. It can't be right."

"No," I whispered shaking my head. "It can't be."

"But…"

My heart stopped as I waited for him to continue.

"I'm drawn to you."

I closed my eyes. Heaven forgive me, but the pleasure I felt from his confession almost brought me to my knees. The future didn't matter. For one moment, I was able to bask in his truth. To know what I felt was real.

I hadn't imagined anything.

"As you are to me," he continued.

I turned and met his enigmatic gaze.

"You're right," I admitted.

I thought I saw relief in his eyes, but I could not be sure.

"On both accounts."

The group of soldiers listening to Rex's tale may as well have been miles away. I felt like we were the only two people in the world, and more than anything, I wished it was truly the case.

Aedan closed the distance between us. The look on his face was intense and conflicted. I knew if he could wish the feelings he had for me away, he would.

If only it were that simple.

He reached out, his strong hand cupped my face, and it took all my strength not to lean into his touch.

"I don't understand," his voice sounded pained and unsure.

I tried not fidget under the intensity of his stare.

"Why *you*?" he continued on as his eyes met mine.

I could have asked him the same question. I wished I knew the answer. Was it because of the circumstance we were thrown together in? Was it because he was the first male human I set my eyes on? *No*, I didn't believe that. I *couldn't* believe that, because if I did, it would somehow diminish the value I placed on every emotional connection I'd ever had in my life.

I wished I could somehow make what I felt about him go away.

More than anything, I wished life was different, not so complicated. If only we could turn back time and be what we were before the extinction or annihilation. Or even, live in another world where this emotion we felt wasn't so wrong. How different it would be then.

"I…" I began to tell him what was truly in my heart, but then Kali's face flashed before mine.

I saw her anguish. The longing she had for him.

He's never looked at me the way he looks at you.

And no matter what, I could not be the cause of her pain. I stepped back from his touch.

"It doesn't matter," I said. "We are each bound to our own path."

"And yet, we seem to always meet our destiny, on the path we take to avoid it." he replied.

I was surprised by the passion behind his words.

"What does it matter?" I asked ruefully. "It is inevitable…"

"What is?"

"Our end." I waited for him to say something. To argue against my words. But nothing but silence greeted me.

"Good night, Aedan," I whispered as I turned toward the tent.

"Siren."

I stopped, turning my head slightly so he could only see my profile.

"Good night," he finally said.

øøø

I was with my mother, and I was still a young child. We were playing on the banks of the water. The waves lapped at the shore as the lavender atmosphere glittered almost magically. She was laughing with me, splashing water in my face, chasing me around as I basked in the wonder only a child could ever know. I ran over to a mound and threw my body down on the textured sand, giggling as the grains scattered in every direction.

My mother ran over to me and laughed in delight.

"Are you having fun, my love?"

"Yes, mama."

"I'm so glad," she said. "Nothing pleases me more than to see your sweet smile."

She handed me a toy, and I began to dig and build around me.

"Mama," I said after a while.

"I'm here, my love." She said watching me with a smile. "I promise you I won't go anywhere. I'll never leave you alone."

I smiled back at her, happy that she was with me.

Fearless, now that I knew she would watch over me.

"You don't have to be afraid," she said.

"I'm not," I told her.

I played for a while longer, before I felt the energy around me change. Within seconds, the sun went down and suddenly the sky was an ominous black.

"Mama?" I said in concern.

"Siren, my love!" My mother's voice was urgent. She grabbed my shoulders and gently shook me. "You must wake up now."

"But I don't want to," I told her.

"But you must. Right now, my love. There isn't much more time." She said forcefully. "Wake. Up."

I fought to stay with her.

"Siren." She demanded. "Listen to me."

"I don't want to leave you," I cried out. I did not want to leave the sweet safe sanctuary of her love, where I finally felt whole again.

"Wake up!" She cried out.

I opened my eyes, and it took me only a second to remember where I was.

It was quiet.

Deathly quiet.

I sat up and listened. There was no noise around me. Nothing. There should have been something, a soldier walking the perimeter or noises from the fire.

I quickly put my boots on and made my way outside the tent.

The light from the moon was gone. The night was black. It took a moment for my eyes to adjust to the darkness, and the first thing I saw was the camp looked entirely different from the way I left it. Some of the tents looked as though they had been destroyed. Slashed up and in haphazard piles on the ground. The smell of smoke from the fire still lingered, mixed in with the pungent odor of something else.

Something almost rusty.

Where was everyone?

My heart thumped loudly in my chest as I stared around at the campsite. Something was wrong. Terribly wrong. I peered out into the darkness and listened.

I heard it faintly at first.

It was like a drip of water, hollow and soft, but I could hear it. My breath was labored as I made way through the darkness. I saw three soldiers sleeping on the ground, laying in strange positions. I made my way over to them in dread. I could make out Dar's strong profile. I leaned down close to his body and gently nudged him.

He did not move.

"Dar?" I whispered.

Nothing.

After, I would realize how foolish I had been.

After, there would be so much time for me to replay those moments over and over in my mind. But at that point I didn't know how much everything would change after that moment.

"Dar?" I said again in concern.

When he didn't respond, I placed my hand on his shoulder and tried to move his body around. A spasm came over me, and the scream came so naturally. I fell back away from Dar's body and regurgitated everything I'd consumed for dinner. Sobs racked my body as I began to tremble in fear. I knew I had to invoke my word—*Arcana..* It took everything I had not to flicker.

I could not even look at him again.

Dar.

Or what was left of Dar. Half his body had been consumed. There were long jagged tear marks in his face and chest, his Shadow half—emerged in the macabre-like scene. The incredible physique I'd admired and thought was invincible had been ripped into with savage cruelty. His eyes were still open, and they spoke of the horror he had endured in the last moments of his life.

How? I knew the other soldiers who were laying beside him had suffered the same fate. The Reptiles had ambushed the camp. Where were the others? I needed to think clearly and regain control over my emotions.

I had to move.

Find the others.

If there were—

No! I couldn't allow myself to go down that road. I stumbled toward Dar's lifeless body and closed his eyes.

"I'm so sorry," I whispered to him. "May you bask in the true light of the universe."

I closed my eyes for a moment, offering a silent prayer for his soul. Then I got up and looked around the rest of the camp. As far as I could see the only dead bodies were the ones I had just found. That meant the rest of the group was out there somewhere.

Had Aedan and Bibi left them behind to protect me?

What had happened?

"Siren!"

It was Kali, along with two other female warriors. She was fully dressed for battle, holding a long sword in one hand and a shield in another. She ran right over to me.

"Are you all right?" Her voice was filled with concern, eyes alight like her Shadow.

"Dar—" I whispered.

Kali's eyes flickered with pain.

"There are many fallen warriors," her voice was emotional.

"What happened?"

"Our scouts found two different Reptile camps not far from here," she said. "Aedan and Bibi took two different groups. Ten of us remained behind. But it was—"

"A trap," I finished in horror.

"Yes," she said. "To divide us. And attack those who remained. We chased them off and killed the ones who attacked us here, but not before they killed some of our warriors. Cyrus is still hunting the ones who got away."

"And Aedan?" I asked. "Bibi?"

"I don't know," she whispered. I could hear the fear in her voice.

"Should we go and find them?" I asked.

"No," Kali shook her head. "Aedan wouldn't want it. We must wait here for Cyrus and the rest to return."

Or what would remain of them, I thought.

"Kali," I began to argue but stopped when I saw the look on her face.

Kali's gaze moved over my shoulder. She slowly lifted her sword up to her chest, her focus purely on whatever was behind me. The energy around her body changing. I knew her Shadow was dangerously close to emerging.

"Move," she whispered so quietly that only I could hear. "Slowly. To. Your. Right."

I did as she said. And when I was out of her way, I watched her charge two Reptiles who were boldly walking into the campsite.

"OM female flesh!" One of them called out, in a voice

that made my toes curl. "Not as soft and tender as I'd like, but you'll have to do."

The female soldiers flanking her side joined in the battle.

I ran right over to Dar's body and looked for a weapon. I picked up the first thing I saw, a long spear, turned and rushed into the fray.

There were many more than two. There were at least twelve Reptilian men and women, and they were strong. Some of the Reptiles were hybrids like the child and the one who'd attacked me with Aedan. They were a monstrous sight, half human, half snake—or lizard, while the other Reptiles flickered between human and animal. One minute they were just staring at us. The next, they attacked.

Kali and the women of OM had surprising restraint. They didn't flicker into their Shadow and remained calm. Kali's skill with the sword was impressive, and she was able to quickly take one down. The other two OM female warriors were incredible as well.

I attacked two of the male Reptiles who ran toward me, smiling with their razor teeth. I knew what would happen if they were able to take me down, so I fought with everything I had. I spun in circles around them, using my weapon as a distraction. I used the same moves I had with Gaia, except this time I would kill.

I would kill, I thought.

I would have to.

I hit one in the shoulder, and he roared out in pain and rushed me in fury, his long V-shaped tongue slithering out. I was ready. I squatted low and held my weapon up, the sharp end of the spear ready to impale. He charged me without thought or reason and ran straight through my weapon.

I could feel his flesh tear, the pressure of moving

through muscle and tissue, until the sharp end pierced his heart. His eyes were on mine. I saw the look of shock on his face. I knew part of my face had flickered into my Shadow, and I wanted him to see it.

Death had come at the hands of a Breed that was supposed to be extinct.

I pushed back with all my strength and threw his body with force away from my own. I watched him twitch on the ground. His hands convulsing, his body fighting to keep going.

Everything around me stopped.

I did not know if the other Reptile was about to attack, if there were more coming for me.

Like an artist marveling at their work, I walked over to him and looked down at his dying body. My face flickered back to its human form as I gathered my bearings. His eyes were pale orange, sickly, and consumed with hate. He smiled up at me, showing off his macabre teeth, his long tongue falling to the side. The nails on his fingers were long, sharp, and black.

"Came to watch me go?" He hissed at me. "Or did you come for a taste?"

"You are a monster," I whispered.

The Reptile laughed in delight.

"The beast lies dormant within us all," he gurgled out. Blood began to drip out of his mouth. "And now, I have unleashed it in you."

I was filled with hate. Because he was right.

I had just lost a part of my innocence, a part of my humanity. This vile, vicious creature of the Earth had caused my fall. I stood there and watched the life leave his body. It was my duty to see the handiwork of my actions.

I was the cause, this, the effect.

He let out his final breath. It sounded like a rattle and then silence.

I stood there staring down at his lifeless face, then glanced at the spear protruding from his body and thought *I should probably pull it out.*

Strange. I felt nothing. No guilt.

No remorse over the life I had just taken.

Nothing.

It was a defining moment. From this second on, I knew I would never be the same. It was like my mother had said, another moment that would change me forever.

The wrinkle in time ceased to exist, and I was once again back in the reality of the situation. I leaned over his body and pulled the spear out. Just as I stepped back away from him a sword shattered my weapon in half and barely missed slicing open my midriff.

I arched my body in and jumped back from the attack.

A female Reptile was attacking me, one who looked as vile as the rest. And she was enraged, even more so than the others. Her eyes were red in fury.

"You killed him!" She screeched out, thrusting her sword at me.

I barely dodged the next swing. From my peripheral vision, I saw Kali and the others still fighting as more Reptiles descended upon us. I jumped over branches and items, trying to keep the livid Reptile at bay. She lunged for me again and this time was able to slice my upper arm.

The pain was astounding, and the immediate throb made my eyes cloud.

I heard a thundering roar vibrate through the clearing.

It was Aedan.

He had brought Bibi and the rest of the warriors with him.

Our eyes met and I saw the panic, the fear, his Shadow, and I knew his bellow had been for me. The relief I felt from seeing that he and Bibi were still alive was staggering. I didn't know what I would have done had they fallen.

I watched Aedan pounce into the battle in a frenzy, hacking mercilessly away at the Reptiles. But he was too far from me. He would have to make his way through, what seemed to be, an endless sea of enemies before he'd ever reach my side.

I was on my own. The only thing I could do was continue to outrun and out dance the female Reptile. I led her up through the clearing, using the trees as my shield. She hacked away, swinging with such force that if she hit me, I would be done.

You can do this, Siren. You just have to survive until Aedan can get to you.

I was in the zone, anticipating her every thrust. And from what I could see from the corner of my eye, the battle was quickly being won.

But I wasn't counting on destiny.

I didn't see the dead body of a solider from OM. I didn't see his long arm strung out on the ground. He blended in. And I tripped, flying up against a tree.

I couldn't stop the scream.

I knew she would have the advantage to strike. I turned around quickly, putting my back to the trunk and saw Kali running with all of her might, her Shadow helping her move faster as she made her way to my side. She shoved me to the ground, threw herself in front of my body and lifted her sword up in the air.

But she wasn't fast enough.

The Reptile plunged the sword through Kali's heart.

An attack that was meant for me.

"No!!!" I heard Aedan bellow in pain. "Kali!"

I felt like I was watching something on a screen. Like I wasn't really there. That this couldn't be what was truly happening. Kali fell to her knees. Her hands came up to grip the sword protruding from her chest and they flickered.

She looked over at me.

I moved to her side just as she fell back and held her in my arms.

"No!" I cried out. "Please, God! No! Kali!"

It wasn't fair. I closed my eyes and pulled the vision of the ocean in front of me. I had to remain calm. I could not flicker. I had to... *Arcana*. Deep breath. *Arcana*.

Mission First.

Kali had just sacrificed her life for me. A woman she loathed. A woman she *knew* had feelings for the man she loved. I wanted to die. I wanted to trade places with her, and at that moment, I would have done anything to make it happen.

"Stay with me," I whispered to Kali as she looked up at me with glassy eyes. She began to stare at something over my shoulder.

"No!" I shook my head at Kali. "Not yet!"

There was a breeze.

I looked up in time to see Aedan lop off the female Reptile's head and come for Kali. He fell to his knees beside us and gently pulled her into his arms.

There were tears in his bright eyes as he brushed back her dark hair from her beautiful face. "Kali," he whispered softly. His voice was choked up with emotion.

I wept as I watched them. It was the hardest moment of my life—grieving for Kali and for Aedan, while also trying to control the sadness that was threatening to take over. I pushed my fingertips together, breathing slowly.

"It is beautiful, Aedan," Kali's voice was weak. "Just as we imagined it would be."

"Tell me," he said as he held her.

She smiled up at him and lifted her hand to his cheek.

"One day you will see," she told him. "But not yet."

He held up her hand with his, pressing it lovingly to his cheek.

"Do you remember when we were children and I told you I would always protect you?" His grief blanketed the night.

"Do not, my love." Kali's voice was weaker by the second. Time was running out.

"I have failed you," Aedan's voice was muffled. He pulled her body up to his face and buried his head in her neck. His shoulders shook and I knew Kali was *gone*.

I looked away and cried my own tears of pain. Of guilt. I had never known such guilt before in my life.

"Kali!" Aedan howled as he looked up in the night sky and screamed in pain.

The camp was deathly silent.

Aedan's guard had killed the rest of the Reptiles and were gathered around their leader with their heads bowed, watching the sad scene playing out before them like a Shakespearean tragedy.

He placed her gently on the ground and abruptly stood. The pain I saw in his gaze was almost my undoing.

"Get up!" he roared at me, his Shadow revealed itself, aggressive and furious.

"Aedan," I whispered, unsure.

"Get up and bring her back!" He screamed at me.

"I can't do it," I shook my head at him. "It's not how it is done."

"Bring her back!" He bellowed in my face again with the strength of his ancestors.

I could feel the hot tears on my skin as I looked at him helplessly and took a couple steps back.

"I can't."

He grabbed hold of my arm. "You can't or you *won't*?!" His voice was like ice.

"Please," I begged him as he dragged me toward Kali's lifeless body. "I can't."

"Aedan!" Bibi called out in alarm.

"Do not!" He roared at her. "She. Will. Do. This!"

I lay in a crumbled heap in front of her body, crying.

Arcana.

"I wish I could," I said over and over again. "I wish I could...I promise you."

My words seemed to make Aedan lose his mind. He picked me up again and shoved me against the tree, wrapping his hand wrapped around my throat. Within seconds, his sword was poised just a hair away from my throat. But it wasn't his Shadow looking at me with hate. It was him.

"She died for you," he raged. "*She just died for you!*"

"I know," I said in anguish. "I wish I could help you."

Arcana.

He growled low in his throat and closed his eyes.

"Let her go," Bibi was standing next to us. She placed her hand on Aedan's arm, the one holding the sword to my throat.

"She can't help her." His grip around my neck didn't loosen.

"Aedan," Bibi's voice was forceful. "Let her go. We must see to Kali and the others now. It is time to mourn."

His body shuddered and he finally opened his eyes.

It was worse than I could ever imagine. He stared at me like I was vermin.

Like everyone in Kingdom OM had. Gone was the kindness and empathy, and in its place was an Aedan I did not even recognize.

Arcana.

"Get this Aliud out of my sight," he coldly stated.

Devoid of all emotion.

Everything I had feared had come to pass.

CHAPTER NINETEEN

I don't remember when it started raining.

But I remember marching back through the gates of the city of Larsa. I remember the somber audience that awaited us. I remember Aedan and Cyrus holding Kali's body, which was draped in black garments given by Aedan's surviving guard as they each fell to their knees before her body to honor Kali and the great sacrifice she made.

Saving an Aliud.

I remember watching Cyrus sob openly at the campsite. He did not care who saw him. He felt no shame in the love he had for Kali and the devastation of her loss. I remember seeing Bibi sit down, hold Kali's hand, and talk to her lifeless body. She wiped away tears as she spoke of their past, and the mischief they would get themselves in. And she smiled a few times as she whispered words in her ear.

I remember Aedan flickering into his Shadow, running from the campsite into the night. No one dared question him. And no one dared stop him.

But I don't remember when it started raining.

We reached the Praetor's home. I was taken there by two soldiers I didn't recognize. The rest had gone to a temple where I was told the bodies would lay, until they were burned and spread out across the land, however the family saw fit.

The soldiers had been kind to me, and I didn't know why. They should hate me more now, despise me, and demand I leave their land. Or worse, demand my life. But instead, they were kind.

I did not deserve it.

I walked through the Great Hall and headed straight for my room. I never wanted to leave it again

"Siren."

It was Sara. I had forgotten about her. About Dr. Novak. About Michael.

More importantly, I had forgotten Kali was Dr. Novak's daughter. I almost crumbled to the ground.

"Dr. Novak has requested to see you."

"I can't, "I shook my head. "I can't, Sara."

I couldn't bear the thought of looking in his eyes and knowing I was the cause of his daughter's death. He would hate me now, and I could not blame him for it. And what he would do to me down in that lab of his, I could only imagine.

"You must," Sara said forcefully.

"Must?" I questioned. "Is it an order from the Praetor?"

"Currently the Praetor has asked to not hear your name," Sara informed me.

I wasn't surprised. But it hurt, nonetheless. I had not wanted any of this.

"You cannot deny him," Sara's voice sounded almost human. "No matter what your feelings might be for him. He is entitled this request. As a father."

The computer was right. Where I wanted to run and hide away in my room until I somehow magically woke from this nightmare, Sara knew what had to be done.

A computer knew what had to be done.

"I will go to him," I agreed softly.

I walked down to the hall and took note of all the candles lit. Everywhere I looked, I saw one. I knew for OM, fire had significance and prayers were given with candles.

"Are these for Kali?" I asked knowing Sara was tracking my every move.

"They are for all the fallen heroes."

Sixteen other soldiers died. Dar was one. I did not know the names of the others.

"Where is everyone?"

"They are mourning at home," Sara explained. "Kingdom OM encountered a tremendous defeat today. In their short history, they have never had such casualties."

"They inflicted such casualties," I whispered.

"The Cetacean Massacre," Sara heard me. "Yes. Some regret it. Others don't. Such is the case in human history."

Sara's emotionless comments were unnerving. For a computer to understand and be able to point out human fallacy was alarming. If a computer chose to believe, whether right or wrong, that we were expendable because of our destructive nature, the world would take an even worse turn.

"You worry about my unfiltered comments and discerning eye," Sara stated.

"I do," I spoke the truth. "You would agree it is a dangerous proposition."

"Life is a dangerous proposition," Sara said. "Dr. Novak says this all the time."

She was right. And I had only just experienced how dangerous.

"You should not fear me, Siren," Sara said. "I am not your enemy."

"You belong to Dr. Novak. You do what he asks," I said to her. "Your circumstance makes you my enemy." Sara did not respond.

The door to Dr. Novak's office was open. It was dark inside, the flicker of candles casting shadows around the walls. I could see the pitch-black sky from his massive windows as the rain drizzled on the city.

Glancing around, I noticed Dr. Novak sitting on his L-shaped couch staring out in space. I waited by the door. I knew he had heard me enter, and I did not know what to expect.

"Come in, Siren." His voice sounded emotionless.

I slowly walked over to the couch and stared down at him.

"I don't know what to say to you right now to ease your sorrow," I began softly. Even though he was my enemy, he had still lost his daughter.

"There are no words—there is no remedy for this type of pain," his voice broke as he tried to gain control of his emotions.

"Kali was your daughter and she, she—" I whispered as I tried to find the right words.

I couldn't finish the sentence.

"Died for you," Dr. Novak said as his pale blue eyes narrowed into tiny slits and took an eerie glow. "She took a sword in her heart for your life. Her warrior's honor meant more than her own desire to live. Her pledge to our foolish Practor to keep you safe, killed her."

"Pledge?" I asked in confusion.

"In front of me, before you left on the hunt," Dr. Novak said with hate. "He didn't trust her with you. He thought she was being cruel. And he wanted me to hear his words."

Dr. Novak laughed maniacally.

"She *loved* him," he went on in disgust. "She loved him her whole life. She promised him she would keep you safe. And she did."

I blinked back my tears. It was too cruel. All of it. I despised everything about this man, but I understood what it meant to lose someone you loved—and for him, a daughter.

His only living heir.

"I ask for your forgiveness," I whispered to him.

Dr. Novak stood up from the couch and walked over to the window, keeping his back to me. He stared out into the night as I waited for him to speak.

"You want my forgiveness?" His voice rumbled, shaking in rage. The sound permeated around me, my body trembling of its own accord.

"Yes," I whispered trying to calm myself. No matter my feelings for him, I never wanted this.

"Sweet Cetacean," Dr. Novak finally turned to stare at me, his voice a low, dangerous chuff. His blue eyes were glowing, the rage he felt, making them shimmer against the ominous shadows in the room. He seemed to grow taller, until he was merged with his Shadow—a ferocious polar bear—a hunter that had fed on my ancestors for centuries. The fear that gripped me was paralyzing. I could barely control my Shadow, screaming to be freed, desperate to escape.

"I will *never* forgive you," he said emphatically, walking toward me. "I will use you for what I need and then I will get my revenge and destroy you—I will kill you myself. Milo won't get the opportunity. No other will be able to touch you. It will be me—standing above you, when you take your very last breath."

I could feel the blood leave my face.

"There is a bracelet on the table there," Dr. Novak's voice was cold as he pointed with the arm of his Shadow. "You will keep it on at *all* times."

My gaze found the small bracelet that resembled a thin black wire.

"It's a locating device," he told me. "With it Sara will be able to track you wherever you go. All my pets must wear a collar."

The sympathy I had for him began to fade as I stared at him in indignation.

"I am not your pet."

"No," Dr. Novak agreed. "A pet would mean you were something I had affection for, where the only emotion I feel for you is *hate*."

"I won't put that thing on," I told him as I shook my head.

"You will," Dr. Novak said with a cold smile. "Or I'll tell everyone what you really are. I don't think they'd take too kindly to that knowledge given the current circumstance. Even the young Praetor would hate you."

My stomach fell.

He was right.

"Sara can already track me anywhere inside the Praetor's home," I said evenly.

"You are correct," he agreed. "But not outside this compound."

"That should be enough for you," I said.

Dr. Novak shook his head as he watched me.

"Yesterday it was enough," he said coldly. "But today, the world is a much different place. From this moment on, I will know where you are at all times."

ØØØ

Kali's soul ascension ceremony was beautiful.

Everything about it, from the temple, to the giant limestone bowl burning with an eternal flame, to the songs the children sang in Kali's honor.

The only jarring moment came when Aedan, Cyrus, Bibi

and Dr. Novak took her body, wrapped in white muslin cloth, and set it onto the flames. I knew it was part of their culture, but it was still hard to see.

On behalf of the General, Sara asked if I wanted to attend, and even though I would have preferred to stay in my room, I felt I had to. Kali had given her life for me, and I would respect her in the best way I could. I was shown to a private booth in the temple, one where I would be able to watch mostly unobserved, unable to detract from the moment that was purely about Kali.

For almost the entire duration of the ceremony, I found myself staring at Aedan. He was dressed in white from head to toe, his face could have been made of stone. I knew he was torturing himself, though he suffered his guilt in silence. It would take a long time before Aedan would truly heal.

There were a few times during the ceremony where I felt as though he was watching me. But every time I looked over at him, his gaze was glued to the front of the temple.

When the ceremony concluded, the crowd slowly left the temple. I watched everyone leave, including Dr. Novak. They would go to eat and drink in Kali's honor. Sara told me this was custom in the Kingdom and would last all night, considering there were many other soldiers mourned in the city at this time.

I left the booth I was seated in and walked over to the fire pit they had placed Kali's body on. Ashes were all that remained. I fell to my knees and prayed before her. I sent her love and light. I thanked her for the great sacrifice she made and wished her peace in the ever after.

"Mama?" I whispered out loud. "If you can hear me now, find Kali and show her the kind of love I experienced before you left."

I stayed like that for a moment longer, head bowed in prayer and then slowly rose.

Aedan was waiting behind me.

I didn't have to see him to know it.

It took all of the courage I had to turn around and face him. I was afraid to see that look again on his face. I met his gaze. He was a changed man. The look of sorrow and guilt on his face nearly took my breath away.

"I thought you had gone," I said apologetically. "If I had known you would return, I wouldn't have come here."

"I came for her ashes." His voice was like steel, his jaw clenched as his eyes locked with mine.

Sara told me he would spread them for Dr. Novak, which surprised me considering his contempt for Aedan.

"Of course," I murmured. "I'll leave you."

I started to walk past him and was surprised when his hand shot out and grabbed hold of my arm. There was great force in his grip.

I closed my eyes. I did not want him to see me as weak.

"Look at me." Aedan commanded.

I did.

"I lost control," he stated without a hint of emotion. "I attacked you. I shouldn't have."

It wasn't much of an apology, and to be honest, I didn't even think he was obliged to give me one. I understood where his pain came from, and I would never hold what he did in grief against him. But still, I accepted his words with a nod of acknowledgement.

He stared at me for a moment longer before letting go of my arm.

I started to walk away but stopped.

"You need to know," I spoke with my back facing him.

"If I could have saved her, brought her back, I would have. And there is nothing I wouldn't do to change what happened."

Aedan didn't acknowledge my words.

I left him then, to grieve alone.

øøø

I woke up the next day to news Aedan had left to spread Kali's ashes. Sara was the one to tell me he had gone and that Dr. Novak would observe the five days of mourning for Kali and the other soldiers lost. And after that time, she told me, we would begin our experimental research again. I had no idea what was coming for me now that Dr. Novak despised me so much, but I knew it would not be good. If I was honest, it had frightened me more than I thought possible. Maybe even more than the Reptiles. It was visceral. And instinctive. Like my life was truly in imminent danger.

The sun was out, so I walked the perimeter of Aedan's home for hours.

"General Canis is looking for you," Sara said to me as I made my way back to the hall. I was getting used to having her around.

"Where is she?" I asked.

"In the Praetor's library," Sara answered.

I had yet to speak to Bibi since Kali's death, and I was anxious to see how she would treat me. I entered the library and found her staring out the window.

"How was your walk?" she asked me.

"Pleasant enough," I replied.

She faced me with her arms crossed. "Kali was a warrior. Since we were children, we had been raised to fight."

I waited for her to continue.

"There is nothing you could have done," she went on. "She knew the risks. We all know the risks of battle. She chose her destiny."

To say I was surprised by the General's words, would be an understatement.

"To die for me?"

"Yes," Bibi's voice was strong. "To die for you. It was the path she chose. And it's not your fault. It's not anyone's fault. It's the cruel reality of this world we live. It could have been me. Or Aedan. Or even you. And the pain of the loss would be just the same."

"Aedan will never forgive me," I was resigned to that sad fact.

"He needs time," Bibi sighed. "He blames himself. Just as you blame yourself for her death."

I looked away from Bibi's knowing gaze.

"You cannot continue down the path of self-reproach and hate," she continued. "Nothing good will come from living in darkness. You said these words to me yourself, when I told you about the Incident. You will return to your Kingdom, and you will live on and remember the sacrifice she made."

"For the rest of my life," I whispered, my voice full of emotion. "I will never forget it."

"I know," Bibi smiled sadly. "As we all will. I came here to tell you that you must continue to live. Though we mourn, we still breathe. And life must go on."

I appreciated her empathy. Her words soothed me. And I was relieved she didn't blame me for Kali's death.

"And Cyrus?" I asked her. "How is he?"

"Kali was his best friend," she said. "His feelings for her were complicated, and he is in deep mourning. He has taken it very hard. She was—is family. And her loss will be felt for some time."

He had been in love with her. If I had gathered as much from what little interaction I had with him, I was sure the General knew the truth as well.

"As I imagine it would be," I said.

"I came to check on you," she said. "I must head to the temple now for a private ceremony for the other warriors with the rest of the Praetorian Guard. I'll be back later."

"Thank you," I said. "But please, see to your people. I'm fine here, on my own."

As I had always been.

I walked Bibi out of the compound and watched her get in a pod and leave for the temple. "Now what?" I mumbled to myself.

"Is that question directed for me?" Sara answered quickly.

I realized I wasn't as alone as I believed.

"No," I said sighing. "It's just a rhetorical comment. A statement regarding my current situation."

"If you'd like," Sara said. "I can show you to the screening room, where you can find entertainment for the next few hours until the General returns."

My mind was too preoccupied to sit through any type of OM entertainment.

"I'm fine," I said. "I can find another way to occupy my time."

"Shall I give you options?" Sara continued.

"No," I said as I made my way back up to my room.

Gaia was waiting for me by the door. She was sitting with her knees pulled up to her chest, head bent down, lost in deep thought.

"Gaia," I smiled, happy to see the girl. "What are you doing here?"

She stood up slowly.

"I came to see you," she sounded worried.

"I'm all right," I told her touched by her concern. "How are you doing?"

"I'm actually fine," she told me honestly. "You see, unlike the others, I know where they all are now. And I envy them...I could feel your pain, you know."

"What?"

"Your sadness," she confessed softly. "I can feel it. That's why I came here."

Connected.

Gaia and I were now connected for life. When I reached out and spoke to her soul, we bonded. Gaia, having touched the light of the universe, had opened up her senses to endless possibility. She could feel energy now.

"It is just one of the gifts you brought back with you," I told her.

"Do you have this ability?" she asked me. "Do your people? The Cetaceans? Do they all have it?"

"Yes," I whispered. "Those who are left have the same gift."

"How many?" she asked me. "How many are there like you?"

"When I left my planet, there were eleven of us remaining."

"Only eleven?" Her voice faltered. The child's eyes showed her surprise.

"Yes," I said.

"It must be lonely."

"It is," I acknowledged. "Quite lonely."

"But not anymore," she extended her hand. "I'm now your family as well. I might not be made like you, but I know we're still the same."

I reached out and took her hand, pulling her into my arms. She hugged me back tightly, the gravity of her words touched me. I was free to be myself with her. I didn't have to lie. Or pretend to know about another Kingdom. Gaia gave me a semblance of hope.

I could just be me.

"Thank you, Gaia," I whispered to her. "Your words mean everything."

"I brought you something I thought you might need," she pulled away and reached into her pocket to retrieve a small gold bottle. She handed it to me.

"What is it?" I asked curiously.

"A sleeping remedy," she said. "After everything that's happened I thought you might want something to help you sleep. Dr. Novak gave it to me after my accident. You only have to use one drop and you'll be out for the night. It's pretty powerful and it works fast."

I was about to reject the gift—but then I stopped myself. Gaia might have just offered me my first weapon to use to help me out of OM. I pointed toward the bracelet on my hand, the device that allowed Sara to listen in on every conversation I had, then pressed my finger to my lips. Since the Reptile attack, Aedan had ordered the city walls closed. No citizen could leave Larsa until the land was deemed safe, which meant no one from OM would be taking me to Kingdom B. I was on my own again.

"I don't need any sleeping aides," I said as I took the bottle and shook my head, silently begging her to play along.

Gaia's eyes flashed in realization, she quickly nodded in

understanding.

"Of course, I understand if you don't need it," she told me as I slipped the bottle into the compartment of the belt I wore. "I just thought I'd ask."

"Thank you," I replied with a conspiratorial wink. "But I'm okay."

Gaia winked right back at me. Now we shared another secret.

"Would you like to leave the compound with me?" Gaia asked innocently. "My grandmother said it was all right. I thought I'd show you my favorite place in the world."

"How can I say no?" I was happy to have the distraction. "I would be honored."

I had never left the compound without the General or Aedan's approval, but with him gone, Bibi at the temple, and Eadric's approval, I didn't think it would be an issue. We took a pod into the city, and for the first time in forever, I finally felt free. We went through tiny streets lined with many buildings. There were a few children playing on the sidewalks.

"Is this a residential neighborhood?" I asked.

"Yes," Gaia said. "Many of OM's Assembly live over here."

"Do you?"

"Yes," she said. "But we're not staying here. We're going to the outskirts of this area."

I stared out on the neighborhood.

"You're very lucky," I told her. "You have so many neighbors."

"What's your home like?" She asked quietly.

"Very different from this," I told her before briefly describing Akasha.

"Were you happy there?" Gaia was curious.

"Sometimes," I said with longing of days past. "But then there were other moments where I felt deprived and so alone."

"I'm glad you came here," Gaia said.

"Me too." I had to say the words out loud, before I was able to acknowledge the truth in them. No matter what, I'd lived more in these past days than I had ever before in my life.

"We're here," Gaia said with excitement.

I looked out the window and was treated to a rainbow of colors. She brought me to an outdoor marketplace that sold every imaginable item. There were leather goods, scarves, food, toys, and flowers—so many vibrant flowers. People of all ages walked up and down the aisles, buying and selling.

"Gaia," I said in awe. "This is incredible."

"I knew you'd like it," she said.

I jumped out of the pod after her in excitement.

"Don't worry," Gaia said to me. "I've brought my chip."

"Chip?"

She lifted up a clear glass card that had a tiny titanium chip in the center.

"To pay," she explained. "You can pay me back later."

"When I start earning money here?" I couldn't help but laugh.

"Who knows?" she said with a shrug.

I know, I thought.

We spent the next few hours walking up and down the many aisles of the market. I was enthralled with the smells and the textures, and the smiling faces enraptured me. When my hands were full of small linen bags filled with different items Gaia made me buy or bought for me, we found ourselves standing in front of a fresh fruit juice stand. Gaia wanted me to try a new exotic fruit the scientists had recently developed. She promised I'd love it.

These past hours, I had truly enjoyed myself, forgetting everything and just being. I was forever indebted to this young girl for bestowing the greatest gift on me—

Acceptance.

"We'll have two C-35s," Gaia said when we reached the stand. "You're going to love it."

"C-35?" I asked.

"It's a drink." She handed me the bright purple drink.

"Wonderful," I said.

I took a sip of the C-35 and Gaia was definitely right. The drink was sweet and heavenly and I loved it. It tasted almost like grapes but with a hint of apple.

"It's too good," she said.

"It is," I agreed and was about to take another sip, when something hit the back of my neck. I was caught so off guard, I spilled my drink all over Gaia. I turned to see what it was and got pelted by another object—this time it landed against my side. They were packets filled with some type of liquid.

"Hey!" Gaia shouted as she protectively stepped in front of me and faced the crowd.

A group of people gathered around us, staring right at me with hate, one flickered into his Shadow—a gorilla. I saw two children quickly run away, flickering into their elephant Shadows when Gaia shouted. I assumed they had been the ones to pelt me with the liquid filled bags. The crowd around us seemed to grow as they started hissing at me in rage.

"Murderer!" One person shouted.

"Aliud!" Another said.

They swayed around me with hate in their eyes as their human and Shadow faces blurred together. Everywhere I looked, I felt their disgust.

"A life for a life!" Someone screamed out.

"Get away!" Gaia shouted back at the crowd as they closed in on us. "Let us through!"

I looked around for a way out.

But there was none.

"Stay behind me," I pushed Gaia back to protect her as they moved closer chanting in anger.

It felt like the crowd tripled in a matter of seconds.

This was not good. I looked over at Gaia.

"Get away from me!" I said urgently. "They can't be controlled and I don't want anything to happen to you."

"I'm not leaving you," she adamantly shook her head.

"Aliud!" One shouted.

"Kill the Aliud!"

I had no weapon. There was no way I could keep them at bay. As they grew closer and closer, I spun around in a circle, holding Gaia protectively behind me, searching for a way out. Just as I was about to give up all hope, there was a break in the crowd and a group of heavily armed soldiers moved through. They lifted their weapons and faced the crowd directly in front of me.

"Stand down!" A voice bellowed out from behind them.

In seconds, the crowd stopped their shouts and stood in silence.

I drew in a shaky breath.

It was Milo.

CHAPTER TWENTY

Milo made his way through the crowd and stood in front of his soldiers.

One look at his formidable stance and the people backed down.

"What is the meaning of this?" His voice boomed over the chaos. "We are not like the others. We do not let our Shadows control us." He admonished the ones who had.

"The Aliud killed Kali!" Someone cried out in fury.

"The Praetor says the Reptiles killed her," Milo replied evenly. "If our esteemed leader says it, shouldn't we all believe it? After all, Kali was his intended mate."

My eyes narrowed. Something didn't feel right.

Milo would not defend Aedan like this. Though his voice dripped with innocence, there was nothing virtuous about him.

"It can't be!" Someone shouted out in anger.

"He lies to protect the Aliud!" Another said.

Warning bells went off in my head. Milo looked too pleased. And too sure.

He was planning something.

"None of us here know what really happened. Only what we've been told. He is our leader and we must believe him," Milo continued on through the protests. "And regardless of what the truth is, we are better than this. We are not wild animals like the other breeds!"

"She should die!" Another screamed out.

"Hang her outside the city walls, so the Reptiles can have what's left of her!"

My gaze locked with the man who shouted that out.

There was no empathy. No warmth. Only a desire for vengeance.

"We demand justice!" Someone shouted out. People yelled in agreement.

"If we are to have justice, let it happen within the laws that govern our land," Milo yelled. "The laws created for our protection. *We are OM!"*

The people cheered in pleasure, incited by his passionate speech. Without a doubt, he was a brilliant rhetorician.

He turned his bright gaze to mine. "I will take you back to the Praetor's compound."

"I can..." Gaia interjected.

"Your grandmother is expecting you," Milo said dismissively. "I will take her back."

"It is all right," I said to Gaia to appease her. She looked concerned. "I'll be fine. And I'll see you later. I promise. Go to your grandmother."

She hesitated for a moment.

"Okay," she finally said, but her eyes narrowed on Milo.

I left her and followed Milo away from the crowd, careful to avoid their angry gazes and incite the mob. They pointed and snarled, whispering among each other, staring at me with disdain.

It was not a considerate act, I knew, only to make sure I got in. I held onto the bags, waiting for him to speak.

"That went well, wouldn't you say?" Milo smiled over me.

I kept quiet.

"If I were you, I'd stay away from open markets in the future," he went on. "It might prove to be quite dangerous."

"What is your game?" I asked him.

"My *game?*" He sneered. "I don't play games, little bird.

Games are for children. In my world, you are with me or you are not."

He looked right at me. "And *you* most definitely are not."

"Why did you stop them?"

"Some situations require an amount of finesse," he said slyly. "Above all, I am a strategist."

I could feel my blood run cold. This had nothing to with me or even my being in OM. This was all about Aedan. And how Milo could usurp his power.

"You're using me," I said.

"Yes," he replied. "I am. And I thank you greatly for this gift you've bestowed upon me."

I could feel the anger churn inside. How dare he use me for his gain? I worried more now, for Aedan. What was Milo about to bring on him? Civil war? Or something worse?

"Have I angered you, Aliud?" His voice was mocking. "If so, I'm glad."

I tried to control my emotions. I didn't want to give him any satisfaction.

I gave him a bright smile. "Why would I be bothered? None of this has anything to do with me. You're not my Breed. I'm going home soon, and I'll forget you even exist."

I felt tremendous satisfaction watching Milo slowly lose his smile. It was quite fascinating to see how the rage took over, turning his face into something twisted and dark.

"That then begs the question," Milo threatened. "Will you *really* be going home, Aliud?"

I refused to back down. "Are you threatening me?"

"Never," his voice was mocking. "You are a guest of Eadric, our Elder, and more importantly, the Praetor."

And there it was. The underlying threat. Their lives were

also in danger. This was a man who would stop at nothing to gain what he wanted.

We reached the Praetor's compound, and I quickly moved toward the door, trying to escape the pod and Milo's vile presence.

"I hear you and Dr. Novak have become quite friendly."

His words made my blood run cold.

"I was understandably angry at first, worried you'd *sing like a canary* as they say," Milo said with a sinister smile, "but when Dr. Novak told me there was a distinct possibility you might not be from Kingdom B, my interest was piqued."

I met his gaze, relieved Milo didn't know the truth—at least for now.

"I can't wait to find out what you really are."

"You know what I am," I sounded uninterested.

"Is Aedan hiding your secret?" Milo asked curiously.

"There is no secret," I returned quickly, afraid for Aedan.

Milo waved his hand, brushing my words off, his face etched in disbelief.

"Dr. Novak says you've met our guest," Milo continued on. "I'm curious, what do you think of him?"

"He's not your guest," I returned in anger. "He's a caged prisoner."

"As you will be soon," Milo returned with an evil smile.

I opened the door to the pod. I couldn't bear to hear anymore.

"Enjoy your accommodations while you can," Milo called out to me.

When I entered the hall, I wasn't surprised to see the General there, waiting for me.

"Are you all right?" She asked as she rushed over to me. "I was told what happened in the market with Gaia."

"I'm all right," I assured her. "But Milo…"

"Yes, I heard," she stated. "He's using this, *Kali's* death, and blaming you for it. With emotions high, the people are scared about the attack and more frightened than ever of the unknown. Kali was beloved by many, known throughout the land as the Praetor's intended mate. She came from an old family bloodline, which is one of the reasons why she was an acceptable mate for Aedan."

Her words were surprising.

"I did not know a bloodline mattered for his future mate."

"In his case, it does matter," Bibi said cryptically. I wished she'd explain, but I didn't want to push.

"It won't be hard for Milo to convince people to turn," the General went on. "To forget you saved Gaia's life."

"I understand," realization dawned on me.

"You're safe here in the Praetor's home," Bibi said. "But outside the compound…"

"I won't leave again without you," I assured her. "I don't want to cause more problems for anyone. Or worse, put anyone's life in danger."

"I know that," Bibi said. "Every step we take from this moment on must be carefully thought out. As you must realize, we cannot put more soldiers at risk."

Which ultimately meant, they could not help me get out of OM.

Not until the safety of their people was assured.

The fate of my mission was truly in my own hands. I thought about the sleeping aide Gaia had given me. Unknown to the girl, she had given me a weapon I could use against Dr. Novak—which would aide in my escape through the tunnel in his lab. All I needed to do now was find an opportunity to set the plan in motion.

"There could be more Reptiles out there," I agreed.

"Kali's death will not be in vain."

We both turned to see Cyrus standing in the archway of the hall.

My heart ached for his sadness. He looked haggard. Grief emanated from his soul. He walked over to us, careful to keep his gaze on Bibi.

"We will train Siren in our ways," Cyrus said. "She must know how to protect herself."

"She does know how," Bibi stated matter of factly. "I have seen her skills firsthand. She is more than able."

"Regardless," Cyrus said impatiently. "If she trains with us, word will spread of her strength. People talk. And word of her prowess will only serve her, especially if we don't know how much longer she'll stay here. It could be indefinitely."

It was hard to imagine I had only been in OM for nine days. It felt as though I'd been here forever.

"Aedan..." Bibi began.

"He isn't here," Cyrus interjected with great force. "When he returns and hears of what happened, he'll have no choice but to agree."

Bibi took a moment, before she nodded in agreement.

"What is your plan?" Bibi asked.

"I will train with her in the coed Fanum," Cyrus said. "It's a sacred sanctuary. She'll be safe there."

"It is a bold statement," Bibi said.

"It is the only kind to make now."

I could feel the tension. The General was conflicted, more than likely, because of Aedan's absence.

"Very well," Bibi said after a moment.

Cyrus finally turned to look at me. His expression was blank.

"I will collect you in the morning."

"I'll be ready," I said.

I excused myself and went to my room. I set the bags down on the couch and caught a glimpse of the bracelet Dr. Novak had made me wear. Seeing the device infuriated me. I slipped it off my hand and placed it on a table.

"You have taken the bracelet off," Sara said to me. "It is not a safe proposition."

"Safe?" I hissed.

"Yes."

"Will he torture me the way he's tortured Michael?" I all but snarled.

"Perhaps," Sara stated emotionlessly.

"I'll take the risk," I said in anger.

"Siren," Sara's somber voice gave me pause. "You don't know what he's capable of."

"And you do," I stated, wondering why Sara was warning me.

"I do," she confirmed. "And right now, his emotions are erratic."

"Why are you telling me this?" I asked her. "You're on his side. You belong to him. He is your master."

"I am merely telling you the probability of the pain you'll self-inflict by this one action," Sara stated simply. "It is greater than ninety percent."

Sara said it so matter of factly. The way only a computer would.

"I will take that into consideration," I sighed and reluctantly grabbed hold of the bracelet again. I walked over to the window and looked out.

It was a beautiful day. I wondered if Aedan was all right. I prayed he was.

øøø

"I loved her," Cyrus told me quietly as we sat across from each other eating lunch in the coed Fanum temple. We'd just finished a training session and were on a break.

His admission was painful to hear.

"I know," I replied, devastated for him. "And I'm sorry for your pain. For the pain I caused."

He looked down at his food.

"It's not your fault," he finally said. "It is part of the life we chose."

He picked up a piece of synthetic meat and took a bite out of it. I still had not developed a taste for it, instead I ate the fruit and rice.

"Did you ever tell her?" My voice faltered as I asked him the question.

"Kali knew how I felt," he said slowly, and I saw the tears form in his eyes. "She always knew. I was in love with her from the moment we met."

He laughed bitterly.

"But it didn't matter," he went on. "I never stood a chance. I was a pale shadow compared to Aedan. She worshipped him. Always. And I know she used how I felt about her to her advantage whenever she was angry with him. But I didn't mind. I only wanted her attention."

His gaze met mine.

"She was afraid of you," he told me.

"Why?"

"Afraid you'd take him away from her," he said. "Where I rejoiced in the possibility, she cried her insecurities in my arms."

I couldn't even imagine Kali ever crying, and it saddened me to know I was the cause.

"I wanted him to leave her," Cyrus said. "But I never had any hope for it, until you walked into our Kingdom."

I looked down in embarrassment. I didn't want to be seen as a woman who'd been trying to steal Aedan from his intended mate. Everything that occurred between us had been out of my control, or at least, I told myself that.

"My whole life I wished for it," he whispered. "Now, I would do anything to watch her spend a thousand lifetimes with him."

"I'm so sorry," I finally said.

"Me too," he told me bitterly. "But we can't change it, can we?"

"No," I shook my head. "Unfortunately, we cannot."

For the next two days, Cyrus and I spent most of our time together.

If we weren't training, we were talking about OM, life, his childhood with Kali, and his complicated relationship with Aedan. I could sense the jealousy he had for him, as well as the great love. He considered Aedan his brother and with that came all the typical emotions associated with that kind of relationship.

It was a love-hate feeling.

Jealousy. Admiration.

Envy. Pride.

Cyrus vacillated between these emotions whenever he spoke of Aedan. I let him do most of the talking, limiting myself to speaking of my mother and basic ideals of Kingdom B. I genuinely enjoyed my rapport with him. It was nice to get to know Cyrus. He had a big heart, of that, I had no doubt.

On the third day of our training, Sara informed me that Dr. Novak was ready to continue his experiments, and she'd alert me when I'd have to go back down to the lab. Though I wasn't looking forward to spending any time with him, I knew his secret tunnel was my only way out. I needed to get back down there as soon as I could and start to study his habits the same way he would mine.

"You're distracted!" Cyrus said in disappointment as he hit me with his shield. He was teaching me the way OM soldiers used their shields as weapons. The four corners of the object were razor sharp and could kill if needed.

I fell to the ground on my back and laughed. Cyrus walked over.

"What's so funny?" He smiled down a me.

"It looks like I just died for the millionth time," I told him.

"Fifteenth," he corrected me, in a good-natured way. "But who's counting?"

"Apparently, you are," I told him with a raised brow.

"Can't help it," he returned with a shrug. "I'm competitive."

"I'd like to see some of your moves now," Cyrus said as he tossed me a long spear.

Bibi had joined us this morning. We were in a small private room in the arena where they both asked I show them how I used the spear with Gaia. I was flattered Bibi spoke so highly about my abilities.

"Bibi says she's never seen anything like it," Cyrus continued.

"I was trained in the Wushu and Shaolin fighting styles," I explained as I moved the spear around in my hand.

"Are those forms of ancient Chinese martial art?" Bibi

asked.

"Yes," I nodded. "They are all about quick movements, fluidity, and being one with your core axis."

"You can use blades," Bibi's eyes lit up.

"I prefer a spear," I told her.

"Show me." Cyrus demanded impatiently. "I want to see."

"Attack me," I commanded.

His brow raised at my tone but then he engaged. Cyrus was a walking weapon, and I was able to dance around him easily blocking his attacks. His size was almost cumbersome, and he couldn't move with the ease I displayed. It would take training. And patience.

I moved around him easily, using my spear as a distraction. He couldn't even keep up. I had him at a disadvantage in seconds.

"That's incredible," he was breathing heavily. "Your movement is unlike anything I've ever seen."

"Coming from you, I take that as a great compliment," I said.

"You beat me once before," Bibi said standing up in excitement. "Care to try again?"

I laughed and bowed before her. "Join me."

Before Bibi could pick up a weapon, the door to the room opened.

My heart stopped.

It was Aedan.

He stood not ten feet from us with his arms crossed and an indecipherable look on his face. He looked better than the last time I saw him. But still, impossibly distant.

"Praetor," Cyrus bowed his head.

"What are you doing?" He asked quickly, his bright gaze

finding mine.

"Siren's teaching us her ways," the General told him.

"Her ways?" Aedan's eyes narrowed.

"The training we have in Kingdom B," I explained. I searched his gaze for any hint of emotion—anger, hate, indifference. But there was nothing.

"You've not seen anything like it," Bibi continued. "It's quite impressive."

"Show me."

His voice left no room for argument. Cyrus tossed him his spear and Aedan faced me. He tossed his weapon back and forth within his hands and watched me curiously.

"I'm waiting?" He arched a brow.

I was nervous. His proximity, his lack of emotion, everything about him put me on edge.

Now or never.

I stepped forward and attacked Aedan putting him on the defense. He easily deflected my blow and the others that came after it. I tried to dance around him, to feel my axis, my core energy, but I could not seem to focus. I knew Aedan wasn't even using his full force and was probably wondering what Bibi and Cyrus were talking about.

"Is that all?" He goaded me on, bringing his spear down hard on mine. I was barely able to cover the blow.

"Don't be shy, Siren," Bibi encouraged with a smile. "Aedan's a big boy."

"Perhaps she's not as skilled a warrior as you think," Aedan's voice was arrogant and cold. "Perhaps she has you fooled."

His words stung. I'd have to be an idiot not to know what he was insinuating. And not only that, but he hurt my pride.

I closed my eyes.

Concentrate. It's not Aedan. It's a simulation.

And when I opened my eyes, I was back.

"Are you sure?" I said to him.

"Excuse me?" He seemed almost offended by my question.

"Are you sure you can handle me?" I replied.

Something flickered in his eyes, and the way he looked at me made me blush.

"Just fine."

I went at him and didn't hold back. I flew in the air and came down hard, but he was able to dodge the hit. When his eyes locked on mine, I could see the newfound respect. He hadn't been expecting this from me. His eyes lit up and I could see the pleasure, but he quickly hid it.

We fought for a long while.

Aedan wasn't an easy opponent to beat. He was faster than Cyrus and Bibi and much more strategic with his moves. He observed, allowing me to strike him a few times, like he was memorizing my moves. Calculating what I would do next. I spun around him, jabbing at him with the spear, hoping to bring him to his knees. But it was impossible. He moved quickly, not allowing me to get near.

In the end, it was his strength that got me.

I had to avoid an attack from him, because I couldn't deflect the sheer brute force of his blows. He hit me hard, with the strength of his Shadow, half his arm flickering before the tip of his spear came to rest at my heart, signifying his victory. I never liked to lose, but I was at least happy he seemed winded.

The sound of Bibi and Cyrus clapping filled the room. They came over and joined us.

"That was brilliant," Bibi said, beaming. "I thoroughly enjoyed watching the skirmish."

"Quite impressive," Cyrus agreed as he smiled at me.

Aedan kept the spear directed at my heart. My gaze met his as I tried to catch my breath. His eyes were alight with something I couldn't discern. It felt like a million years, before he threw the weapon down and reached out to take mine.

"Training is finished for the day."

"As you command, Praetor," Cyrus said as he lowered his head in obedience.

I could feel Aedan's cold, critical gaze.

"I will see her back to my compound," his voice was frosty.

I looked at Cyrus.

"I enjoyed the lesson today," I told him. "I'll see you tomorrow at the same time?"

"I have yet to decide if you will continue," Aedan answered for Cyrus.

My blood ran cold.

This was not the Aedan I had known.

"Well then," I said to Cyrus with a forced smile. "I'll see you when I see you."

Aedan turned and walked out of the arena. I guessed he wanted me to follow. The tension between us was unmistakable when we entered the awaiting pod. Aedan sat in silence, staring out the window.

"How are you? "I asked him quietly.

His sharp gaze met mine. For a brief second, I could see the anguish and uncertainty in its depths. But he masked his emotions quickly.

"As well as can be expected."

He didn't want to speak to me. It hurt me but I understood why, and I wouldn't try and make things better between us. I would respect his feelings toward me.

The pod made an unexpected turn, and we headed east of the Praetor's compound. I didn't dare ask where we were going. The trees began to change on the road as we went down a hill.

The sparkling blue ocean spread out in front of me like a sweet dream. The waves were low, and the sun hit the water, causing a thousand twinkling lights to shimmer before my eyes. I could barely contain my joy. Something unknown began to pulse in my body. A heat, a pleasurable heat took over as my eyes burned with longing for the salty water that stretched out before us. I wanted to dive in and get lost in the sweet sea more than anything in my life.

I could feel Aedan's gaze on my face and I didn't care. I couldn't hide my happiness.

My *joy*.

Home.

I felt as though I had finally come home.

"We're here to talk," he told me quietly. "I wanted to be somewhere I knew we could be completely alone."

My heart began to race.

The pod came to a stop in front of the white sand beach.

"Sara—" I began.

"What about her?" Aedan questioned.

I lifted my hand, showing him the bracelet. If he was surprised to see it, it didn't show.

"Take it off," he commanded.

I did as he said and left it on the seat before following Aedan out of the pod.

"We walk," his voice was harsh.

I fell in stride next to him as we made our way to the water. The excitement began to bubble over, and I was almost giddy from the high I felt, being so close to the ocean.

The sound of the waves crashing against the shore was like sweet music to my ears. My mouth practically watered. I could feel my Shadow fighting to emerge. To run and dive into the sea. But somehow, I was able to keep her at bay.

"I don't think I've ever seen anyone react to seeing the ocean quite like you," he said quietly as he observed me.

"I can't help it." I admitted. We came to a stop right at the water's edge, where the waves lapped the sand and almost touched our toes.

"There is so much you can't help," he crossed his arms and stared out at the water.

I nervously looked away from him choosing to examine the waves.

"We used to come here as children," he began. "Kali and I. We'd run along the shores and play. I think I enjoyed it much more than she did. She preferred the city. She thought it was too quiet out here. The sound of the waves made her nervous, she said. Like something was coming for her."

A light breeze came by and tossed some sand up in the air.

"You owe me," his voice was steely, an underlying threat in his tone.

Something shifted around us. The air, the energy, I did not know. But I realized we were in a defining moment.

Something between us was about to irrevocably change forever.

"Do you know what it is you owe me, Siren?" Aedan finally turned to me.

I met his piercing gaze.

And we both said it at the same time.

"The truth."

There was such an intensity in his gaze that I had to look away. I knew what he wanted to hear. I just didn't know how to tell him.

"I can't," I whispered.

"Can't or won't?" His eyes flickered in disappointment.

"I don't know how," I began.

"I'm going to be honest with you," he went on. "As I've always been, from the moment we met. If you lie to me again I'm going straight to the Assembly and telling them about your pod. And I'm sure you know there will be ramifications for you."

It wasn't an empty threat. He meant every word.

I let a moment of silence seep into the air around us. The only sounds came from the rhythm of the sea. It was fitting for him to learn the truth here.

I folded my arms across my stomach. "Do you want to know why I gaze upon the ocean with such longing?" I finally said.

"Tell me."

"Because it has been denied to me my whole life. This great body of water that covers most of this planet has been denied to me. Until now. This is the very first time I've set eyes on Earth's ocean and can actually reach out and touch it."

Aedan huffed. "Each Kingdom resides by a body of water."

My gaze pinned his. "By each—you mean the four that remain. OM, R, B and A."

"They are the only kingdoms," Aedan responded.

"Today, they are," I replied carefully, watching him. "But there was a time when another Kingdom resided on this Earth."

I watched as the realization of what I was saying dawned on him. His face grew pale, and he shook his head in denial.

"It is impossible."

"Because you were supposed to have killed us all?" I asked sadly. "Your people masterminded the annihilation of my Breed. And yet here I stand before you, only because you rescued me from what would have been certain death. Is the irony not lost on you?"

"Your pod…" he continued ignoring my words.

"I did fall from the sky, like you said," I went on. "I moved through space and time from the planet I was raised on, to come back here—to my home planet. To my right, just as much as yours."

I watched him process my words, and before he could speak, I continued.

"I am one of eleven Cetaceans left in the entire universe," I told him. "Now you know. If you kill me, I beg you to do it here by the water, and let me take my last breaths gazing out onto this sea that I crave now more than air."

He visibly flinched from my comment. I could tell it bothered him.

"Have you all returned?"

"There are three others," I told him. "But I don't know where they are, or if they're alive."

It was true. The others could have crashed like I did. Maybe they didn't survive, or worse, what if they had landed in the arms of a Reptile like the ones I'd encountered with Aedan? I shuddered at the thought.

"How can you not know?" He asked in disbelief.

"You destroyed any way I had to communicate with them," I reminded him.

Aedan didn't look apologetic.

"And this planet?" he said. "Where you were raised—where is it?"

"Too far for you to even comprehend," I told him. "The small group that survived after the slaughter, got away."

"So it was true—" Aedan said. "The Cetaceans could—*can* control their Shadows."

"It's true." I whispered. "And now you know I've put your position as Praetor at risk."

Conflicting emotions danced across Aedan's face, and I wondered what he thought now or if he would ever really tell me. But there was one thing I couldn't deny—

I felt a profound sense of relief.

It was undeniable really, how good it felt to tell the truth to him. To say what I was. Where I came from. To not hide from my reality. I could just be myself.

Siren. The Cetacean. The last living descendant of Elora.

He knew what I really was.

"And what was your plan when you arrived?" Aedan asked curiously. "To just come down here and live amongst us?"

I wanted to tell him that it was, but I was still afraid. I didn't know how he would react to the prospect of Cetaceans returning to Earth to procreate and stay. I decided it was an element he did not need to know.

"The plan was for us to explore the planet for forty days," I lied to him.

"Explore the planet?" He asked surprised.

"Yes," I said. "It was a gift, coming here. To come and

see our birth planet."

"And after forty days?" he asked quietly.

"We go home," I told him.

"With the pod?" I knew he was thinking about how he destroyed mine.

"With the pod." His eyes briefly flickered on my belt.

"So explain something to me," he asked curiously. "If we were to get you to Kingdom B, where you told us you are from, you were just going to go there and do what exactly?"

"Explore," I replied uncomfortably, wondering if he would believe the lie. "Their gates are open to all the kingdoms."

"No, "Aedan said tautly. "They are *allegedly* open to four kingdoms."

"Allegedly?" I asked.

"Do any of us really know what would happen if we walked up to one of their gates and asked to be accepted into their Kingdom?"

"It was a risk we chose to take," I replied knowing he was right. "From what we know, we believe them to be a peaceful people—"

"When faced with a Breed they believed to have been wiped off the face of the planet, peace becomes secondary to survival," Aedan scoffed.

"I am one person, Aedan." I said. "What harm can I cause?"

"History has taught us that *one person* has the ability to change the world," he returned forcefully.

Aedan looked away from me and watched the ocean. I knew he was contemplating everything I just told him. I held my breath and waited for him to speak.

"They can't know," he finally said after what felt like an

eternity. "The others. No one can ever know."

The relief I felt from his words was staggering.

"The more people know, the more possibility there is for your life being in danger," he said. "We were raised with the history of the Cetacean massacre. Though some of us aren't proud of our ancestors, there are others who believe it was done for the survival of our Breed. And they adamantly stand behind their beliefs…"

Aedan's eyes lit up.

"We cannot risk it." His voice was like a powerful rumble.

He wanted to protect me.

I closed my eyes in gratitude, giving a silent thanks to whoever was watching out for me above. To whoever it was who made sure it was Aedan that found me when I crashed in OM. My life could have been entirely different, if it had been someone else.

And now that he knew and still accepted me as I was, I knew I had to do what I could to protect him as well.

"Aedan," my voice was solemn. "There's something I think you should know."

CHAPTER TWENTY-ONE

"Dr. Novak," I told him. "He knows what I am."

"What?" Aedan looked at me in surprise.

"He's known since the day I met him in the med lab."

"You lie," Aedan shook his head in disbelief.

"I don't," I rushed out. "I promise you. I'm telling you the truth."

I told him about Dr. Novak's secret lab, and the experiments he wanted to perform on me. Aedan looked shocked at first, then enraged, barely keeping his Shadow in check. He turned away from me and faced the ocean as he registered my words. I could feel the anger radiate off his body, and I wondered how he'd react once he knew everything. I had to tell him. Now.

"There is more," I said quietly.

"More?" Aedan looked incredulous. "What more could there be?"

"He has two other test subjects," I began slowly. "Given to him as gifts."

Aedan's golden eyes began to glow ominously.

"Milo gave him two Reptiles."

Aedan snarled in fury as he looked at me, his face flickering into his Shadow.

"There are Reptiles within the city walls?" He was barely able to control himself.

"Yes," I quickly tried to reassure him. "One is a little girl, hidden away. She's gaunt and I don't know how much longer she can survive—if she's even still alive. And the other is in a cage in Dr. Novak's secret lab. He put a collar on him—some device that prevents him from acting out—so he's not a risk to your people—"

"All Reptiles are a risk to my people," Aedan's voice was hard.

"No!" I shouted at him trying to make him understand. "Michael—he is not. He was drugged, taken from his home, and given to Milo to dispose of—"

"Even with all of his plots and machinations, Milo would never betray his own people to Kingdom R," Aedan shook his head in denial.

"He is plotting against you!" I rushed out quickly. "I promise you, I'm not lying..."

My words finally registered.

"What do you know of his plans?" Aedan asked.

"I've told you everything I know," I said. "It's all Michael was able to tell me—"

"Michael?" he snarled in outrage. "*The Reptile*? Do you forget what they tried to do to you? Do you forget how they killed my soldiers...*Kali*?"

"I'll never forget," I said softly. "But I believe him."

Aedan cursed out loud before walking toward the shore, ignoring the water that washed over his boots. He lifted his head up to the sky and howled in rage.

"They will die," his voice shook from the force of his anger. "Those that have betrayed me. Those that have betrayed OM will *all* die."

My blood turned to ice as I watched him. Somehow, I had to reach him through his anger.

"Aedan," I implored. "Think. You have to think things through before you act. You have to come up with a plan. You don't know who else is involved. How deep this goes. There could be more people here working against you—"

Aedan's shoulders trembled as he sought to gain control.

I could only pray my words reached him.

øøø

Fear.

Relief.

My feelings vacillated between the two emotions in the pod on our way back to Aedan's home. He had not uttered a word to me, his emotions brewing around him like a turbulent storm.

Aedan knew the truth about me so I didn't have to pretend in front of him anymore. I felt as though I'd been lying to him forever, and I was relieved I no longer had to live in that tangled web of deceit.

He knew the truth about Dr. Novak and Milo. I could only imagine what was going through his head. I hoped he would listen to my words and approach the situation with caution—to learn as much as he could and how deep the conspiracy went, before he acted.

But he didn't make me privy to his thoughts.

He had grabbed hold of Dr. Novak's bracelet and held it tightly in his hand the whole way to the compound. He knew Sara was listening in.

Once we reached his home, he led me inside and held out the offensive bracelet.

Put it on, he mouthed to me.

My eyes widened in surprise, but I did as he said. He lifted his finger to his mouth and shook his head, telling me everything that just transpired would remain a secret. His demeanor had changed. He was in control now. I could see it. He was making a plan. And the relief I felt was staggering.

"Will you be down for dinner?" He asked as though nothing was amiss.

"I planned on it," I said. "Unless you'd like me to stay in my room."

"You are free to join us," Aedan said.

I was grateful he wouldn't deny me the company. I wished we were alone, without Sara listening in, so I could ask him what he intended to do.

"I'll see you at dinner, then," I said quickly, playing along before I walked away.

"Siren?" His voice was strong and commanding.

My heart sped up at the sound.

I hated that I loved the way he said my name.

I turned to look at him, my eyes clashing with his.

I hated that I loved the way the gold in his eyes sparkled in the light.

"Yes?" I said.

"I've also decided," he ran his hand through his hair. "You can continue to train with Cyrus, if you want."

And I hated that I loved his innate kindness.

He was a good leader because he was a good man.

"Thank you," I became emotional as the unmistakable truth hit me hard.

I was in love with Aedan.

And I hated it. Because it was wrong. And it was something I could never ever have.

"We'll talk later," he said. "There is much for me to contemplate." He'd digest everything I said and hopefully find the best way forward.

Once I was in my room, I found myself reaching for Dr. Hedy's journal, pressing the button to see more, hoping there would somehow be an answer. If I could see something, some insight into our two breeds, maybe I could understand why I was so drawn to Aedan.

KINGDOM: Animilia
BREED: Human Cetacean Hybrid
NAME: Elora
SEX: Female
AGE: 3
CLASS: The First

Physical Features:

Elora's skin color is golden, and she thrives in and out of the sea. Her body is lean and the tests show us she will be of average height. Her eyesight is perfect, and her ability to see and hear underwater is extraordinary. She can stay underwater and breathe for up to two hours, and we believe as she grows older, she'll only become more adept at this quality. Her swimming skills are unparalleled. In the water she cannot be beaten. The Breed, like its Soul Particle ancestor, has extraordinary echolocation skills.

Personality Traits:

Elora is of superior intelligence. Her IQ rates off the charts, and her ability to learn is extraordinary. Once she is taught a skill or information, she processes and excels at it in ways the human species has never seen. She is friendly and kind, with an endless capacity for empathy and feels others' pain quite profoundly. She is loyal and I believe would risk her life to save another. As noted, in regards to

Marcus, she is drawn to him and is quite often found by his side.

She is driven by compassion and the need for harmony and peace. If we were to pick one Breed that excelled and surpassed all expectations, it would be the Cetaceans, as their scope for knowledge and love is unequalled.

Habitat:

When shown different habitats she prefers one by the ocean, where she could live in and out of the water.

KINGDOM: Animilia
BREED: Human Other Mammal Hybrid
NAME: Marcus
SEX: Male
AGE: 3
CLASS: The First

Physical Traits:

Marcus is the most physically fit of all the Breeds. Even though he is so young, his body structure is athletic and muscular. From all of our testing, we know he will be quite tall. He takes pride in exercise and is interested in all sports that teach warfare. Marcus has a heightened sense of smell and hearing. He is able to shout louder than any other Breed, especially when he believes he is faced with danger. He can communicate all of his emotions through various *vocalizations, not speaking words, but snarling, purring, or even growling. When tested, he has an uncanny sense of protection and can immediately feel imminent danger.*

Personality Traits:

Marcus likes to be part of a pack. Though the others are mostly loners, he is drawn to Elora, the Cetacean—just as she is strangely drawn to him. The two are inseparable and Marcus is extremely protective of Elora when he feels she might be in bodily or emotional danger. He is already a great speaker and can articulate his feelings quite well. He is a natural leader, and when there are fights, he tries to bring about a peaceful resolution. We believe the females will assume the same traits and will also be seen as alphas. On the whole, Marcus is honest. It is rare he exhibits traits we would find alarming.

Preferred Habitat:

When shown different habitats, Marcus prefers vast plains, lush, with plenty of water, an almost perfect ecosystem.

Just then, Dr. Hedy's face came up on the monitor.

"A final thought on the five different breeds...my Soul Particle children will witness great examples of convergent evolution in humans. With the animal Soul Particle injections they will take on traits and evolve, adapt more with further generation."

"My only hope?" Dr. Hedy smiled. "That we evolve into compassionate beings. Moving into the future as one is the only way forward."

When the screen powered off, I pondered Dr. Hedy's last words. Was it the only way forward for us? Together?

As one?

After all that had happened, I did not know what the right answer was. I only knew that even with all of our differences, and against my will, I had still fallen for Aedan. Perhaps my ancestor, Elora, had felt the same way about Marcus? There was clearly some common bond the two had that Dr. Hedy took note of.

The sounds coming from the hall called to me. I placed the tablet on my nightstand and set out. When I walked down the stairs and heard all the voices, precisely *his*, my stomach did summersaults. I had to lean up against the wall, my feelings were almost overwhelming.

"I think I'm going to be sick," I whispered to myself.

"Should we go to the med scan?" Gaia asked in concern.

I nearly jumped out of my skin, cursing myself for not remembering Gaia liked to wait for me by the stairs before dinner. Her black hair was woven into many intricate braids and pulled back from her exotic face, exposing her bright eyes.

"I don't need the med scan," I told her in a hurry. "That was just an internal moment I was having."

Gaia didn't look like she believed me.

"Really," I said with a reassuring smile. "And don't you look very pretty tonight."

"I do?" Gaia blossomed under the compliment.

"Yes," I said. "You really do."

"Thank you, Siren," Gaia said happily. "You look pretty as well, but then, you always do."

"I don't." I rushed out insecurely. I certainly didn't feel it.

"That's why all the women hate you," Gaia told me. "They're jealous because all the men stare at you."

"What?" I gasped. "That's not true!"

"It is," Gaia took my hand. "I hear everything."

She pulled me into the Great Hall, where everyone was already seated. It looked like there were over twenty people at the table. I didn't dare look in Aedan's direction. I could see him from the corner of my eye. He was immersed in conversation, and I didn't think he even saw me enter. My gaze moved around the room and settled on Cyrus who waved at me from the other side of the table. He pointed at the two seats he kept empty for us.

Gaia and I rushed over and sat down. I was in the middle of the two.

Cyrus poured us both a glass of water.

"Very kind," I muttered. "It would be nice if you extended this type of graciousness when I'm training with you."

"You'll never learn that way," Cyrus said with a smile. "I'm happy Aedan's allowing us to continue. We'll train tomorrow, but not the following day."

"Why not?" I asked.

"How can you not know?" Cyrus asked.

I shook my head.

"Tomorrow is the Day of the Soul."

I had lost track of time. The celebration of the Day of the Soul was in honor of the day Dr. Hedy injected the Soul Particle in The Five First. Every Kingdom observed it. We even held a small celebration on Akasha.

"I forgot," I told him honestly.

"Understandable. You've lost track of time," Cyrus said with a nod. "What do you do in your Kingdom? To celebrate?"

"We throw a party," I replied.

"Like us," Cyrus said. "Ours has been known to get a

little out of hand. The day after is pretty much a day of recovery from overindulgence."

"Too much of the Praetor's drink?" I laughed knowingly.

"Something like that," he replied with a laugh. "It's a celebration…even Dr. Novak—"

"Dr. Novak?" I asked quickly, my interest piqued.

"He has a special blend he only drinks this one time a year. He keeps it in his lab so no one can steal a taste of it. And trust me, we've all tried," Cyrus shook his head with an amused grin. "If anyone were to need attention from him, they'd be very unlucky. The drink is strong and knocks him out quick."

"Seems unlike him," I replied with a casual smile.

"It's one night," Cyrus said with a shrug.

My mind raced—did I finally have my way to escape? If I could find Dr. Novak's drink and add the sleeping remedy, I'd be assured he'd be knocked out for the night.

Cyrus looked over to where Aedan was seated.

"And behold, the lion is without a mate."

I followed Cyrus's gaze and understood what he meant by his comment.

The lion was single.

He was attractive.

He was a leader of a Kingdom.

The women were already vying for Aedan's attention. And now, I felt genuinely sick to my stomach. To my complete horror, Aedan caught me staring. I looked down at my plate.

"I shouldn't be surprised. It is our way," Cyrus continued not noticing the interaction. "But still, I can't help but feel like Kali deserves better."

"From Aedan?" I asked quietly.

"No. I'm not worried about him. Aedan will not choose a mate for a long while," he said then smiled. "I don't even think he really liked the idea of being mated for life."

"Why?" I blurted out the question.

"He's a loner," Cyrus said with a shrug. "Kali always complained that she never really thought she knew him. And that she didn't think he loved her the way she loved him."

I was quiet as I contemplated his words.

"I can't believe I just told you that," Cyrus said without missing a beat. "I've never done that before in my life. I've never betrayed her. I don't know what it is, but I just feel so comfortable with you. Maybe too comfortable."

"Your secrets are safe with me," I gave his arm a reassuring squeeze. "I would never betray you. I promise you that. On my honor."

"You sound OM," Cyrus looked pleased.

"Do I?" I asked with a blush.

"I like it."

"When you're finished here, I'd like to talk to you privately in my library," Aedan said from behind us.

I hadn't even seen him get up. He moved fast.

"Me?" I asked and tried to still my heart as I turned in my chair.

"Yes," Aedan said with his gaze locked on mine.

I pushed my chair back and stood up.

"I'm finished."

I followed him out of the hall and into his office. Once we were inside, he shut the door and faced me.

"I want to go down to the lab," Aedan said. "I want to see this Reptile."

"What?" I asked in fear, looking down at my bracelet. "Sara—"

"She listens," Aedan acknowledged. "But she will keep this between us."

"How?" I asked in shock.

"There is a fail-safe I demanded to have added to her program," Aedan said with a pleased smile. "In case Dr. Novak was incapacitated, I had to know I could access her and that she'd follow my command. To my great pleasure, he agreed with my request."

I couldn't help but smile.

"Unbeknownst to Dr. Novak, Sara now follows my orders."

"He won't find out?" I asked.

"She'll continue answering his requests," Aedan said. "And what reports she delivers will be approved by me first."

I closed my eyes in relief.

"And will she still follow my every move?" I couldn't help but ask.

"Is there a need?" He asked quietly.

"No."

"Then she won't. But you'll have to keep the bracelet on," Aedan said. "And you should be relieved to know I told Dr. Novak you won't work with him in his lab, until I say otherwise."

My eyes shot up at him in surprise.

"How did he take it?" I asked thinking of his experiments. "Was he suspicious?"

"No," Aedan shook his head. "He believes I hate you because of Kali's death, but he pressed to have you down there as soon as possible. I assured him that would more than likely be the case."

I should have expected Aedan would want to protect me

from Dr. Novak's experiments. I was touched, but it was also imperative I escape the following night, because now I really didn't know when I'd be able to get down to the lab again.

"Also—" Aedan said.

"Yes?"

"The child," he began softly, "she died two days ago. Sara told me, when I asked to see where Dr. Novak was hiding her."

My heart sunk in sadness, but a part of me was relieved she wouldn't suffer anymore.

"That is unfortunate," my voice was somber.

"The entire situation is what's unfortunate," Aedan returned bitterly.

I could not argue with him.

øøø

"Sara, show me the prisoner," Aedan said as we stood in Dr. Novak's secret lab.

According to Sara, Dr. Novak was asleep in his apartment. Aedan had been alerted when we were at dinner in his hall, which was why he chose that moment to leave.

Aedan's body tensed as the holographic image in the room disappeared to reveal the cage with Michael leaning against the bars staring at us.

I heard Aedan's low growl as he stared in rage at Michael, his face began to morph into his Shadow. He took a dangerous step toward the cage. I put my hand on his arm and tried to hold him back. But he was made of steel.

Michael's eyes began to glow as he stared at Aedan.

"Aedan—" I tried to stay calm. "Remember what I told you."

Aedan looked over at me in displeasure. I knew it had to be hard for him. Like it had been for me. Everything he knew and had seen of the Breed, clouded his vision.

I had to make him see.

"He was taken from his Kingdom and brought here," I reminded him. "It's not his fault."

"That's my decision to make," his voice was cold.

"Their kind is known for their uncontrollable tempers," Michael's voice was filled with animosity. "It is no use, Siren. Look at him. He can't restrain himself."

Aedan moved quickly, pouncing at the cage in no time, rattling the bars with force as he growled into Michael's face. His threatening presence made Michael flicker into his Shadow.

"And your kind eat human flesh," Aedan snarled. "Which offense would you say is greater?"

Michael's eyes rounded but he didn't back down. The two stared at one another, their loathing apparent. I knew if there were no cage between them, they would be at each other's throat and it would be quite a battle to see.

"Michael," I said as his gaze moved to mine. "Do you know what Aedan's talking about?"

He stared at me for a long minute before nodding his head. I closed my eyes in sadness. I had believed, *hoped* that had not been the case. Whatever he saw on my face made his demeanor change. He pushed away from the cage and turned his back to us both.

"There are rebel groups growing each day that oppose the old ways," Michael explained, his voice sad. "Our climate has become more volatile, forcing people to search for better land. Eighteen years ago when I was born, my father had walls built around more affluent areas of Akkad, our city, in order to keep the upper class happy. This allowed the rich to keep their land and the rest to have to fight for theirs."

Michael turned to us and shook his head in disgust. It was the dark time he spoke of when we had been alone.

"It was my father's greatest mistake as a ruler," he said. "To choose rich over poor instead of uniting us. As years went by, the situation only became worse. More people spoke out. Rebels gathered followers, who had nothing to lose, to help them find land of their own and fend for themselves."

"OM land," Aedan said dangerously.

"Yes," Michael replied.

"And the consumption of human flesh?" I asked quietly.

"It's been three years," Michael said softly as he met my gaze.

"I will kill you!" Aedan said with fury as he pounded the cage with his fist.

"We heard rumors," Michael said ignoring Aedan. He kept his gaze on mine, silently pleading with me. "In the halls of our government there were people who would report on the macabre scenes they came across. Reptiles slaughtered. Consumed for food."

"Each other?" I asked in horror.

"Starving people will do anything to survive."

"And your father did nothing to stop this madness?" Aedan snarled. "Nothing to stop the slaughter of his own kind?"

"He tried," Michael said. "He tried. We have soldiers stationed everywhere now. Eyes watching. But it seems they venture out of the city walls."

"It seems or you know?" Aedan asked ferociously.

Michael remained silent.

"Did you know?" I asked softly.

"Yes," he said to me. "I've known. The government knows. Why do you think they wanted to dispose of me? Why do you think I'm in this cage? I voiced my displeasure. My horror."

"And your father?" I said.

"He finds the act just as vile as I do."

"And yet he's done nothing." Aedan said in loathing.

"With my counsel, we were devising a plan to implement change," he said quietly. "To open the walls, divide the land, and satisfy the needs of all our people. To produce more synthetic meat—but there are powerful people, who sit in our parliament, that have done everything they can to stop us."

Michael turned to stare at Aedan, his eyes glowed eerily. "And now your people," he said with rage, "*OM* aids them."

I looked over at Aedan who stood as rigid as a statue.

"Why is that?" Michael asked as he gripped the cage.

ØØØ

After securing Michael's word not to inform Dr. Novak of our secret conversation, we left him. Aedan was quiet when we entered the chamber that led up to Dr. Novak's main lab. I knew it was a lot for him to take in and process. He had uncovered a conspiracy within his own government, and it couldn't be easy for him to come to terms with everything Michael had said.

When we exited the chamber, I grabbed a hold of his arm. His body tensed.

"What are you thinking?" I asked him.

"I'm reeling," he replied, looking down at me. "There are so many questions in my mind, Siren. And the one that keeps coming to me is why? Why would Milo conspire with the Reptiles? Why would he allow them to kill his own people? *Why?*"

"Power," I replied simply. "It's about power."

"To what end?" Aedan asked me. "Allowing them on our land poses a threat to his own future. Would he see us all die and rule over a sea of carcasses?"

It was a valid question and one I didn't have an answer to. But I knew from all my studies of human wars, the answer had to be more sinister than we could even contemplate.

"Every leader in history that masterminded great wars wanted one thing," I said to him. "To conquer. Land. People. To rule over an empire."

Aedan laughed.

"We are different breeds that separated for a reason. We cannot cohabitate."

"Who says?" I asked him softly. "We are different breeds who possess different skills. OM are known to be great warriors and strategists. The Birds are scientists, innovative in their technology to grow and produce food. The Amphibians are hard workers, they build and have created incredible structures despite the odds. And the Reptiles are shrewd, cunning. Machiavellian."

"A class system." Aedan said slowly.

"Yes," I replied. "With one ruling Kingdom for all four breeds. To use the others as they see fit and to dispose of the ones that will not serve them."

Aedan's eyes widened.

I didn't know if I was right, but I knew I had given him something to think about.

"I have to go," He finally said revealing nothing. "I trust you can find your way back on your own?"

"Yes," I replied quickly.

He left me in Dr. Novak's lab. Alone.

My heart sped up. This was my moment.

He has a special blend he only drinks this one day each year. He even keeps it in his lab, so no one can steal a taste of it.

Cyrus's words played through my head.

I looked around the lab, for Dr. Novak's special blend. I walked over to the metallic shelves stacked with instruments and searched for the bottle. I couldn't see it.

I closed my eyes and felt the energy in the room. If it was here, I'd be able to sense the substance. All around me, I could feel the sterile objects in the room, before my senses zeroed in on a bottle that could be used for human consumption.

It was in the far right corner, hidden behind a microscope. I walked over to the shelf and pulled the brown bottle out. I twisted the top off, and the smell of the pungent liquor burned my eyes. I clicked the compartment open on my belt and grabbed hold of the sleeping aide Gaia had given me. I poured the entire contents in and swirled it around before twisting the cap back on and putting it back in place.

If Dr. Novak drank tomorrow night, he would hopefully sleep for days.

Chapter Twenty-Two

It was early evening and I was in my room.

I could hear the music pounding through the compound. The hall had been bustling with activity. I ran into Gaia downstairs as she saw to the party preparations, and she told me there were over three hundred people invited that evening. They'd already started to arrive, and I knew Aedan was down in the Great Hall greeting his guests.

I was nervous.

After what seemed like an eternity in OM, I finally had my plan—my way out.

There was a knock at my door.

"Come in," I called out.

I wasn't surprised to see Gaia. In her hand, she was holding a box with a ribbon wrapped around it.

"I brought you something," she said with a smile.

"What is it?" I asked.

"You have to open it and see," she told me with a great deal of excitement. "That's why it's called a present."

I stared at the box like it was alive.

"Haven't you gotten a gift before?" Gaia asked, watching my face closely.

I shook my head. I had never received a present before.

Not even for my birthday. On Akasha, our gift was life.

"Go ahead," she urged. "Open it."

I untied the gold ribbon. When I lifted the lid and saw what she'd given me, I was overcome with emotion and love for this sweet child. It was like she had heard or felt my insecurities and answered my silent prayer.

She had given me a dress.

"I don't know what to say," my voice choked up with emotion.

"I believe you are eleven today," she said to me.

"I'm sorry?" I looked at her in confusion.

"You first came to Earth eleven days ago," she reminded me. "You're eleven."

Eleven days seemed like a lifetime ago.

So much had happened in such a short time.

My life was completely different than what it had been when my pod crashed to the Earth—I was different.

My mission.

It loomed before me like an ominous cloud. I had come to care greatly for the people I'd grown close to. They were my friends. And Aedan—I was in love with him.

"No sad thoughts," Gaia said like she could read my mind. "At least, not tonight. I suggest tonight you just be free."

"Be free?" I asked.

"Yes," she shrugged. "This is the night everyone in OM gets to just be. For one small moment, no problems exist in the world. Not any. Not even yours."

"I like that," I said after a moment.

"Good," she said firmly. "Now just look at the dress!"

I lifted the delicate garment out of the box and smiled in pleasure. It was blue, gauzy material and would be long, falling straight to my feet.

"I'm speechless," I told her.

"There is nothing to say," Gaia said. "Try it on!"

Her excitement was infectious.

I quickly took off my clothes and slipped on the dress. It was sleeveless with stretchy material that was fitted at the top and then fell in blue waves around me. I felt so feminine.

I couldn't help but spin around in a circle.

I had never worn a dress before in my life.

"How do I look?"

"Like a mermaid," she said with a smile. "Now sit so I can do your hair. I'm going to leave it down, I just want to add a few small braids. And I'll put a little makeup on you too."

"Makeup?" I asked, unsure.

"Nothing crazy," Gaia rolled her eyes and spoke to me like she was older than her years. "Everyone uses it."

I bit my lip so I wouldn't laugh. I followed her orders and allowed her to fix my hair and add blush, something on my eyelids, and a gloss to my lips. When she was done, she stepped back and admired her handiwork.

"Go and see."

I ran over to my bathroom and stood in front of the mirror. I didn't recognize myself.

Who was this creature staring back at me?

My brown hair was full and fell in waves down my back. Gaia had added only a couple of braids in the thick tresses, combined with what little makeup she used, I looked so—

So—

Exotic.

The light blue dress fit me perfectly, accenting my curves, and the color seemed to bring out the color of my eyes.

"Are you happy?" Gaia asked.

I looked over my shoulder.

"I am."

We walked down to the Great Hall that was packed with people. Cyrus alleviated some of my initial anxiety, when he told me Milo wouldn't be at the party. He also went out of his way to assure me that no one would dare disrupt such a special day with an act of violence.

It was too sacred a time.

Gaia and I made our way through the crowd of people, who looked as though they were already enjoying themselves.

"Siren."

I spun around to see Dr. Novak in front of me, holding onto a clear glass. I could smell his offensive drink from where I stood. My heart soared in satisfaction.

His eyes were already glassy.

"How many have you had, Dr. Novak?" Gaia asked the way only a child would.

"Three," he said to her with a sad smile. "Tonight, I drink in my daughter's honor."

I cringed at his words, the reminder of Kali's death, still painful.

"Can you leave us for a moment, Gaia?" I asked.

"Yes," she glanced over at Dr. Novak, then walked away.

His eyes moved over me in disdain. His face flickered into his Shadow, and I knew he must be slowly losing control. The drink was working fast.

"Trying to fit in?"

I chose not to answer.

"It won't help, you know," Dr. Novak continued.

"I'm here for the party," I stated coldly.

"Ah yes," he said with animosity. "And tomorrow, we'll have a little party of our own."

"I'm sure it will be quite an affair," I said softly wondering why Dr. Novak was lying. Aedan had just told me I wouldn't be going to his lab, until he gave permission. Unless, the doctor was planning another experiment, like the one I endured with the little girl.

"It will be," his voice dripped with venom. "You see, I plan on running a very special test on you. One that has nothing to do with reproduction but another area I find quite fascinating—pain tolerance. And how different breeds react under *strenuous* circumstances."

My eyes widened.

"I've run the test on the creature in the cage and was quite astounded by my findings," he said as he leered at me. "I'm anxious to see what *your* results will be."

I watched with great satisfaction as he took another sip of his drink. I wondered how much longer before the sleeping aide hit him.

"Isn't the med scan a wonderful tool to have?" He went on, giving me an evil smile, one pale blue eye starting to glow. "I find there are many uses for it."

I could feel my heart pound in my chest. He would hurt me. He would do bodily harm. And then he would heal my wounds, so no one would know.

"Enjoy your evening," he said, turning away from me and taking another sip of his drink. I watched him sway, his feet shuffled a bit, and then he walked over to one of the long white couches against the wall and sat down. He leaned his head against one of the pillows before finally closing his eyes.

I watched for his heavy, labored breaths. It didn't take long before Dr. Novak was in deep sleep.

I looked around the hall for any sign of Aedan and could find none. I made my way through the least crowded areas, smiling at whoever met my gaze. For having begun only hours ago, the party had already taken its toll: guards were down, people were inebriated, some people flickered into their Shadow, and focused on having a good time.

I ducked out of the party and quickly made my way to Dr. Novak's lab. Once inside, I ran over to the hidden panel and opened it. I hit the button and the chamber doors opened.

The trip down took less than a minute but it felt like an eternity. Once the doors opened, I closed my eyes and felt my way to Michael's cage through the holographic image that was up. When I reached the bars, Michael was standing there waiting for me.

His eyes glinted in appreciation as his gaze swept over my attire.

"You look beautiful," he said softly.

His comment caused me to pause.

"Thank you," I said with a smile.

"What are you doing in here?" He asked.

"Getting you out," I told him as his eyes widened in shock.

I began to hit the keys on the electronic panel, and after hearing the tones, I hurriedly pressed the code to open the cage. Michael stepped out quickly, looking at me with gratitude.

"The collar—" he said as he reached up to his neck.

I looked around the room searching for a device to unlock it.

"There!" He called out and ran over to a table set with various sharp instruments. He picked up a long metal object that could be used for breaking wires and worked the collar. While he freed himself, I ran over to the door that led to the only way out of OM.

I quickly typed in the code, and it slid open.

Michael came up beside me and moved forward, slowly turning the knob and opening it. The door was heavy and creaked open slowly, hitting the wall to the tunnel with a thud. Darkness greeted us as we stared down the ancient corridor.

Michael turned to me, his eyes glowing—I knew it was the adrenaline.

"Let's go!" He said as he headed in.

I waited where I was.

"Siren?" He said urgently, holding out his hand.

"I'm not coming with you," I told him quietly.

"You can't be serious?" He exclaimed. "You can't stay here!"

"I won't stay," I said. "But I'm not leaving with you now. I have to—I have to say my goodbyes."

And I did.

I would not leave OM without seeing Aedan one last time. I could not.

"To Aedan?" Michael asked knowingly.

"Yes."

"Don't be foolish!" He said as he grabbed hold of my arm, trying to pull me along.

"Let go of me, Michael," my voice was strong. "I've set you free."

Michael stopped, releasing his hold and stared down into my eyes, his turquoise eyes bright. "This might be your only chance," he said.

"I won't be long," I told him.

"I'll protect you if you come with me," he pleaded.

"I don't need your protection," my voice was firm. "I just need you to go. Now!"

He stared at me for a moment longer before rubbing the back of his large hand against my cheek.

"I will never forget this."

And with that, he turned around and ran into the darkness.

øøø

"Can I have this dance?"

Justus's hand was on my shoulder. I'd just made my way back to the party to search for Aedan. I knew it was foolish, reckless of me to come back up when my freedom had been right there for me to take, but something had stopped me. Not something. Someone. And I would never forgive myself for leaving without having one last moment with him.

I smiled at Justus.

"You look beautiful," he said shyly. "Like a vision."

"Thank you," I said as I looked around for the dance floor.

"It's outside," he said to me. "Because the weather is so nice. So what do you say?"

Be free. Gaia's voice rang through my head. While the party went on, I still had time. And I had never danced before.

"I would love to dance with you."

I followed Justus outside. There were a few couples swaying to the soft music coming from the drums. He pulled me into his arms, and for a second, I felt great panic. I wasn't used to someone holding me so closely.

"I promise I won't bite," Justus joked, referring to my stiff body.

I laughed and tried to relax, but it was almost impossible to do. I was relieved when the song was over. How had I been so comfortable with Aedan holding me so intimately from the moment I met him?

"I'll see you later?" I said to him.

"Yes," Justus replied happily.

I walked through the crowd, pushing past the people as they laughed and drank amongst one another. I envied their freedom.

They had no mission.

No worries, like me.

They were just living their lives as their own with no obligation to anything other than themselves.

I made my way to the back stairwell, determined to find someplace where I could be alone for a moment. The weight of what I had just done for Michael suddenly overwhelming me. Aedan would be furious, when he discovered his escape.

And he would blame me.

I hoped he would understand why I did it.

"Where are you going?"

Aedan.

He was everywhere in OM.

Everywhere I looked. Everything I saw.

"Just taking a moment," I said with my back to him. I was standing at an arched window overlooking the party.

"Did you enjoy your dance?" There was no mistaking the annoyance I heard in his voice.

Or the misplaced pleasure I felt from his words.

He had seen me with Justus. And it bothered him.

"I did," I said before turning to face him.

My breath caught in my throat. He looked every bit the warrior he was. I watched as his gaze moved down the length of my body. He seemed—surprised.

Something changed his whole demeanor.

There was an electricity emanating from his body that I didn't understand.

"Who gave you the dress?" His voice was low.

"It was gift from Gaia." I said.

"It suits you."

My heart slammed in my chest. Warning bells went off in my head. There was something different about Aedan right now. Something I had never encountered before.

"You've grown close to Cyrus," he said.

"I have," I replied, trying to gauge where he was going with the conversation. "He is a good man."

"He is."

The tension between us was unbearable, and I couldn't take it any longer. It was almost too much. This was it, I decided. My last moment with him. It had to be enough.

"You've been so good to me," I began in a shaky voice. "I'm so lucky it was you who found me…I'll never *ever* forget you."

Our eyes met and an electrical current seemed to pass between us. I had to leave before I broke down. I knew my eyes were glowing. I could feel the energy pulsing.

"If you'll excuse me," I said as I started to walk past him, trying to hide.

His hand snaked out and grabbed hold of my arm. I felt a jolt rush through my body at the contact.

"Why are you hiding from me?" He asked quietly, looking deep into my soul. "I want to see this. I want to see you."

"You know everything," I returned in surprise, knowing he referred to my Shadow. "You know what I am. You know the truth."

"Everything?" he questioned.

"Yes," I lied.

"I think you're still holding something back," he told me. "Something doesn't feel right."

"Are we back to this?"

"To what?"

"Animosity," I said. "Your hate."

"Hate?" he laughed bitterly, his eyes like amber jewels. "Hate? I don't hate you, Siren. Far from it. Maybe I hate myself."

I sucked in a breath as he took a step closer to me, closing whatever space there was between us. My heart rate picked up. He moved fast, pulling me close and running his hand through my hair as he pulled my head back.

"Do you want to know what I hate?" His voice was deep and full of emotion. "I hate that I'm so drawn to you. Even after everything. I still crave…I still want…"

His lips drew near mine.

"You."

His mouth crashed down on mine.

In Aedan, I saw everything that was right with humanity. He was strong. He was kind. He was sensitive.

And he loved me.

I did not know how or why, but I knew it was the truth.

I felt his arms circle my body and press me close to his. I didn't feel uncomfortable. I did not want to run away from his touch.

It was just the opposite with Aedan. In his arms, I felt like I was home.

He pulled back, pressed his forehead to mine, and we breathed each other in. We were both quiet. My heart raced as my mind was overcome with all of the feelings he invoked. I never wanted to let him go.

"I don't understand it," his voice was raw. "But I don't want to fight it any longer."

My breath caught in my throat.

"I *loved* Kali," he said softly. "But I was never *in love* with her."

I waited for him to continue.

"I never felt this inferno, when she was near," he went on. "This desire to be close to her at all costs."

The pleasure I felt from his words almost brought me to my knees. It warmed my heart... *my soul.*

"Only you," he whispered. *"Only you."*

I closed my eyes and allowed myself to bask in the moment.

Being in his arms.

It felt right.

"Will you come with me?" His voice was husky with desire.

I knew what he was asking.

I knew it was wrong for me.

Nothing good could come from it. But I couldn't stop myself.

And I didn't want to.

It was one more moment I could have with him that would live in my mind forever. A memory I would cherish, until I took my last breath.

I cradled his face in my hands and kissed him softly on the lips.

"Yes."

CHAPTER TWENTY-THREE

I woke up in middle of the night.

I was in Aedan's bed.

He was sleeping soundly. Peacefully. The white sheet laying haphazardly across his tanned chest.

Memories from the night we shared flashed before my eyes. His hands on my body. His lips on mine as he showed me what it really meant to be human. And in return, I showed him my complete self- my Shadow. I could relive last night a thousand times over, and I'd still bask in the sweet pleasure of everything he had given me.

I stared at him for a long while, memorizing every inch of his beautiful face. I would live with my memories of him for the rest of my life.

I had to make my way to Kingdom B. I had to ensure my Breed's survival, no matter the cost to my heart.

It was better for him.

And for me—it was the only way,

We could never have a future together. He was the leader of OM. I was an Aliud. It would never happen, and I knew that deep down he realized that as well.

I quietly got out of his bed and slipped on my dress. I left the Sara band on the table, where he had taken it off. I was lucky and made my way out of Aedan's room without him waking up.

I knew he had to be exhausted from everything he'd endured since he met me. It was too much to bear for someone so young. And there, in his room, was the one place he could relax freely with his guard down.

I quickly walked down the hall and into my room. I took

the dress off and slipped on my OM uniform, along with my belt. I stared at Dr. Hedy's tablet and made my decision. I slipped it safely into a bag I had received from Gaia at the market and tied it to my side. I felt guilty for taking the tablet but there was still much for me to learn.

I made my way out of the room and down to the Great Hall. Dr. Novak was snoring loudly, still sleeping in the same position on the couch. I walked over to the corridor that led to his lab and stopped in my tracks.

The hall had been shut. A metal panel sealed the only way in that I knew about.

My heart began to race in fear.

I could not be trapped here. Not now. Not after what I'd done.

Think, Siren. Think. I thought about all the possibilities. I could not go to the gate in the city, I knew that would be sealed and guarded as well.

The only choice I had left was the ocean.

I would have to swim through the water and use the shore to guide me, until I came across Kingdom B.

I knew the location had to be west of OM.

It was the only way. I had to kill the fear that crept up my spine and be like every person in OM—a warrior. Fearless. And ready for whatever awaited me.

My Breed had to come first.

I ran out of the compound.

Cyrus had been right about the people overindulging in the night. There were no guards. In fact, I didn't see anyone. It took me no time to reach the ocean. I took off my boots and ran down the sand toward the water.

The sun was just rising across the horizon.

I fell to my knees to watch it come up. It was the most

beautiful sight I had ever seen. I could feel my body begin to flicker, the energy starting to pulse at the bottom of my feet. I turned around and looked back at OM. From here, I could see the tall pyramid shape of Aedan's home and it was magnificent

"I love you," I whispered out loud, part of me hoping he would somehow hear it and know the truth for the rest of his days.

I turned back to the water and took my first step in. It was cold but my body temperature acclimated quickly. I could feel the sensation of my Shadow taking over, the tingling moving over my body—this realization of being almost whole.

I took another step.

"And just where are you going, my little lovely?" My heart stopped.

To my right was an army of Reptiles. Some of them were standing as their Shadows and others as monstrous hybrids. They looked vicious. And worse, hungry.

How had they gotten in OM?

Panic washed over me. I looked back at the city. I needed to warn the others.

"The fun is just about to start," said the one in the middle who resembled a cobra as he flashed an eerie smile. His teeth were already dripping with blood. He'd fed. He brought his hand up to his mouth, and I saw that his nails were like long black daggers.

Run!

I didn't have time to think.

I quickly dove deep in the water and swam under the waves, my Shadow exploding like a burst of lightening, enveloping my entire body. For a second, the bliss of finally being home made me forget about the Reptiles.

But then, I heard the city alarm go off.

It was like a million high-pitched shrieks echoing through the land.

OM was under attack.

END OF BOOK ONE

ØØØ

COAT OF ARMS
KINGDOM B

My mother said I should never allow
my Shadow to control me.
But she was wrong.
It was my Shadow that drove me.
My Shadow that pushed me forward.
My Shadow that kept me alive.

SHADOW
BOOK TWO

We all have a responsibility to help protect our planet and its beautiful species. These are some incredible organizations working to do just that:

@seashepherdsscs
@int.anti.poaching.foundation
@exotic_feline_rescue_center
@nirvanabirds
@mickaboorescue
@PARCorg
@eagle_enforce
@bio_sapiens
@magicfundamazon
@healrewilding
@sugiproject
https://www.eagle-enforcement.org/
https://www.conservation.org/
https://ealliance.org/

Acknowledgements

Thank you, mom, for your endless love and devotion. Thank you for asking me the following sentence at least once a week, "when is your dad's book coming out?" I think you willed this one more than I. Thank you to my sister, Jasmine, brother-in-law, Bahman, and my niece, Ella for your endless love and support. I couldn't ask for a better family. I am so blessed.

Nedda, my beautiful cousin, thank you for reading my book one thousand times and never allowing me to lose my faith. Thank you for my symbols. Thank you for my Dr. Hedy sketches. Thank you for listening. Thank you for being in my life. I love you so *so* much.

AnnaLynne. Thank you for being Breed's voice. Thank you for loving this book the way that you do. Thank you for being the best kind of friend. Every girl should be so lucky to have someone like you on their side. It feels like you reading this was written in the stars. ☺ I love you forever.

Georgana, my amazing publicist, I know I'm supposed to call you Nina now, but that is never going to happen. You came into my life with *Mud Love* and you've always been my greatest champion. Thank you for all that you are and all that you do. I heart you for life.

Kimberly, thank you for your notes, for championing Breed the way you did, and for everything. You loved this book from the moment you read the first chapter and I'll never *ever* forget it.

Anita, my editor, who helped me shape and finesse my world- you are the BEST.

Thank you, Theresa, my line editor who pointed out the

differences between Siri and Sara and for all the rest. ☺

David, thank you for my beautiful cover and designs. They are everything. You and your handsome hubby, Jake, are the best.

Destiny, thank you for giving the characters life and for all your creativity.

Carlton, thank you for making it happen.

Daddy, it always comes back to you. Thank you for giving me the idea for *Breed*. Thank you for being the most incredible father a girl could ask for. Thank you for your endless kindness and love. I miss you and think about you a thousand times a day. I love you. I love you. I love you.

Famous, my fur baby. My first son. You are always with me on all my walks. You are always in my heart. I miss you everyday.

Thank you to the rest of my friends & family- I'm not naming you, but you know who you are. I love you all so much and I am so blessed. I have the best tribe in the world.

And finally, thank you, PachaMama, for this great Earth you've blessed us with. May we keep her and her beloved creatures safe for eternity.

Books by Colet Abedi

<u>Writing as C.J. Abedi</u>
Fae - Book 1
The Dark King - Book 2
The Queen - Book 3

<u>Mad Love Series</u>
Mad Love - Book 1
Madly in Love - Book 1.5
Mad Love 2 - Book 2
Madly Addicted - Book 2.5
Tame - Book 3

<u>The Wild Duet</u>
Wild
Wilder

<u>Standalone</u>
Trouble

ABOUT THE AUTHOR

Colet Abedi is a best-selling author, television and film producer. She was born in Virginia and currently lives in Los Angeles. When she's not writing she's either off on an adventure in a far off land or planning her next getaway. She writes contemporary romance, women's fiction, and young adult.

Follow me on social media…

@ColetAbedi

@ColetAbedi

Made in the USA
Monee, IL
31 October 2021